THEORETICAL PERSPECTIVES IN LAW

Series Editor

ALEXANDER TSESIS
Professor and D'Alemberte Chair in Constitutional Law, Florida State University College of Law

Dignity and Judicial Authority

Rachel Bayefsky

THEORETICAL PERSPECTIVES IN LAW

The *Theoretical Perspectives in Law* series publishes works that explore a diversity of topics pertinent to jurisprudence, statutory review, constitutional principles, substantive entitlements, procedural justice, legal history, and policymaking. The series is committed to intellectual diversity.

Books in this series parse, critique, expand, and elaborate theoretical approaches to broad ranges of legal topics. Authors' works explain the principles, priorities, sensibilities, perspectives, traditions, or social conditions that drive evolution of law. Authors write of how sovereignty, wealth, connection, privilege, culture, and popular discourse influence legal concepts, rules of decision, procedural justice, and substantive fairness. The series further examines how law impacts sociology, politics, traditions, and culture and, in turn, how they impact precedents, policy priorities, administrative tactics, separation of powers, and representative governance.

Theoretical Perspectives in Law offers a forum for pursuit of contested matters in legal theory that impact contemporary society. Approaches range from empirical, to normative, to positivist. The basic concept may be said to articulate core, rule of law principles in subjects that range from constitutional law to property law.

Authors in the series advance fields of knowledge by elaborating, parsing, analyzing and criticizing text, history, norms, doctrines, and structure. They thereby provide readers with substantive and structural frameworks to be used in research and teaching. Comprehensive studies enable authors and readers to explore challenges facing a variety of current affairs. A dive into legal theory, ultimately and perhaps idealistically, seeks to evaluate and effectuate fairness and justice.

Dignity and Judicial Authority

RACHEL BAYEFSKY
Associate Professor of Law,
University of Virginia School of Law

OXFORD
UNIVERSITY PRESS

OXFORD
UNIVERSITY PRESS

Oxford University Press is a department of the University of Oxford. It furthers the University's objective of excellence in research, scholarship, and education by publishing worldwide. Oxford is a registered trade mark of Oxford University Press in the UK and certain other countries.

Published in the United States of America by Oxford University Press
198 Madison Avenue, New York, NY 10016, United States of America.

Library of Congress Cataloging-in-Publication Data
Names: Bayefsky, Rachel, 1987– author.
Title: Dignity and judicial authority / Rachel Bayefsky.
Description: New York : Oxford University Press, 2024. |
Series: Theoretical perspectives in law series |
Includes bibliographical references and index.
Identifiers: LCCN 2024017270 (print) | LCCN 2024017271 (ebook) |
ISBN 9780197750322 (hardback) | ISBN 9780197750339 (epub) |
ISBN 9780197750346 (updf) | ISBN 9780197750353 (online)
Subjects: LCSH: Respect for persons—Law and legislation. |
Torts. | Judicial process. | Courts.
Classification: LCC K3249 .B39 2024 (print) | LCC K3249 (ebook) |
DDC 347/.012—dc23/eng/20240416
LC record available at https://lccn.loc.gov/2024017270
LC ebook record available at https://lccn.loc.gov/2024017271

DOI: 10.1093/oso/9780197750322.001.0001

For my Bubbi and Zaidi, Evelyn and Aba Bayefsky

Contents

Acknowledgments

Many mentors, colleagues, and friends have contributed to my work on dignity over the course of over a decade, and it is possible to name only a few. I would first like to thank Dr. Mark Philp, my DPhil supervisor when I was at the University of Oxford, for his insight and unflagging confidence in the project. Professor Alexander Tsesis, the editor of this book series, has been a wonderful intellectual interlocutor and friend. I am grateful to my colleagues at the University of Virginia School of Law, particularly Professors Ken Abraham, Risa Goluboff, and Debbie Hellman; to my Yale Law School professors Doug Kysar, Jerry Mashaw, and Reva Siegel; to my mentors as a Climenko Fellow at Harvard Law School, Professors Dick Fallon and John Goldberg; and to my teacher at Yale College, Professor Steven Smith. I learned a great deal about judicial authority from the three judges for whom I clerked: Justice Ruth Bader Ginsburg, Chief Judge Robert A. Katzmann, and Judge Jed S. Rakoff.

In writing this book, I have drawn on some of my previous work on dignity, particularly the following pieces: *Dignity, Honour, and Human Rights: Kant's Perspective*, 41 Political Theory 809 (2013); *Psychological Harm and Constitutional Standing*, 81 Brook. L. Rev. 1555 (2016); *Constitutional Injury and Tangibility*, 59 Wm. & Mary L. Rev. 2285 (2018); *Remedies and Respect: Rethinking the Role of Federal Judicial Relief*, 109 Georgetown L.J. 1263 (2021); and *Public-Law Litigation at a Crossroads: Article III Standing and "Tester" Plaintiffs*, 99 N.Y.U. L. Rev. Online 128 (2024).

For generously reading part or all of the manuscript, I thank Ken Abraham, Peter Bozzo, Debbie Hellman, George Rutherglen, Steve Schaus, and Rich Schragger. The editors at Oxford University Press have been terrific, including Jamie Berezin, Lisa Butts, Getsy Kirubai, and Brian Stone.

For research assistance, I thank Henry Adams, Elizabeth Adler, Isaiah Affron, Rachel Anderson, Grayson Buttler, Hannah Genender, Julia Grant, Dillon Grimm, Harry Hild, Natasha Holtman, Julia Stamper, Adam Younger, and especially Lauren Emmerich and Gamliel Yerushalmi.

My lawyer friends Peter Bozzo, Geoff Shaw, and Meng Jia Yang have enriched both my life and this book with their thoughtfulness and kindness. The same is true of my childhood friends Jordana Federman, Arianna Schudrich, and Alexandra Wald (now Bortz).

Finally, I thank my family—including its newest member, Michael Francus—for their encouragement, support, and love.

Introduction

"Dignity" is a rallying cry of social and political movements worldwide. "We walk for human dignity," read signs held by marchers in the American civil rights movement. "We demand dignity, respect, union rights, living wages for all," a union placard states. Calls for dignity also feature prominently in movements promoting women's equality, greater acceptance of same-sex relationships, and global movements for national independence. Something about the idea that people have dignity, or must be treated with dignity, strikes a chord in a wide variety of geographic and cultural settings.

Dignity is not only a social and political concept, but also a legal one. Rights to dignity are enshrined in constitutions around the world. Examples include the German Basic Law's provision that "Human dignity shall be inviolable. To respect and protect it shall be the duty of all state authority";[1] Israel's Basic Law protecting "human dignity and liberty";[2] and the South African Constitution's inclusion of "Human Dignity" in the Bill of Rights.[3] The significance of dignity is deeply woven into the international human rights regime, as exemplified in the Universal Declaration of Human Rights' pronouncement that "[a]ll human beings are born free and equal in dignity and rights."[4]

Dignity is less prominent as a legal value in the United States, but it appears in America nonetheless. Perhaps most conspicuously, the US Supreme Court's jurisprudence on same-sex relations has appealed to dignity. The Court has characterized bans on same-sex marriage as forms of "indignity"[5] and "humiliat[ion]."[6] More generally, American courts have drawn on the

[1] Grundgesetz [GG] [Basic Law], art. 1(1), translation at https://www.gesetze-im-internet.de/englisch_gg/englisch_gg.html.

[2] Basic Law: Human Dignity and Liberty (Isr.), https://m.knesset.gov.il/EN/activity/documents/BasicLawsPDF/BasicLawLiberty.pdf.

[3] S. Afr. Const. § 10, 1996.

[4] G.A. Res. 217 (III) A, Universal Declaration of Human Rights, art. 1 (Dec. 10, 1948).

[5] United States v. Windsor, 570 U.S. 744, 768 (2013).

[6] Obergefell v. Hodges, 576 U.S. 644, 668 (2015).

Dignity and Judicial Authority. Rachel Bayefsky, Oxford University Press.
DOI: 10.1093/oso/9780197750322.001.0001

language of dignity, respect, and stigma in contexts ranging from racial discrimination to disability rights to tort suits involving battery, defamation, and invasion of privacy. Legislators, too, invoke dignity as a basis for their activities, proposing or passing such laws as "Dignity for Incarcerated Women," "Death with Dignity," and "Dignity in Aging."

Though many political and legal actors agree that dignity is important, there is much less consensus on dignity's meaning and implications. Indeed, dignity can be found on multiple sides of heated debates. Does legalized abortion violate the dignity of fetal life or uphold the dignity of women? Does affirmative action advance the dignity of minorities or stigmatize them? Do restrictions on offensive speech infringe on the dignity of potential speakers or help to create a respectful environment?

Given the ideological malleability of dignity, one might question whether it is well suited for the legal sphere. Law, after all, requires specificity, line-drawing, and rules that the public can follow. Dignity, by contrast, is notoriously slippery. Moreover, law centrally involves the exercise of authority. Should government officials be empowered to advance their visions of dignity through the coercive mechanisms of the state? In particular, dignitary concerns have been invoked in several countries to restrict certain behaviors, such as pornography and hate speech.[7] Some might worry that appeals to dignity in law encourage heavy-handed or arbitrary governance. As one writer has put it, "[t]he notion of dignity can easily become a screen behind which paternalism or moralism are elevated above freedom in legal decision-making."[8]

In light of these concerns about the use of dignity in law, one might also question whether *courts* are proper candidates for the advancement of dignitary goals. In an article on the US Supreme Court's same-sex marriage jurisprudence titled "The Dangers of a Constitutional 'Right to Dignity,'" a commentator expressed trepidation about "empowering judges to decide whose dignity trumps when the interests of citizens with very different conceptions of dignity clash."[9] Why should judges, who stand at some remove from the political process, be authorized to further their visions of dignity through cases that govern the public at large?

[7] *See* Christopher McCrudden, *Human Dignity and Judicial Interpretation of Human Rights*, 19 Eur. J. Int'l L. 655, 702–04, 718–19 (2008).

[8] David Feldman, *Human Dignity as a Legal Value: Part I*, 1999 Public Law 682.

[9] Jeffrey Rosen, *The Dangers of a Constitutional 'Right to Dignity,'* The Atlantic (Apr. 29, 2015), https://www.theatlantic.com/politics/archive/2015/04/the-dangerous-doctrine-of-dignity/391796.

Yet critiques of dignity, substantial as they are, cannot erase the intuition that dignity and related ideas like respect, stigma, and humiliation are meaningful features of moral and political experience. Moreover, dignity is difficult for the law to ignore. Dignity is embedded in existing laws, including statutory enactments and the common law. Courts are tasked with interpreting and applying legal provisions related to dignity and adjacent concepts. For example, an offensive touch can qualify as battery if it "offends a reasonable sense of personal dignity,"[10] and liability for the privacy tort of "intrusion upon seclusion" often depends on whether the "intrusion would be highly offensive to a reasonable person."[11] Judges and juries have a role in elucidating these standards and applying them to particular cases. Even if a legal doctrine or statutory provision does not explicitly mention dignity, courts may be faced with scenarios that raise dignitary considerations. For example, judicial decisions on the legality of strip searches or accommodations for people with disabilities affect people's dignity even when judges do not set out to rule with dignity in mind.

The question remains, then, how courts should approach controversies in which dignity is at stake. Courts' responses to this question teach us, in turn, about the contours of judicial power and the bounds of the judicial role. How should courts identify dignitary violations from an evidentiary perspective? How should they respond when opposing parties claim the mantle of dignity? When does the effort to promote dignity stray beyond judges' competence and threaten judicial legitimacy?

Not every social problem is a legal problem, and not every legal problem is one that courts may tackle. Defining the types of harm that courts are entitled to redress, and specifying how they may redress them, is a key step in delineating judicial authority. Dignitary harm is especially revealing vis-à-vis the bounds of judicial power, as it bears on courts' ability to incorporate malleable and culturally charged concepts into their jurisprudence.

This book therefore examines the relationship between dignity and judicial authority. The book has four main goals. The first is to demonstrate that the idea of dignity opens a vista onto fundamental questions about the proper role of courts in a constitutional democracy. Debates about dignity are sites for social and ideological contestation. Judicial involvement in efforts to define and promote dignity sheds light on the role courts should play in an

[10] Restatement (Second) of Torts § 19 (Am. L. Inst. 1965).
[11] Restatement (Second) of Torts § 652B (Am L. Inst. 1977).

environment of political and cultural conflict. For example, some might take the view that the promotion of dignity is not a task for courts—instead, it is a job for other social institutions such as legislatures, community organizations, and families. Disputes over whether it is "court-like" for judicial institutions to advance dignity raise the question of what courts should be doing: Allocating material resources? Maintaining order and public safety? Furthering social reconciliation? These questions are not simply about the concept of dignity; they concern the basic issue of what citizens in a constitutional democracy can properly expect from courts, and what courts can legitimately provide.

The book's second goal is to offer a defense of judicial institutions as an appropriate site for the furtherance of dignitary aims. More specifically, I argue that the identification and rectification of dignitary harms are tasks that properly fall within judicial authority. In making this argument, I focus primarily on federal and state courts in the United States, while drawing on some comparative perspectives from outside the United States for illumination. The geographic focus on the United States stems both from the interest in cabining the inquiry and from the fact that American lawyers and scholars are currently debating the legitimacy of judicial institutions and the bounds of their authority. I propose that the identification and remediation of dignitary harm are legally sound and normatively desirable tasks for American courts.

That argument raises the question of what "dignity" means, and the book's third aim is to clarify the idea of dignity itself. Though it is not possible to devise a single "correct" understanding of "dignity," a coherent cluster of concepts surrounds dignity and accounts for several of its legal manifestations. As understood in this book, dignity is a relational concept; it concerns the place of individuals in a social world. Promoting dignity involves protection of the social self. In particular, dignity involves *respect for status*, the *absence of domination*, and the ability to exercise *control over self-presentation* to others. From a normative perspective, courts properly serve as sites for the promotion of dignity in the sense that they appropriately rectify unjustified status demotion, arbitrary forms of domination, and actions that wrongly undermine people's ability to control their self-presentation.

The book's fourth goal is to explain how, as a practical matter, judicial institutions in the United States can advance dignity. Pragmatic issues of this kind are not simply afterthoughts; they are deeply intertwined with the substantive issue of courts' authority to promote dignity. For instance, if insoluble line-drawing problems plague efforts to integrate dignity into courts' decision-making, then one might question whether the rectification of dignitary harm is properly within the judicial bailiwick. I argue that dignitary values can be practically implemented, and I provide examples of ways in which courts can identify and redress dignitary harm in the real world. For instance, in constitutional standing doctrine, courts can recognize dignitary harm as "injury in fact" sufficient to open federal courthouse doors while cabining the circle of plaintiffs who could assert this harm. In the law of remedies, courts can impose relief that expresses respect for the party whose rights were violated—such as punitive damages, "symbolic" nominal damages, or even compelled apologies—without committing themselves to providing unlimited relief. Promoting dignity in these domains requires the structured exercise of judgment, but that is an endemic feature of the judicial task and is not unique to dignity.

Thus, in exploring the relationship between dignity and courts, the book illuminates both the nature of dignity and the authority of courts. In the past several years, dignity has been the subject of increasing interest from philosophers, historians, and legal theorists.[12] Existing treatments of dignity's legal role reflect, however, a strong emphasis on comparative constitutionalism, international law, and theories of rights.[13] The general focus of the existing literature is on dignity as a conceptual basis for rights, especially constitutional rights, or as a principle guiding the interpretation of constitutional rights.

This book, in addition to contributing to the growing debate about dignity and its implications, engages in a distinctive legal inquiry. Its focus is on the consequences of dignity not for theories of rights, but for institutions—notably courts in constitutional democracies, especially the United States. Centered on judicial authority, the book explains what dignity can tell us about the promise and limitations of the judicial role. Relatedly, I elaborate on how courts can promote dignity in a concrete sense. The book thus emphasizes the intersection between dignity and doctrinal determinations about harm, remedies, and jurisdiction. To do this, I drill down both into

[12] *See, e.g.*, ERIN DALY & JAMES R. MAY, DIGNITY LAW: GLOBAL RECOGNITION, CASES, AND PERSPECTIVES (2020); MICHAEL ROSEN, DIGNITY: ITS HISTORY AND MEANING (2012); JEREMY WALDRON, DIGNITY, RANK, AND RIGHTS (2012).

[13] *See, e.g.*, STEPHEN RILEY, HUMAN DIGNITY AND LAW: LEGAL AND PHILOSOPHICAL INVESTIGATIONS (2018); AHARON BARAK, HUMAN DIGNITY: THE CONSTITUTIONAL VALUE AND THE CONSTITUTIONAL RIGHT (2015); ERIN DALY, DIGNITY RIGHTS: COURTS, CONSTITUTIONS, AND THE WORTH OF THE HUMAN PERSON (2021).

conceptual theories of dignitary interests and, beyond the realm of theory, the intricacies of legal doctrine. The goals are to widen dignity's capacity to inform legal decision-making and to shed new light on the boundaries of judicial power.

*

This book has three parts. Part I, Defining Dignity, clears the conceptual terrain by analyzing the idea of dignity and by introducing the problems of judicial authority that dignitary issues help to illustrate. Parts II and III then examine the impact of dignitary concerns on two areas that bear on the scope of judicial authority: the bounds of legally actionable harm, and the identification of suitable remedies. Part II, Dignitary Harm, explores the conditions under which courts do and should treat dignitary harm as the basis for legal protection. Part III, Dignity and Remedies, delves into normative and practical questions regarding judicial remedies for dignitary violations.

More specifically, Chapter 1 unravels the concept of dignity by exploring its philosophical and historical underpinnings—for instance, the Roman concept of *dignitas*, Kant's views on dignity, and dignity's place in the international human rights regime. The chapter then explains how dignity functions in current legal debates, focusing on the American legal system. Dignity serves as both a site for and a mediator of deep divergences about values and worldviews. In other words, dignity functions as a focal point for the expression of social disagreement in law. Thus, the concept should not be dismissed as counterproductive simply because it is susceptible to differing, and ideologically charged, interpretations.

Chapter 2 proposes a working understanding of dignity—"relational dignity"—that aims both to keep faith with dignity's historical roots and to inform contemporary legal regimes. A common thread running through many references to dignity is protection of the social self. Dignity is social and relational; to respect dignity is to maintain the conditions necessary for people to occupy a certain place in a communal world. In particular, dignity (as understood here) involves *respect for status*, the *absence of domination*, and the ability to exercise *control over self-presentation* to others. The chapter fleshes out several aspects of this idea of dignity. Notably, dignity here is not conceptualized in "subjective" terms. A person's dignity is violated, for example, only when her *rightful* status is attacked—not when a person's idiosyncratic view of her own status is challenged.

Part I, therefore, examines dignity's historical and conceptual roots, and it proposes a working understanding of dignity. The book then moves on to explore issues critical to the relationship between dignity and judicial authority: dignity as a legally actionable harm (Part II) and judicial remedies for dignitary harm (Part III). Not all real-world detrimental effects amount to legal wrongs, and not all legal violations are ones that courts may redress. Thus, the concepts of harm and remedy help to delineate the power of judicial institutions.

To begin Part II, Chapter 3 investigates the place of dignitary harm in constitutional standing doctrine. Article III of the US Constitution limits federal-court jurisdiction to "Cases" and "Controversies." The Supreme Court has interpreted this requirement to mean that plaintiffs seeking to enter federal courts must suffer an "injury in fact" that is "particularized" in the sense that it is incurred by plaintiffs themselves, and "concrete" in the sense of being "real." When harm is physical or economic in nature, courts readily recognize the harm as "real." But what about when harm involves more "intangible" types of harm, such as stigma or disrespect? The chapter argues for greater recognition of dignitary harm as injury in fact in the constitutional standing analysis. And it contends that dignitary harm can qualify as injury in fact without opening the floodgates of federal jurisdiction to any plaintiff alleging offense.

Chapter 4 tackles the interplay between dignitary harm and tort law, and its ramifications for issues of judicial power and competence. It highlights various tort claims that are particularly likely to safeguard dignitary interests. An example is battery committed through offensive contact that does not cause physical harm, such as spitting in someone's face. The chapter then addresses questions arising from the challenge of adjudicating tort claims based on dignitary harm. In particular, the chapter examines the historical pedigree of dignitary claims in tort law; the matter of how courts can sift actionable from nonactionable dignitary claims; and the vexed relationship between dignity in tort law and the First Amendment. The chapter argues that dignitary values should not be subordinated to First Amendment aims.

Part III turns to the question of judicial remedies for dignitary harm. How can courts provide relief for dignitary harm, and how (if at all) is this judicial function justified? Do judicial remedies for dignitary harm themselves damage dignity—for example, by tarnishing defendants' reputations or intruding too deeply into defendants' personal spheres?

The first chapter in Part III, Chapter 5, defends the notion that courts should provide relief for dignitary harm and explains how they can do so. Judicial remedies for dignitary harm are consonant with the broader remedial goal of restoring or maintaining the plaintiff's "rightful position." Moreover, plaintiffs' goals in litigation can include advancing their nonmonetary interest in vindication, and courts should not ignore this interest when they are granting remedies. Relief for dignitary harm can take numerous forms, including compensatory damages for dignitary harm, punitive damages, nominal damages, and declaratory judgments. The chapter indicates how each of these remedies can help to redress dignitary harm. Further, courts need not provide infinitely expansive relief for dignitary harm. Considerations such as efficiency could outweigh the goal of promoting dignity through the law of remedies.

Continuing with Part III's theme of remedies, Chapter 6 examines a type of judicial remedy that raises fundamental questions about the bounds of judicial authority: court-mandated apologies. In the United States, court-ordered apologies are not common, but they occur in some cases, such as certain criminal cases and attorney discipline proceedings. In other cases, parties may be heavily incentivized to apologize even if they are not formally forced; for instance, judges often impose lower sentences on criminal defendants who express remorse. The chapter examines the relationship between court-mandated apologies and dignity. On the one hand, an apology from the defendant can vindicate the plaintiff's dignity. On the other hand, court-ordered apologies risk violating the dignity of the defendant, and they raise First Amendment compelled-speech concerns. I argue against a blanket ban on court-mandated apologies, and I explore implications of these apologies for the topic of judicial encroachment on individual conscience.

The book concludes by reflecting on the possibilities and limits of judicial institutions in promoting dignity. Dignity may be a messy idea, but the concept mirrors the complexity and controversy of our social world. It may be tempting to seek to cast courts out of the fray. But the better approach is to acknowledge that courts already make determinations about harm and remedies that influence society's ability to pursue dignitary goals. Judicial power can and should be harnessed to help construct a society that instantiates dignitary values more effectively.

PART I
DEFINING DIGNITY

What is dignity? Here a roadblock looms. One of the most common charges against dignity is that it has a dizzying array of meanings and uses, too many for the concept to be coherent or serviceable. If dignity can mean practically anything and can be used to support a vast panoply of political and legal causes, then what is the point of invoking it? Still less—the critique runs—should dignity shape the actions of societal institutions such as courts.

Dignity is indeed a complex and multifaceted concept, but that does not mean any attempt to explicate the idea is doomed to failure. Chapter 1 begins to unravel dignity's threads by reviewing key features of the concept's philosophical and historical development. The chapter then explains how dignity functions in legal debates, with a particular emphasis on the American constitutional system. There, dignity serves as a focal point for the expression of social disagreement in law. The multiple meanings of dignity speak to the persistence of cultural and political conflicts. But they also permit dignity to play a mediating role in such conflicts, by focusing attention on dignitary dimensions of a dispute that those with different perspectives may be able to acknowledge.

Chapter 2 proposes an understanding of dignity that is tethered to dignity's intellectual pedigree and that can play a useful role in the project of integrating dignity into judicial decisions. On this understanding, dignity critically involves protection of the social self. To respect dignity is to create or sustain the conditions necessary for people to interact with fellow human beings in a certain way. The interactions in question generally share these features: respect for status, the absence of domination, and the ability to exercise control over one's self-presentation to others. The account of dignity offered here is meant to provide a springboard for analysis of the relationship between dignity and judicial authority.

1

Mapping Dignity

At the outset, it is helpful to provide a sense of how dignity has developed and which interests it can be harnessed to protect. This chapter proceeds by explaining dignity's historical roots and providing a taxonomy to categorize different understandings of dignity. Then, the chapter highlights the role of dignity in high-profile constitutional debates. In several debates, the language of dignity is a medium through which individuals express profound social disagreements. This does not mean dignity is incoherent. Rather, its usage reflects underlying normative disputes that inform legal doctrine.

Dignity's Roots

Dignity is a legal idea, but it also extends beyond law to the domains of philosophy, religion, and culture. Within each of these domains, dignity has a history; it is connected to certain forms of social organization that arose at specific times and places. The objective here is not to canvass every understanding of dignity across these vast expanses, but to identify intellectual traditions that have helped to shape the concept and create the associations that exist today.

The Roman Concept of Dignitas

The "obvious etymological connection of 'dignity' with the Latin term *dignitas*"[1] reflects Roman influence on the development of the concept of dignity. As Miriam Griffin has written of dignity in Roman thought, "*[d]ignitas* is an attribute signifying a certain standing or rank in the community; it rests on a particular office or status, and on the prestige that accrues to

[1] Miriam Griffin, *Dignity in Roman and Stoic Thought, in* Dignity: A History 47 (Remy Debes ed., 2017).

Dignity and Judicial Authority. Rachel Bayefsky, Oxford University Press.
DOI: 10.1093/oso/9780197750322.003.0001

its holder. . . . It is long term and it is inheritable by descendants."[2] So understood, dignity in Roman times was intimately connected to high status in a social and political hierarchy.[3]

Dignity in Roman thought involved not only a status, but also a form of self-presentation to the outside world.[4] Griffin suggests that "dignitas" "is, probably, etymologically connected with *decus*, comely and fitting appearance."[5] Dignity was related to the majestic or noble bearing suitable for those possessing high status in Roman life.

The close association between dignity in Roman thought and elevated rank is not merely a vestige of the ancient world. Among the definitions of dignity in the *Merriam-Webster Dictionary* is "high rank, office, or position."[6] We still hold ceremonies to recognize those with power or high social status—inaugurations, military exercises, coronations, bestowal of honorary degrees—and use clothing and language that we take to reflect the dignity of the occasion and its honorees. Moreover, we expect those occupying high offices to present themselves to the world with a degree of dignity that befits their station. When such individuals fail to do so, we may call them undignified.[7]

Yet dignity in Roman thought was not exclusively a function of either social status or outward presentation. First, Roman dignity was partly associated with a standard of behavior that went beyond outward appearances and spoke to a person's morality and virtue.[8] Thus, *dignitas* played the kind of dual role that "honor" plays in the current day: It was connected to high status, but it was also linked to the quality of being "honorable" in the sense of living up to valuable ideals.

Second, Roman dignity could at times attach to people as members of humanity rather than as participants in a social hierarchy. As Michael Rosen has pointed out, Cicero—likely in a continuation of Stoic thought—connected human dignity to the quality of not being bound exclusively by the drive to satisfy bodily needs.[9] In Cicero's view, "sensual pleasure is wholly unworthy

[2] *Id.* at 50.

[3] Teresa Iglesias, *Bedrock Truths and the Dignity of the Individual*, 4 Logos 114, 120 (2001) ("[p]olitical *offices*, and as a consequence the *persons holding them*, like that of a senator, or the emperor, had *dignitas*").

[4] Griffin, note 1, at 50.

[5] *Id.*

[6] *Dignity*, Merriam-Webster Dictionary, https://www.merriam-webster.com/dictionary/dignity.

[7] *See* Michael Rosen, Dignity: Its History and Meaning 13 (2012).

[8] Griffin, note 1, at 53.

[9] Rosen, note 7, at 11–12.

of the human race."[10] This account of dignity is hierarchical in that human dignity may be contrasted with the inferior rank of nonhuman animals.[11] Moreover, people vary in their focus on satisfying bodily needs. But the notion of humanity's dignity facilitates more egalitarian visions of dignity as between human beings, since dignity becomes a quality that human beings possess independent of social status.

To summarize, then, the Roman idea of *dignitas* furnishes a powerful basis for the connection between dignity and high social status. Further, Roman thinking on dignity emphasizes social self-presentation—the ways that individuals carry themselves in front of others. At the same time, Roman thought contains the seeds of a form of dignity that attaches to human beings on a more egalitarian and less socially contingent basis.

Religious Accounts of Dignity

Religious views of dignity are as varied and complex as the world's faith traditions. Though it is impossible to characterize religious ideas of dignity in a brief and neatly packaged way, a few broad themes can be discerned.[12]

According to many religious traditions, dignity stems from or inheres in the connection between human beings and the divine. The notion that human beings have dignity because they are made in the "image of God," for example, runs deep in Jewish[13] and Christian[14] traditions. With respect to Islamic conceptions of dignity, Mustafa Shah has observed that "the Qur'an's overall message is one of salvation and within this context the concern for human dignity is not only presented as a given within the text, but it is intricately anchored to notions of divine imperative and command."[15] Dignity in

[10] *Id.* at 12; *see* Griffin, note 1, at 56–60 (analyzing notions of humanity's distinctive traits held by the Stoics and Cicero).

[11] For discussion of the relationship between human dignity and nonhuman animals, see, for example, George Kateb, Human Dignity 160–61 (2011).

[12] *See* Aharon Barak, Human Dignity: The Constitutional Value and the Constitutional Right 18–23 (2015).

[13] *See, e.g.*, Yair Lorberbaum, *Human Dignity in the Jewish Tradition*, *in* The Cambridge Handbook of Human Dignity 136 (Marcus Düwell, Jens Braarvig, Roger Brownsword & Dietmar Mieth eds., 2014).

[14] *See, e.g.*, David Hollenbach, *Human Dignity in Catholic Thought*, *in* The Cambridge Handbook of Human Dignity 252 (Marcus Düwell, Jens Braarvig, Roger Brownsword & Dietmar Mieth eds., 2014); Oswald Bayer, *Martin Luther's Conception of Human Dignity*, *in* The Cambridge Handbook of Human Dignity 101 (Marcus Düwell, Jens Braarvig, Roger Brownsword & Dietmar Mieth eds., 2014).

[15] Mustafa Shah, *Islamic Conceptions of Dignity: Historical Trajectories and Paradigms*, *in* Dignity: A History 108 (Remy Debes ed., 2017).

religious traditions is frequently based on qualities that human beings possess by virtue of their relationship with, or subservience to, a higher being.

Relatedly, dignity in religious traditions is often associated with humanity's station within the divinely ordained structure of existence. For example, Rosen describes "[t]he Aquinian conception of 'dignity' as the value something has in virtue of occupying its proper place within a divine order."[16] Moreover, dignity in religious thought is not necessarily an intrinsic quality of all human beings; it may attach to adherents of certain faiths[17] or to individuals who live up to religious demands.[18] Jens Braarvig suggests that dignity in classical Buddhism (though not in other forms of Buddhism) is an "*inner* dignity, that can be attained by religious practice, but it is not an *inherent* dignity."[19]

Dignity in religious thought has a complex relationship with egalitarianism. On the one hand, religious ideas of dignity provide powerful fuel for the view that all human beings are equal before God. On the other hand, religious understandings of dignity may be associated with hierarchy, at least at certain points in history. According to one interpretation, "[f]or the Catholic Church in the nineteenth century, all members of society have dignity, but their dignity consists in their playing the role that is appropriate to their station within a hierarchical social order, one in which some are 'nobler than others.'"[20] Another author writes that "human dignity in Hinduism is an ambiguous and perhaps even paradoxical concept: on the one hand, all living beings (not solely human beings) are thought to possess *inherent* dignity, but on the other hand we find that in the social realm dignity appears in *degrees*."[21]

Of course, religious traditions are internally complex and subject to development over time, and dignity is by no means immune from these influences. One example comes from Catholic thought, which adopted more egalitarian understandings of dignity by the mid-twentieth century.[22]

[16] Rosen, note 7, at 47–48.

[17] *See* Bonnie Kent, *In the Image of God: Dignity after the Fall*, *in* Dignity: A History 95 (Remy Debes ed., 2017).

[18] *See id.*

[19] Jens Braarvig, *Buddhism: Inner Dignity and Absolute Altruism*, *in* The Cambridge Handbook of Human Dignity 172 (Marcus Düwell, Jens Braarvig, Roger Brownsword & Dietmar Mieth eds., 2014).

[20] Rosen, note 7, at 49.

[21] Jens Braarvig, *Hinduism: The Universal Self in a Class Society*, *in* The Cambridge Handbook of Human Dignity 163 (Marcus Düwell, Jens Braarvig, Roger Brownsword & Dietmar Mieth eds., 2014).

[22] Hollenbach, note 14, at 252; Rosen, note 7, at 51–53.

Theological traditions exist in a dynamic relationship with historical events and changing philosophical currents, and religious thinking on the nature of dignity is no exception.

Dignity and Kant

Kant is frequently considered a key figure in the development of today's ideas about dignity.[23] Indeed, he has been called the "father of the modern concept of human dignity."[24] Kant is often associated with an idea of dignity as inherent worth.[25] In the *Groundwork of the Metaphysic of Morals*, Kant distinguished between things with a "price," which "can be replaced with something else, as its *equivalent*," and things with a "dignity," which is "elevated above any price, and hence allows of no equivalent."[26] According to Kant, "morality, and humanity insofar as it is capable of morality, is that which alone has dignity."[27] These passages are commonly interpreted to endorse a vision of dignity that serves as a precursor to the modern human rights regime: dignity as the intrinsic worth that each human being possesses independent of social situation or personal attributes. Kantian dignity is often linked to the view, in Christopher McCrudden's words, "that individuals should be treated as ends and not simply as means to an end."[28]

Moreover, Kantian dignity is frequently tied to concepts of autonomy, freedom, and independence. As McCrudden notes: "[W]hether rightly or wrongly, the conception of dignity most closely associated with Kant is the idea of dignity as autonomy; that is, the idea that to treat people with dignity is to treat them as autonomous individuals able to choose their destiny."[29] In this sense, Kantian dignity may be viewed as an outgrowth of the

[23] *See* Rachel Bayefsky, *Dignity, Honor, and Human Rights: Kant's Perspective*, 41 Political Theory 809, 811 (2013). Portions of the discussion here draw on my article on Kant. *See also* Christopher McCrudden, *Human Dignity and Judicial Interpretation of Human Rights*, 19 Eur. J. Int'l L. 655, 659 (2008).

[24] Giovanni Bognetti, *The Concept of Human Dignity in European and US Constitutionalism*, *in* European and US Constitutionalism 89 (G. Nolte ed., 2005).

[25] *See* Jeremy Waldron, Dignity, Rank, and Rights 24 (2012).

[26] Immanuel Kant, Groundwork of the Metaphysic of Morals IV.434, at 97 (Mary Gregor & Jens Timmermann trans., Cambridge University Press 2011) (1785).

[27] *Id.* IV.435, at 99.

[28] McCrudden, note 23, at 659. Contemporary understandings of "Kantian" philosophy in the human rights regime may diverge from Kant's own approach, which arguably treated *humanity* rather than individual human beings as an end in itself. *See, e.g.*, Christine M. Korsgaard, Creating the Kingdom of Ends 109–111 (1996).

[29] McCrudden, note 23, at 659–60.

dignity invoked by Renaissance writers such as Pico della Mirandola, who connected dignity with free will.[30]

Yet dignity for Kant is more complicated than the linkage of his philosophy to human rights or freedom would suggest, for a few reasons. First, Kant's philosophy raises the question of which attribute of human beings serves as the basis for dignity: Reason? Moral capacity? Moral acts? The choice among relevant attributes could lead to substantially different accounts of human dignity. Moreover, not everyone possesses rational or moral capacities to the same degree. Should we decline to ascribe dignity, for example, to people with severe disabilities or to infants?

Second, Kant placed value on a quality called the "love of honor," which involved not only seeking to follow the moral law but also refusing to demean oneself in the eyes of others.[31] For Kant, dignity served as the basis for a mandate of self-respect—and "dignified" behavior evincing self-respect—in addition to the basis for a moral claim to respect from others. In other words, dignity required the dignity-bearer to behave in a dignified manner; it did not solely require others to treat the dignity-bearer respectfully.

The complexities in Kant's account of dignity raise questions about how his philosophy relates to current visions of dignity as egalitarian and rooted in human freedom. Dignity for Kant was about more than the equal value of each human being. It was also about the obligation to obey the moral law, as well as the rational faculties that render such obedience possible.

Nonetheless, Kant's philosophy is a critical reference point for modern accounts of dignity—even for those who may be reluctant to sign on to all particulars of his ethical or metaphysical views. Kant's understanding of rational or moral beings as "ends in themselves" continues to serve as a rallying cry for those fighting for recognition of every person's worth regardless of status or group membership. Yet the nuances in Kant's account of dignity underscore the richness and variability of the concept of dignity. Which quality of human beings grounds their dignity? What is the connection (if any) between possessing dignity and behaving in a dignified way? Differences in applying the concept of dignity stem at least partially from divergent answers to these kinds of questions. Thus, the complexity of Kant's ideas about dignity helps to set the stage for dignity's wide-ranging contemporary applications.

[30] Giovanni Pico Della Mirandola, Oration on the Dignity of Man (A. Robert Caponigri trans., 1996).

[31] Bayefsky, note 23, at 824–25.

Dignity and Postwar Human Rights Traditions

Dignity has been a mainstay of the international human rights regime at least since the conclusion of World War II. Dignity in this iteration is known as "human dignity": the value or worth that each person possesses simply by virtue of being a human being, and that supports a right to be treated in accordance with that value or worth. The Universal Declaration of Human Rights, adopted in 1948, proclaims that "[a]ll human beings are born free and equal in dignity and rights."[32] The Geneva Conventions of 1949 prohibit "outrages upon personal dignity, in particular humiliating and degrading treatment."[33] As these instruments suggest, World War II significantly influenced the focus on dignity in the human rights regime. The Nazis treated Jews as subhuman and therefore fit for annihilation. The affirmation of human dignity as a fundamental value served to repudiate the ideas that animated the Nazi regime.

Following World War II, dignity became "commonplace in new international human rights and humanitarian law instruments."[34] As scholars including Erin Daly and Christopher McCrudden have documented, references to dignity appear throughout the international human rights regime, such as in leading treaties on civil and political rights; economic, social, and cultural rights; and racial discrimination.[35] According to former president of the Israeli Supreme Court Aharon Barak, "[h]uman dignity is seen today as one of the general principles of international law."[36]

In addition to being enshrined in international human rights documents, human dignity plays a role in numerous national constitutions.[37] For example, the German Basic Law, enacted in 1949, states that "[h]uman dignity shall be inviolable. To respect and protect it shall be the duty of all state authority."[38] Israel has a "Basic Law" indicating that "[e]very human being is entitled to protection of his life, body and dignity."[39] The South

[32] G.A. Res. 217 (III) A, Universal Declaration of Human Rights, art. 1 (Dec. 10, 1948).

[33] *E.g.*, Geneva Convention Relative to the Treatment of Prisoners of War, art. 3 (Aug. 12, 1949), 6 U.S.T. 3316, 75 U.N.T.S. 135.

[34] McCrudden, note 23, at 668.

[35] Erin Daly, Dignity Rights: Courts, Constitutions, and the Worth of the Human Person 15 (2021); McCrudden, note 23, at 669.

[36] Barak, note 12, at 37.

[37] *Id.* at 110.

[38] Grundgesetz [GG] [Basic Law], art. 1(1), translation at https://www.gesetze-im-internet.de/englisch_gg/englisch_gg.html.

[39] Basic Law: Human Dignity and Liberty (Isr.), https://m.knesset.gov.il/EN/activity/documents/BasicLawsPDF/BasicLawLiberty.pdf.

African Constitution, adopted in 1996, has a provision titled "Human dignity": "Everyone has inherent dignity and the right to have their dignity respected and protected."[40] The Swiss Constitution states that "[h]uman dignity must be respected and protected."[41] The US Constitution does not refer to dignity, but (as discussed later in this chapter) some American judicial rulings have identified dignity as a value informing constitutional interpretation.

Conceptually, dignity in the international human rights regime and in comparative constitutionalism serves multiple roles. First, human dignity is sometimes conceived as the *basis* for human rights—the reason why human beings possess human rights. Second, human dignity may be characterized as a particular *type of right*, in the sense that all people have the right to be treated with dignity. The notion that prisoners of war must be treated with dignity, for example, falls into this category. Third, human dignity may be understood as a constitutional *value*; dignity is an aid to be used in interpreting constitutional provisions, including those identifying certain human rights and delineating their scope. Fourth, dignity may serve as a constraint on individual liberty or rights. Dignity may be invoked to bolster restrictions on forms of behavior deemed to violate dignity or to be "undignified." Examples range from bans on the showing of pornographic films to bans (in France) on "entertainment" consisting of tossing people with dwarfism in front of a public audience.[42]

Accordingly, dignity serves multiple roles in the human rights regime and in contemporary constitutionalism. When it comes to translating broad pronouncements about dignity into specific prescriptions for behavior, the practices of states and other entities differ widely. For instance, courts in Canada, Hungary, and South Africa have upheld restrictions on hate speech on the basis that the relevant speech violates the dignity of its targets; such an approach would likely find less sympathy on the US Supreme Court.[43] The means of protecting women's dignity also diverge in different political and cultural systems.[44]

The diversity in dignity's applications may be understood as either a "plus" or a "minus." On the "plus" side, dignity might be considered a locus of

40 S. Afr. Const. § 10, 1996.
41 Bundesverfassung [BV] [Constitution] Apr. 18, 1999, SR 101, art. 7 (Switz.).
42 *See* McCrudden, note 23, at 702–06.
43 *Id.* at 703–04.
44 *Id.* at 674 n.148.

"overlapping consensus"[45] among those with different philosophical views. In other words, many might agree on the importance of human dignity without necessarily agreeing on why or how dignity should be protected. On the "minus" side, dignity might be viewed as an empty vessel, a mere placeholder for values that are given true content only in much more specific contexts. Indeed, references to dignity might be viewed as counterproductive insofar as they create the illusion of consensus where none exists. To help inform the debate over dignity's conceptual value, I catalog the varieties of dignity and examine certain applications of dignity in American constitutionalism.

The Varieties of Dignity

Having identified clusters of historical traditions from which dignity arose, I turn to a taxonomy of visions of dignity. Though different forms of dignity interact and overlap, categorizing ideas of dignity along various dimensions helps to clarify "dignity talk."

The Object of Dignity

The object of dignity is the entity to which dignity attaches, the dignity-bearer. The object of dignity could be individual human beings, giving rise to the locution "human dignity." The object could be a position or status; in an older usage, "dignity" could refer to a high rank. The object could also be a group: "the dignity of the British people." Or the object could be an abstract noun: "the dignity of labor."

The Basis for Dignity

The basis for dignity is the quality by virtue of which an entity possesses dignity. There are multiple possible bases for *human* dignity, in particular. Human beings might have dignity by virtue of being members of the human

[45] On the idea of "overlapping consensus," see JOHN RAWLS, POLITICAL LIBERALISM 144–45 (2005).

species, or possessing qualities such as the capacity to reason or to act morally, or behaving in a certain way, or standing in a particular relation to God.

The Kind of Treatment that Dignity Demands

Dignity may serve as the basis for people to demand a certain type of treatment from others.[46] Alternatively, the dignity-bearer may be required to behave in a particular manner.

When dignity spurs a call for a form of treatment from others, the type of treatment that dignity demands is often expressed in terms of rights, or in terms of an entitlement to respect. On some views, an entitlement to be treated with dignity is a minimal notion, akin to the right not to be subjected to the most demeaning forms of treatment. The role of dignity in prohibitions on torture speaks to an understanding of dignity as the basis for minimally decent treatment. On other accounts, an entitlement to be treated with dignity has broader implications; for instance, recognition of a person's dignity may spur obligations of equal treatment in political, economic, or social spheres.

Dignity may also be a matter of obligatory behavior on the part of the dignity-bearer. Individuals—or at least those with a certain rank or position—must behave in a "dignified" way or refrain from behaving in a manner that is "beneath their dignity." Dignified behavior is usually contrasted with frivolity or even levity; thus, "dignity" is connected to "weight" or "gravity."

Can Dignity Be Lost?

If dignity attaches to each member of the human species by virtue of membership in the species, then human beings cannot lose their dignity. In the human rights regime, human dignity is inherent: It is the worth that all human beings possess due to their humanity and therefore cannot be lost. One might take the view, however, that harsh treatment strips people of their dignity, suggesting that dignity can be lost.[47] There is no necessary

[46] *See* STEPHEN DARWALL, THE SECOND-PERSON STANDPOINT 120–21 (2006).
[47] COLIN BIRD, HUMAN DIGNITY AND POLITICAL CRITICISM 238 (2021).

contradiction here, as the word "dignity" may be used in different ways. Some might say "human beings should not be treated in a manner that does not accord with their inherent human dignity"; others might say "human beings should not be treated in a manner that leaves people bereft of their dignity." Chapter 2 discusses in greater depth the stakes of choosing between these ways of speaking about dignity.

Another possibility is that people can lose their dignity through their own behavior. For example, if dignity is understood in terms of a certain form of conduct, then one may lose dignity by behaving in a frivolous way and making a spectacle of oneself.

The Relationship between Dignity and Equality

Dignity is often invoked alongside equality. This connection is not self-evident. Indeed, for much of its history, dignity was associated with hierarchy and attached to those with a high societal status. The Latin term *dignitas*, "signifying a certain standing or rank in the community,"[48] scarcely rings of egalitarianism. According to Jeremy Waldron, the modern era witnessed the democratization of dignity, from a feature of high-status individuals to one shared by everyone.[49] The reimagining of dignity, on this account, signifies a change in fundamental values in the modern age. Yet some modern versions of dignity retain inegalitarian features. People are still often expected to behave with the dignity that befits their societal roles and to treat those with high status in distinctive ways.

To summarize, the dimensions of dignity just mentioned—such as its object, basis, and implications for treatment and conduct—help to distinguish among different visions of dignity. The variation in understandings of dignity might be viewed as evidence of the concept's lack of utility. But one could draw similar distinctions with respect to other theoretical and legal concepts, such as autonomy, privacy, and equality. Complexity is not equivalent to incoherence.

[48] Griffin, note 1, at 50.
[49] Waldron, note 25, at 34.

Dignity and Conflict over Values in American Constitutional Debates

Thus far, the focus has been on mapping varieties of dignity in several social and political contexts. The next part of the chapter turns to law and the role of dignity in legal debates. The emphasis will be on certain legal debates in the United States, as a prelude to discussions of the relationship between dignity and judicial authority in American courts.

The word "dignity" does not appear in the US Constitution. In this respect, American constitutionalism stands in sharp contrast to several constitutional regimes elsewhere in the world, where dignity plays a foundational role. Dignity appears in other areas of American law—including the "dignitary torts" discussed in Chapter 4—but it does not, by and large, play a leading role in legal doctrines in the United States. Nevertheless, dignity is a value that has entered into American legal debates in constitutional and other settings, either explicitly or implicitly. Actors in the legal system reference dignity to air deep-seated views about values they deem critical.

In illustrating dignity's function as a locus for the expression of disputes over social values in law, I concentrate in this chapter on American constitutional interpretation. Later chapters will explore other settings in which dignity arises, such as tort law (Chapter 4) and remedies (Chapter 5). The claim is not that dignity plays a central role in US constitutional interpretation, but that the intersection between dignity and constitutional law illuminates meaningful features of prominent American constitutional debates.

US Supreme Court justices have invoked dignity or related concepts in interpreting certain constitutional provisions.[50] In the equal protection context, *Brown v. Board of Education* is frequently understood to reflect concern with the dignity of Black schoolchildren. The *Brown* opinion famously referred to these children's "feeling of inferiority as to their status in the community" when attending segregated schools.[51] These feelings stemmed, the *Brown* Court explained, from the demeaning social meaning

[50] Leslie Meltzer Henry, *The Jurisprudence of Dignity*, 160 U. PA. L. REV. 169, 172–73 & nn.18–26 (2011); Vicki C. Jackson, *Constitutional Dialogue and Human Dignity: States and Transnational Constitutional Discourse*, 65 MONT. L. REV. 15, 16–17 & n.7 (2004); Reva B. Siegel, *Dignity and the Politics of Protection: Abortion Restrictions under* Casey/Carhart, 117 YALE L.J. 1694, 1736 (2008).

[51] 347 U.S. 483, 494 (1954).

of segregation: "the policy of separating the races is usually interpreted as denoting the inferiority" of Black individuals.[52]

The Supreme Court's jurisprudence on same-sex relations over the past twenty years has also featured prominent references to dignity and to associated concepts such as stigma and humiliation. In *Lawrence v. Texas*, the Supreme Court held unconstitutional a law that criminalized forms of same-sex conduct, reasoning that the law "demean[ed] th[e] existence" of same-sex couples.[53] The Court later referred to the same law as causing "[d]ignitary wounds."[54] In *United States v. Windsor*, the Supreme Court ruled unconstitutional a federal law restricting the federal definition of marriage to a union between a man and a woman, citing "injury and indignity" that qualified as "deprivation of an essential part of the liberty protected by the Fifth Amendment."[55] In *Obergefell v. Hodges*, in declaring there was a constitutional right to same-sex marriage, the Court explained that plaintiffs seeking to have their same-sex marriages recognized "ask for equal dignity in the eyes of the law."[56]

The Supreme Court has invoked dignity outside the discrimination context as well. The Eighth Amendment, the Court has indicated, "prohibits cruel and unusual punishments" and "reaffirms the duty of the government to respect the dignity of all persons."[57] The Fourth Amendment, according to the Court, "guarantees the privacy, dignity, and security of persons against certain arbitrary and invasive acts by officers of the Government."[58] In addressing the relationship between the First Amendment and state-law protections from defamation, the Court observed that "the individual's right to the protection of his own good name reflects no more than our basic concept of the essential dignity and worth of every human being."[59]

Concern for dignity in the US Supreme Court is often thought to emanate from particular justices—notably the now-retired Justice Kennedy. His appeals to dignity, moreover, have been critiqued as vague and

[52] *Id.* (internal quotation marks omitted). For an account of *Brown* that disentangles humiliation and its psychological consequences, see Deborah Hellman, *Equal Protection in the Key of Respect*, 123 Yale L.J. 3036, 3043–3046 (2014).

[53] Lawrence v. Texas, 539 U.S. 558, 578 (2003).

[54] Obergefell v. Hodges, 576 U.S. 644, 678 (2015).

[55] United States v. Windsor, 570 U.S. 744, 768 (2013).

[56] *Obergefell*, 576 U.S. at 681.

[57] Moore v. Texas, 581 U.S. 1, 12 (2017) (internal quotation marks omitted).

[58] Ontario v. Quon, 560 U.S. 746, 755–56 (2010) (internal quotation marks omitted). For discussion of dignity and the Fourth Amendment, see Josh Bowers, *Probable Cause, Constitutional Reasonableness, and the Unrecognized Point of a "Pointless Indignity,"* 66 Stan. L. Rev. 987 (2014).

[59] Gertz v. Robert Welch, Inc., 418 U.S. 323, 341 (1974) (internal quotation marks omitted).

unprincipled.[60] More broadly, references to dignity are sometimes associated with justices attached more to "living constitutionalist" than "formalist" modes of constitutional interpretation such as originalism and textualism. For example, Justice William J. Brennan, known for his nonformalist approach to constitutional interpretation, declared in 1985 that the American Constitution was "a sublime oration on the dignity of man, a bold commitment by a people to the ideal of libertarian dignity protected through law."[61] Chief Justice Earl Warren explained that "[t]he basic concept underlying the Eighth Amendment is nothing less than the dignity of man."[62] For originalist or textualist interpreters, by contrast, the absence of a textual "hook" for dignity, as well as dignity's apparent elasticity, may render the concept a dubious resource in constitutional interpretation.[63]

Yet the language of dignity and related concepts is not the preserve solely of "purposivist" or "living constitutionalist" justices. Invocations of dignity in US constitutional law include Justice Scalia's point that the Fourth Amendment "knock-and-announce rule" protects "privacy and dignity;"[64] Chief Justice Roberts' endorsement of the view that "[o]ne of the principal reasons race is treated as a forbidden classification is that it demeans the dignity and worth of a person to be judged by ancestry instead of by his or her own merit and essential qualities;"[65] and Justice Thomas's statement that treating people "equally before the law without regard to our race" is necessary to "see each other for what we truly are: individuals with unique thoughts, perspectives, and goals, but with equal dignity and equal rights under the law."[66] Indeed, some judicial resistance to the constitutional protection of same-sex relationships invokes the language of disrespect. Justice Alito wrote in dissent in *Obergefell*, the case holding that there was a constitutional right to same-sex marriage: "By imposing its own views on the entire

[60] *See, e.g.*, Jeffrey Rosen, *The Dangers of a Constitutional 'Right to Dignity,'* The Atlantic (Apr. 29, 2015), https://www.theatlantic.com/politics/archive/2015/04/the-dangerous-doctrine-of-dignity/391796. For a summary of critiques of Justice Kennedy's judicial philosophy, see Mitchell N. Berman & David Peters, *Kennedy's Legacy: A Principled Justice*, 46 Hastings Const. L.Q. 311, 315–17 (2019).

[61] Stephen J. Wermiel, *Law and Human Dignity: The Judicial Soul of Justice Brennan*, 7 Wm. & Mary Bill of Rts. J. 223, 223 (1998)(internal quotation marks omitted).

[62] Trop v. Dulles, 356 U.S. 86, 100 (1958) (plurality opinion).

[63] *See, e.g.*, Obergefell v. Hodges, 576 U.S. 644, 694 (2015) (Roberts, C.J., dissenting) ("There is, after all, no 'Companionship and Understanding' or 'Nobility and Dignity' Clause in the Constitution.").

[64] Hudson v. Michigan, 547 U.S. 586, 594 (2006).

[65] Students for Fair Admissions v. President & Fellows of Harvard College, 600 U.S. 181, 220 (2023) (quoting Rice v. Cayetano, 528 U.S. 495, 517 (2000)) [hereinafter *SFFA*].

[66] *Id.* at 277 (Thomas, J., concurring).

country, the majority facilitates the marginalization of the many Americans who have traditional ideas."[67]

Another, different source of references to dignity in Supreme Court jurisprudence is the law of sovereign immunity. There, dignity is marshalled to support restrictions on private suits against sovereign states. The Court has stated, for example, that "[t]he generation that designed and adopted our federal system considered immunity from private suits central to sovereign dignity,"[68] and that "[t]he preeminent purpose of state sovereign immunity is to accord States the dignity that is consistent with their status as sovereign entities."[69] Several opinions endorsing the sovereign dignity of states have been written or joined not only by Justice Kennedy but also by justices associated with the Supreme Court's "formalist" wing (including Justices Scalia,[70] Thomas,[71] Gorsuch,[72] and Barrett[73]). Justice Thomas stated in a 2022 sovereign immunity dissent that a certain cause of action allowing suit against states in their own courts was "uniquely offensive to the States' dignity," and he criticized "attempts by this Court to deny States the dignity owed to them in our system of dual federalism."[74]

The dignity at stake in the Supreme Court's state sovereign immunity jurisprudence attaches to states rather than to human beings and therefore is not the same as "human dignity." Indeed, some applications of state sovereign dignity are controversial. For example, Judith Resnik and Julie Chi-Hye Suk have questioned the invocation of dignity to block suit against states.[75] Nonetheless, Resnik and Suk seek to reinterpret rather than to eliminate respect for sovereignty—so that the judicial practice of adjudicating claims against sovereign states becomes a way to affirm "the status of democratic sovereigns."[76] At any rate, the dignity of sovereign states very much remains part of the Supreme Court's sovereign immunity jurisprudence.

The discussion thus far has highlighted several doctrinal applications of dignity in American constitutional law. I turn now to hot-button areas where

[67] *Obergefell*, 576 U.S. at 742 (Alito, J., dissenting).
[68] Alden v. Maine, 527 U.S. 706, 715 (1999).
[69] Fed. Mar. Comm'n v. S.C. State Ports Auth., 535 U.S. 743, 760 (2002).
[70] *See id.*
[71] *See* Franchise Tax Bd. of Cal. v. Hyatt, 587 U.S. 230, 245 (2019).
[72] *See id.*
[73] *See* Torres v. Tex. Dep't of Pub. Safety, 597 U.S. 580, 602 (2022) (Thomas, J., dissenting, joined by Justices Alito, Gorsuch, and Barrett).
[74] *Id.* at 616, 628.
[75] Judith Resnik & Julie Chi-hye Suk, *Adding Insult to Injury: Questioning the Role of Dignity in Conceptions of Sovereignty*, 55 Stan. L. Rev. 1921, 1927–28 (2003).
[76] *Id.* at 1928.

contestation over the meaning and implications of dignity reflects disagreement about underlying values in constitutional law. Specifically, I focus on abortion, affirmative action, and the relationship between antidiscrimination law and religious liberty or free speech. These issues highlight the different and even opposing uses to which dignity is put.

Abortion

Dignity and related concepts have figured into the Supreme Court's abortion jurisprudence, sometimes overtly but more often lurking beneath the surface. Notably, dignity appears on multiple "sides" of the abortion debate. As Reva Siegel has explained, one version of dignity in the abortion context is "dignity as life."[77] Concurring in the Supreme Court's 2022 *Dobbs* decision overruling *Roe v. Wade*, Justice Kavanaugh observed that "many pro-life advocates forcefully argue that a fetus is a human life. They contend that all human life should be protected as a matter of human dignity and fundamental morality."[78] The Supreme Court has used dignity to refer to fetal life in opinions prior to *Dobbs* as well. In the 2007 case *Gonzales v. Carhart*, for example, the Supreme Court upheld a federal statute regulating abortion procedures—the Partial-Birth Abortion Ban Act of 2003—against constitutional challenge.[79] The Court (per Justice Kennedy) explained that "[t]he Act expresses respect for the dignity of human life."[80]

In terms of the taxonomy laid out earlier in this chapter, "dignity as life" in the abortion setting attaches to human beings, or potential human beings, by virtue of their humanity or potential humanity. Dignity cannot be lost, and it demands forms of treatment that accord respect to fetuses; hence, dignity is at odds with abortion procedures. A view of dignity as fetal life also accords with—and is frequently, though not necessarily, associated with—an understanding that human life has dignity by virtue of the human relationship with God.

A different setting in which dignity is invoked in the abortion context involves the dignity of women forced to carry a pregnancy to term. In the 1992 case *Planned Parenthood v. Casey*, in which the Supreme Court laid out

[77] Siegel, note 50, at 1737–38.
[78] Dobbs v. Jackson Women's Health Org., 597 U.S. 215, 337 (2022) (Kavanaugh, J., concurring).
[79] Gonzales v. Carhart, 550 U.S. 124, 132 (2007).
[80] *Id.* at 157.

the "undue burden" framework for evaluating state regulations of abortion, the Court characterized intimate choices such as whether to bear a child as "central to personal dignity and autonomy."[81] Siegel describes these visions of dignity in terms of "dignity as autonomy" and "dignity as equality."[82] Justice Stevens's partial concurrence in *Casey* reiterated themes of dignity as autonomy—"[t]he authority to make such traumatic and yet empowering decisions" as whether to abort a pregnancy "is an element of basic human dignity"—and dignity as equality: "Part of the constitutional liberty to choose is the equal dignity to which each of us is entitled."[83]

In their joint dissent from the Supreme Court's decision in *Dobbs*, Justices Breyer, Sotomayor, and Kagan discussed women's autonomy and equality in a dignitary register. They decried the "profound loss of autonomy and dignity that coerced pregnancy and birth always impose," and they argued that "[w]hen *Roe* and *Casey* disappear, the loss of power, control, and dignity will be immense."[84] Further, the dissenters wrote, "the expectation of reproductive control is integral to many women's identity and their place in the Nation. That expectation helps define a woman as an equal citizen, with all the rights, privileges, and obligations that status entails. It reflects that she is an autonomous person, and that society and the law recognize her as such."[85] The dissenters thus contended that *Roe* and *Casey* not only had an important practical impact but also served an expressive purpose: They reflected recognition of women's equal status and ability to control their lives.[86] Accordingly, the Court's decision to overrule *Roe* and *Casey*—in the dissenters' view—sent the message that women were not being treated as equal participants in society.

In terms of the taxonomy discussed earlier, the form of dignity at issue in the pro-choice discourse of the *Dobbs* dissent is closely tied to equality and autonomy. The object of dignity is human beings, particularly women as equals of men. Dignity demands a certain form of treatment, in the shape of constitutional principles that recognize women's equality and autonomy in reproductive decision-making.

[81] Planned Parenthood of Se. Pa. v. Casey, 505 U.S. 833, 851 (1992). The relevant portion of the plurality opinion was joined by a majority of justices.

[82] Siegel, note 50, at 1745; *see* Henry, note 50, at 209–10.

[83] *Casey*, 505 U.S. at 916, 920 (Stevens, J., concurring in part and dissenting in part).

[84] Dobbs v. Jackson Women's Health Org., 597 U.S. 215, 398, 409 (2022) (Breyer, Sotomayor & Kagan, JJ., dissenting).

[85] *Id.* at 408–09 (internal quotation marks, citations, and alteration omitted).

[86] *See* Rachel Bayefsky, *Tangibility and Tainted Reliance in* Dobbs, 136 Harv. L. Rev. F. 384, 400 (2023).

Dignity has appeared, then, on what are often considered opposing poles of the abortion debate: the dignity of the fetus versus the dignity of the pregnant individual. Dignity functions as a vehicle through which participants in political and legal debates express views about core societal values. Referring to the dignity of the fetus is a way to underscore that the fetus is not the same as any other bodily tissue and cannot be treated as a thing to be discarded. Referring to the dignity of pregnant women is a way to emphasize that women are fully capable of weighing for themselves the considerations bearing on the decision whether to terminate a pregnancy. As legal controversies surrounding abortion persist in the aftermath of the Supreme Court's decision in *Dobbs*, the implications of dignity will continue to bear on those debates.

Given that dignity is invoked on multiple sides of abortion disputes, one might wonder what dignity has to offer to the law. Does dignity simply cancel itself out? In my view, the answer is "no." Dignity offers a language that opposing parties can both use to express strongly held positions. Dignity-discourse might therefore help to focus debate—here, on the question of how dignity can best be protected in the abortion context. This does not mean that consensus or compromise is forthcoming, but dignity could provide a basis for a more manageable debate.

In particular, dignity offers a means of acknowledging the moral seriousness of parties' differing positions. Perhaps it is not inherently contradictory to recognize both the dignity of fetal life (or potential life) and the dignity of women. On this understanding, characterizing interests in dignitary terms could demonstrate a degree of respect for the cultural and moral understandings that inform (even if they do not determine) divergent legal positions. As one practical suggestion, the law could permit abortion while regulating the disposition of fetal remains. The question of how judges should rule on the substance of abortion restrictions extends beyond the scope of the current discussion. Overall, however, dignity-talk underscores the connection between constitutional law and the societal controversies that form the backdrop to doctrinal debates.

Affirmative Action

Another hotly disputed topic that features discussion of dignity is affirmative action. As the discussion of *Brown v. Board of Education* above suggests, dignity appears in antidiscrimination law and policy. The Supreme Court has noted that "the stigmatizing injury often caused by racial discrimination" is "one of the most serious consequences of discriminatory government action."[87] Discriminatory barriers in employment, education, family life, and elsewhere are plausibly conceived as attacks on the dignity of those subject to the barriers.

To some, affirmative action programs are ways to promote dignity for members of historically oppressed social groups. Affirmative action may be seen as a means to rectify historical injustices that assaulted the dignity of members of marginalized groups,[88] or as a means of correcting for continuing injustices, including "everyday indignities."[89] An example of this perspective comes from Justice Ketanji Brown Jackson's dissent in the Supreme Court's 2023 decision *Students for Fair Admissions*, which held that universities may not make admissions decisions based on race. Justice Jackson stated: "To demand that colleges ignore race in today's admissions practices—and thus disregard the fact that racial disparities may have mattered for where some applicants find themselves today—is . . . an affront to the dignity of those students for whom race matters."[90] Another example comes from Justice Sotomayor's dissent from a 2014 Supreme Court case upholding a voter initiative barring the use of race-based preferences in the admissions process for state universities: "Race matters because of the slights, the snickers, the silent judgments that reinforce that most crippling of thoughts: 'I do not belong here.'"[91] Affirming the dignity of minorities, on this account, requires recognizing the ways in which race has affected their lives, often in stigmatizing ways, and trying to alleviate these negative consequences.

Dignity is also invoked by opponents of affirmative action. In *Students for Fair Admissions*, Chief Justice Roberts, writing for the majority, stated (as earlier noted): "One of the principal reasons race is treated as a forbidden classification is that it demeans the dignity and worth of a person to be judged by ancestry."[92] The majority also critiqued "stereotypes that treat

[87] Allen v. Wright, 468 U.S. 737, 755 (1984).

[88] *See* Adarand Constructors, Inc. v. Pena, 515 U.S. 200, 272 (1995) (Ginsburg, J., dissenting).

[89] For discussion of "everyday indignities," see Terry Smith, *Everyday Indignities: Race, Retaliation, and the Promise of Title VII*, 34 Colum. Hum. Rts. L. Rev. 529 (2003).

[90] *SFFA*, 600 U.S. 181, 397 (2023) (Jackson, J., dissenting).

[91] Schuette v. Coal. to Defend Affirmative Action, Integration & Immigrant Rts. & Fight for Equal. by Any Means Necessary (BAMN), 572 U.S. 291, 381 (2014) (Sotomayor, J., dissenting).

[92] *SFFA*, 600 U.S. at 220 (quoting Rice v. Cayetano, 528 U.S. 495, 517 (2000)). For discussion of the divergent social meanings attached to race-related policies, see Benjamin Eidelson, *Respect, Individualism, and Colorblindness*, 129 Yale L.J. 1600, 1649–69 (2020).

individuals as the product of their race."[93] Justice Thomas has written that affirmative action programs "stamp minorities with a badge of inferiority."[94] Justice O'Connor stated that "[c]lassifications based on race carry a danger of stigmatic harm."[95] On these views, affirmative action is stigmatizing to its beneficiaries because it suggests they cannot succeed otherwise. In this discourse, there are also echoes of the idea that dignity requires people to be treated as ends, not mere means: Minority students should not be tools in the hands of university administrators seeking to create a more "balanced" class but should instead be judged in accordance with their own characteristics.

The divergent references to dignity and stigma in affirmative action debates highlight the variety of interests that dignity protects and the ways in which dignity serves as a vehicle for the expression of deeply rooted values. Despite the heated nature of these debates, the ideas of dignity to which participants refer may be mutually intelligible. As educational and other institutions absorb the Supreme Court's 2023 decision barring race-conscious university admissions policies, dignity might provide a basis for mediation among different positions.

To elaborate: To the extent an institution is legally permitted to pursue diversity in its student body, it could seek to advance this goal in a manner that produces less stigma. For example, universities could try to create a welcoming environment on campus in ways that extend beyond the mere fact of admission. This would help reduce the risk of treating minority students just as means to the end of creating a class that looks more diverse. For similar reasons, admissions officers engaged in recruiting, while speaking about the opportunities the university has to offer, could emphasize educational or career benefits to students rather than the contribution that students would make to the diversity of the institution. Further, *SFFA* left open the possibility that universities could "consider[] an applicant's discussion of how race affected his or her life, be it through discrimination, inspiration, or otherwise."[96] Universities might emphasize in admission essay prompts that they are not requiring students to write about trauma; rather, students are free to write about their experiences—related to race or otherwise—in a way that emphasizes positive aspects of their background and affiliations.

[93] *SFFA*, 600 U.S. at 221 (quoting Miller v. Johnson, 515 U.S. 900, 912 (1995)).
[94] Adarand Constructors, Inc. v. Pena, 515 U.S. 200, 241 (1995) (Thomas, J., concurring in part).
[95] City of Richmond v. J.A. Croson Co., 488 U.S. 469, 493 (1989) (plurality opinion of O'Connor, J.).
[96] *SFFA*, 600 U.S. at 230.

Any given approach is likely to be controversial in terms of the ultimate impact on dignity. The general point is that dignity, though it functions as a locus of social contestation in affirmative action debates, might inform policies that accommodate to some degree competing intuitions about stigma and status-based harm. As schools and employers consider whether and how to pursue diversity in light of *SFFA*, dignitary dynamics should be among the relevant considerations.

Antidiscrimination Law and Religious Liberty/Free Speech

A third area that illustrates contestation over the meaning and implications of dignity in constitutional law concerns the relationship between antidiscrimination law, on the one hand, and religious liberty or free speech protections, on the other. Many of the Supreme Court's decisions expanding equality for same-sex couples, as detailed earlier in this chapter, have drawn on dignity. The Court justified constitutional protections for same-sex relations and marriage on the basis that the challenged laws were demeaning and stigmatizing.[97] Dignity, on this account, is closely tied to equality; it is a feature of all human beings—or at least of all members of the American polity—that demands the elimination of certain disrespectful forms of treatment. At the same time, judicial decisions expanding equality rights have been criticized on the ground that they ostracize individuals with conservative cultural commitments. Justice Alito's dissent in *Obergefell*, charging the majority with (as earlier noted) "facilitat[ing] the marginalization of the many Americans who have traditional ideas,"[98] provides an example.

In recent years, the Supreme Court has attempted to navigate among competing dignitary claims made by LGBTQ individuals and those with traditional, often religiously based, commitments. These conflicts often arise in the context of state antidiscrimination laws prohibiting discrimination based on sexual orientation in commercial settings. For example, in the 2018 case *Masterpiece Cakeshop v. Colorado Civil Rights Commission*, a Colorado baker told a same-sex couple he would not bake them a wedding cake because of his religious opposition to same-sex marriage.[99] The Colorado Civil

[97] *See* Obergefell v. Hodges, 576 U.S. 644, 660 (2015); Lawrence v. Texas, 539 U.S. 558, 567 (2003).
[98] *Obergefell*, 576 U.S. at 742 (Alito, J., dissenting).
[99] 584 U.S. 617, 621 (2018).

Rights Commission ruled that the baker had violated a state law prohibiting discrimination based on sexual orientation. The Supreme Court held that the Commission's actions violated the Free Exercise Clause, citing the Commission's "clear and impermissible hostility toward the sincere religious beliefs that motivated [the baker's] objection."[100]

The Supreme Court appealed in *Masterpiece* to the dignitary interests of both the same-sex couple and the baker. "Our society," the Court explained, "has come to the recognition that gay persons and gay couples cannot be treated as social outcasts or as inferior in dignity and worth."[101] "[N]onetheless," the baker "was entitled to the neutral and respectful consideration of his claims."[102] The baker had not—according to the Supreme Court—received such respectful consideration, in light of remarks that commissioners had made demonstrating "hostility" to religion. Those "official expressions of hostility to religion . . . were inconsistent with what the Free Exercise Clause requires," and so the Commission's order had to be set aside.[103]

The *Masterpiece* case reflects an attempt to harness dignity to support compromise, but it also suggests enduring contestation over dignity's meaning. On the one hand, Justice Kennedy's opinion sought to respect both same-sex couples and those with traditional religious beliefs. The decision stressed that disputes like those presented in *Masterpiece* "must be resolved with tolerance, without undue disrespect to sincere religious beliefs, and without subjecting gay persons to indignities when they seek goods and services in an open market."[104] Perhaps, then, dignity's malleability could play a beneficial role: Those on different sides of conflicts between equality and religious liberty could acknowledge troubling features of disrespectful treatment directed at the "other side." Paying attention to dignity might facilitate such acknowledgment because it puts the focus on "human" elements of people's experiences: real-world denigration, stigma, insult.

Yet *Masterpiece Cakeshop* provides a reminder of contestation as much as it gestures toward possible compromise. Some might balk at creating a dignitary equivalence between the experiences of same-sex couples denied service and the experiences of religious people compelled to provide services or

[100] *Id.* at 634.
[101] *Id.* at 631.
[102] *Id.* at 634.
[103] *Id.* at 639.
[104] *Id.* at 640.

subjected to negative comments about their beliefs. *Masterpiece* underscores the challenges involved in deciding which actions are, in fact, disrespectful. For example, is it disrespectful for a baker to decline to serve a gay couple while referring the couple to another service provider? Is it disrespectful for a government official to highlight negative uses to which religious beliefs have been put in the past—a key part of the evidence of "hostility" adduced by the Court in *Masterpiece*?[105] These questions about the nature of dignity and respect have an irreducibly normative dimension. Debates over the relationship between religious liberty and equality claims show how invocations of dignity can compound conflict over social values in addition to mediating such conflict.

In a subsequent case—the 2023 decision *303 Creative v. Elenis*—the Supreme Court held that Colorado could not require a website designer who objected to same-sex marriage to create wedding websites for same-sex couples. The Court recognized that public accommodations laws, which prevent commercial establishments from discriminating, "vindicate the deprivation of personal dignity that surely accompanies denials of equal access to public establishments."[106] Yet the Court held that First Amendment compelled speech doctrine prevented the State of Colorado from requiring the website designer to "utter what is not in her mind about a question of political and religious significance."[107] Here, the Court permitted the expressive interests of the website designer to trump the dignitary interests of same-sex couples.

As courts navigate the intersection of antidiscrimination law, on the one hand, and religious liberty or freedom of expression, on the other, they will continue to face competing dignitary claims. The Court may not be able to find a "neutral" point from which to adjudicate these debates. The diverging appeals to dignity, however, speak to the concept's power in illuminating the stakes of American constitutional debates.

To conclude, this chapter has introduced the concept of dignity by explaining dignity's roots, categorizing different understandings of dignity, and highlighting the role of dignity in salient constitutional disputes. The aim has been to capture the variety of meanings that dignity possesses while

[105] *See Masterpiece Cakeshop*, 584 U.S. at 635–36. For a skeptical look at the evidence of religious animus in *Masterpiece*, see Leslie Kendrick & Micah Schwartzman, *The Etiquette of Animus*, 132 Harv. L. Rev. 133, 138–45 (2018).

[106] 303 Creative LLC v. Elenis, 600 U.S. 570, 590 (2023) (quoting Heart of Atlanta Motel v. United States, 379 U.S. 241, 250 (1964)).

[107] *Id.* at 596 (internal quotation marks and alterations omitted).

underscoring a critical function that dignity assumes in legal argument: a vehicle for both the expression and management of social disagreement in law. That function does not render dignity an incoherent muddle. Like other concepts, such as autonomy or equality, dignity can assume different meanings and can be invoked by multiple disputants in political or legal debates. In invoking dignity, participants in these debates are giving voice to divergent normative perspectives. We should not expect the underlying normative disagreement to disappear. Yet appeals to dignity could facilitate a more focused collision of perspectives, centered on the question of which practices best further dignitary goals, and for whom.

Despite the multifaceted and contested nature of dignity, it is useful to devise an understanding of dignity that can serve theoretical and legal purposes. Chapter 2 therefore proposes a working account of dignity to guide the book's exploration of the relationship between dignity and judicial authority. In doing so, I build on this chapter's discussion of dignity's historical roots and conceptual dimensions, with the goal of offering a view of dignity that captures an important subset of dignity's historical and theoretical manifestations.

2

Relational Dignity

This chapter provides a working account of dignity to guide reflection about the relationship between dignity and judicial institutions. The account of dignity offered here is not the only possible one. However, the vision of dignity described here is meant to keep faith with significant features of dignity's historical roots and to be compatible with important contemporary social understandings of what it means to treat people with dignity.

The account of dignity offered here is called "relational dignity." By way of brief summary, relational dignity revolves around protection of the social self. To treat people with dignity is to create or sustain the conditions that enable certain forms of social interaction. These forms of social interaction involve respect for status, the absence of domination, and the ability to exercise control over one's self-presentation to others.

Relational dignity is more socially situated than an alternative understanding of dignity that is associated with human rights and Kantian traditions. That understanding treats dignity as the inherent worth attaching to every human being by virtue of being human. Relational dignity does not reject the inherent worth of persons, but it focuses centrally on social relations characterized by certain forms of respectful interaction.

This chapter begins by comparing relational dignity to the Kantian view of dignity as inherent worth, highlighting divergences between these accounts. Next, the chapter explicates the features of social relations that typify a world instantiating relational dignity—namely (as noted) respect for status, absence of domination, and control over self-presentation. Each of these features contributes to a grounded and concrete understanding of dignity. As part of this discussion, I consider the relationship between dignity, objectivity, and social norms: Does the individual or society decide whether dignity is violated? I also address the degree of normative weight attaching to dignity, that is, the extent to which the moral pull of dignity can be overcome by other values. The chapter closes by explaining how relational dignity fits into the typology of dignity provided in Chapter 1—for example, the object and basis of dignity, and the kind of treatment that dignity demands.

Dignity and Judicial Authority. Rachel Bayefsky, Oxford University Press. © Rachel Bayefsky 2024.
DOI: 10.1093/oso/9780197750322.003.0002

Human Dignity and Inherent Worth

A common understanding of dignity—which will serve as a useful foil to relational dignity—is dignity as the inherent worth that each person possesses in equal measure and that grounds a claim to be treated with respect. For example, Erin Daly and James R. May write in a casebook on Dignity Law that "[h]uman dignity encapsulates the notion that every person has inherent equal worth," and it consists of three elements: "each person's humanity means something and has worth"; "each person's worth is equal to every other person's"; and "dignity inheres in the human person; it is not defined or granted by law and cannot be taken away by law."[1] From human dignity, Daly and May explain, flow certain moral and legal rights. "[D]ignity supports a full spectrum of human rights"; "there is a legal right to have one's dignity respected and protected"; and "violations of the right to dignity can be vindicated in court."[2]

The view of dignity as inherent worth—call it the "inherent worth" account—is often traced to Kant.[3] Though Kant's views on dignity were multifaceted (as discussed in Chapter 1), the "Kantian" account of dignity as each person's inherent value has provided powerful moral inspiration for the international human rights regime. That regime has held out hope, even if not yet actualized, for the universal recognition of people's worth and the rejection of conduct that denies their worth, including genocide, slavery, and apartheid.

Why, then, not simply adopt the "inherent worth" vision of dignity? The "inherent worth" view of dignity is not *wrong*. The question is simply what an account of dignity is meant to be used for. The principal aim in this book is to address a set of questions about the relationship between dignity and judicial authority. Under what circumstances may judges adjudicate disputes implicating dignity, and how should they do so? To what extent should judges recognize dignitary harm as legally relevant, and what kind of remedies may judges issue for such harm?

Responding to these types of questions benefits from an account of dignity that goes beyond the inherent-worth view. Such an account must be more specific and granular, and less abstract. If dignity refers to the inherent

[1] Erin Daly & James R. May, Dignity Law: Global Recognition, Cases, and Perspectives xi (2020).

[2] *Id.*

[3] *See, e.g.*, Jeremy Waldron, Dignity, Rank, and Rights 24 (2012).

worth that each human being possesses and that justifies human rights, then analysis of dignity's legal consequences risks collapsing into a more general discussion of fundamental rights and their adjudication. One might take the view, for example, that dignity-as-worth provides the philosophical grounding for equality rights. But after dignity plays a justifying role, legal decision-making concerning these rights need not appeal to dignity. In other words, dignity functions solely as conceptual grounding for a theory of rights and does not play a more active role in legal interpretation or adjudication. This is not a necessary result of adopting an inherent-worth view, but it is a risk.

The goal here is to provide a fuller elaboration of the contents of dignity in real-world circumstances. For this purpose, dignity ought to be understood in terms of a distinctive social experience, not simply as a basis for a commonly invoked set of rights. Other scholars have shared the aim of providing a more socially situated view of dignity. Colin Bird, for example, rejects what he calls "traditional" accounts of human dignity, according to which human agents have an inherent worth that grounds an obligation to be treated with respect.[4] Bird's "revisionist" alternative conceives of dignity as "a transient, vulnerable, and socially extended quality whose emergence depends on the character of concrete, organized, interaction under actually existing regimes."[5] For Bird, human dignity is a quality of social life that is present when people are treated in a certain way and is absent when people are not so treated. Jeremy Waldron also rejects an understanding of dignity as "worth": "although *value beyond price* and *the intrinsic nonnegotiable nonfungible worth that inheres in every human being in virtue of his or her moral capacity* are wonderful and important ideas, there is no particular reason to use our term 'dignity' to convey them."[6] According to Waldron, dignity is more fruitfully understood to refer to the high yet equal rank that people possess in modern society.[7]

Rejecting the "inherent worth" view of dignity does not mean, of course, denying the proposition that people do in fact have inherent worth. Such a denial would be morally repugnant. The point is merely to sound a note of skepticism as to whether dignity is identical to, or reducible to, people's

4 Colin Bird, Human Dignity and Political Criticism 69 (2021).

5 *Id.* at 113.

6 Waldron, note 3, at 24.

7 *Id.* at 34.

inherent worth. Treating dignity as inherent worth risks draining dignity of the content that enables it to capture a distinctive set of social experiences.

In addition to the concern about abstraction, another reason to depart from the "inherent worth" account of dignity has to do with the weight attached to dignity in a moral or legal calculus. According to the "inherent worth" account, dignity is a critical moral value that others have a strong obligation to protect. In fact, the obligation to respect dignity may be an indefeasible one, insofar as dignity is associated with Kantian deontology—specifically, with the view that persons must be treated as ends in themselves rather than as mere means. The "ends, not mere means" injunction is at odds with the practice of weighing dignity against other values, such as utility or efficiency. More broadly, it seems immoral or at least counterintuitive to say "this policy will deny the inherent worth of X number of people, but we should pursue it anyway."

Elevating dignity to the status of an indefeasible or nearly indefeasible value, however, weakens the concept's ability to play a significant role in legal decision-making. Social and political life involves competing values and priorities. Legal actors are tasked with ordering a diverse society inhabited by individuals with varying interests. In tackling issues ranging from the environment to taxation to foreign policy, legal actors are asked to make complex judgments, and multiple options may carry a degree of normative weight. If dignity carries enormous or absolute weight, its utility in legal and political debate will be diminished.

In illustrating these points, I will focus on judicial decision-making. The idea that judges, as compared to other legal actors, should navigate among competing principles may elicit particular skepticism. One might argue that courts should simply apply the law enacted by other legal institutions, which themselves have already weighed various factors. In fact, US Supreme Court justices spar over whether federal judges should engage in "interest balancing" in constitutional interpretation.[8] At the moment, though, numerous doctrinal tests—in constitutional law and other areas—call for weighing competing considerations. Examples include rules of evidence permitting judges to balance probativeness and prejudice;[9] procedural rules allowing

[8] *Compare, e.g.*, N.Y. State Rifle & Pistol Ass'n, Inc. v. Bruen, 597 U.S. 1, 26 (2022) (expressing skepticism that judges should conduct interest balancing in the Second Amendment context), *with id.* at 105–07 (Breyer, J., dissenting) (supporting interest balancing in that context).

[9] Fed. R. Evid. 403.

parties to obtain discovery that the judge deems "relevant to any party's claim or defense and proportional to the needs of the case";[10] motions for preliminary injunctions that require courts to balance the equities;[11] and the application of strict scrutiny to content-based regulations of speech (among other government enactments).[12]

These kinds of tests invite judges to weigh dueling considerations. Further, the activity of weighing several factors may occur in the background of judicial decision-making even if not explicitly enshrined in doctrine. This is not to say there are no absolutes in law. US constitutional law is sometimes said to take a more categorical approach to constitutional rights than the proportionality approach prevalent in other countries.[13] But legal settings that call for judges to weigh competing interests are common in the United States as well.

Given that judges frequently weigh competing considerations, the question is which conception of dignity is best suited to enter into the adjudicatory calculus. "Dignity as inherent worth" views have trouble here. To be sure, it is *possible* to construct a legally potent understanding of dignity based on the "inherent worth" account. For instance, the German Basic Law—that is, the German constitution—states in its first article that "Human dignity shall be inviolable. To respect and protect it shall be the duty of all state authority."[14] This provision has been interpreted to mean that "human dignity is an absolute right. . . . [A]n absolute right cannot be limited; . . . it cannot be balanced in order to protect other constitutional rights or to fulfill a public interest."[15] The German Federal Constitutional Court, in the 2006 *Aviation Security Case*, invalidated a statute authorizing the military to shoot down a hijacked airplane in order to protect innocent individuals on the ground.[16]

[10] Fed. R. Civ. P. 26(b)(1).
[11] Winter v. Nat. Res. Def. Council, 555 U.S. 7, 20 (2008).
[12] *See* City of Austin v. Reagan Nat'l Advert. of Austin, LLC, 596 U.S. 61, 68–69 (2022).
[13] *See* Vicki C. Jackson, *Constitutional Law in an Age of Proportionality*, 124 Yale L.J. 3094, 3128 (2015).
[14] Grundgezetz [GG] [Basic Law], art. 1(1), translation at https://www.gesetze-im-internet.de/englisch_gg/englisch_gg.html.
[15] Aharon Barak, Human Dignity: The Constitutional Value and the Constitutional Right 227 (2015); *see also* Eckart Klein, *Human Dignity in German Law*, *in* The Concept of Human Dignity in Human Rights Discourse 145, 149 (D. Kretzmer & E. Klein eds., 2002) ("[H]uman dignity has an absolute effect. There is . . . no way to balance other legal interests, be they of other individuals or of the community, with the dignity of a person.").
[16] BVerfG, 1 BvR 357/05, Feb. 15, 2006, https://www.bundesverfassungsgericht.de/SharedDocs/Entscheidungen/EN/2006/02/rs20060215_1bvr035705en.html.

The statute, the court reasoned, infringed the dignity of the civilians aboard the aircraft in violation of the first article of the German constitution (in addition to infringing their right to life). The court wrote of the civilians in the plane: "By their killing being used as a means to save others, they are treated as objects . . . [they] are denied the value which is due to a human being for his or her own sake."[17]

The German court's discussion, and the constitutional provision it was interpreting, suggests an "inherent worth" account of dignity, one with heavy Kantian overtones. On this account, individual civilian passengers each have intrinsic worth, equal to the value of civilians on the ground. To shoot down a civilian aircraft, even in the service of protecting other civilians, would be to use human beings as mere means in a manner inconsistent with their intrinsic worth. One might worry—plausibly—that the heavy weight assigned to "dignity as inherent worth" limited the ability of German officials to make difficult decisions accounting for multiple people's interests. An "inherent worth" account of dignity poses challenges for judges attempting to resolve an issue by assigning weight to competing values.

An inherent-worth account is not *necessarily* tied to absolutism. For example, a legal system could treat "inherent-worth dignity" as a constitutional value that colors the interpretation of constitutional rights—for example, "apply the constitutional guarantee of freedom of speech in a manner that recognizes human beings' inherent value." Alternatively, a legal system could permit the inherent worth of some to be balanced against the inherent worth of others. In the German airplane case, the inherent worth of civilians on the ground could have assumed greater weight in the analysis.

Nonetheless, an inherent-worth account of dignity is not a good match for a legal world in which conflicting imperatives are regularly pitted against one another. There may be trade-offs between dignity and liberty, dignity and security. Legal actors should be able to recognize the relevance of dignitary considerations in a variety of circumstances without needing to weigh those considerations extremely heavily, if not absolutely.

What, then, is the alternative to a view of dignity as inherent worth? The alternative presented here is called "relational dignity": Dignity is a feature of

[17] *Id.*

social relations that is present when people are treated in certain respectful ways. The next step is to elaborate on the relational dignity account.

Relational Dignity: An Overview

Relational dignity centers on protection of the social self. To respect dignity is to maintain the conditions necessary for people to interact with their fellow human beings in particular ways. In fleshing out the contents of these forms of interaction, it is useful to consider situations in which dignity is violated. In these situations, people draw on the term "dignity" and on related ideas: humiliation, stigma, degradation, disrespect, disgrace.[18] These visceral terms provide a powerful reminder of what it means to have one's dignity violated. In general, interactions that respect dignity share the following features—which I explain by drawing on examples of what it means to *violate* dignity:

- People's rightful status is respected. For example, racial segregation denies racial minorities' rightful status as equals.
- People are not subject to domination. Drawing on Philip Pettit's terminology, "others do not stand over [a person], able to interfere at will and with relative impunity in his or her affairs"[19]—that is, able to "interfere on an arbitrary basis."[20] By contrast, a prisoner who is subject to the personal whims of a jailer is subject to domination.
- People are able to exercise adequate control over their self-presentation to others. For example, publishing naked photographs of someone else on the Internet without permission denies the photographed person adequate control over her self-presentation.

I now elaborate on each of these criteria. To begin, it is useful to discuss two general features of the relational dignity account: its rejection of a "subjective" view of dignity, and its position on the moral weight attaching to dignity.

[18] For an effort to explicate dignity with reference to its violation, notably through humiliation, see AVISHAI MARGALIT, THE DECENT SOCIETY 88 (1996).
[19] Philip Pettit, *The Domination Complaint*, 46 NOMOS 87, 87 (2005).
[20] PHILIP PETTIT, REPUBLICANISM: A THEORY OF FREEDOM AND GOVERNMENT 55 (1997).

The Subjectivity of Dignity

Is relational dignity defined subjectively or objectively?[21] A subjective definition of dignity means that a person's dignity is violated whenever she perceives her dignity to be violated. On this view, a bullying supervisor's dignity is violated when his employees fail to pay him the deference he believes he is owed, even when the supervisor's demands for deference are morally wrong. According to an objective view of dignity, by contrast, the supervisor's claim that his dignity is being violated is incorrect when his demands for deference are wrong.

To make the analysis more fine-grained, we could distinguish three possibilities. Dignity could be *subjective*, in the sense that individual sensibilities determine whether dignity has been violated. Dignity could be *intersubjective*, in the sense that prevailing social understandings, rather than individual idiosyncrasies, determine whether dignity has been violated. Or dignity could be *objective*, in the sense that there is a truth of the matter about whether dignity has been violated, and that truth extends beyond prevailing social understandings.

As understood here, relational dignity is not a subjective phenomenon. This is evident from qualifiers such as "*rightful* status" and "*adequate* control" in the description of dignity above. The bullying supervisor makes a claim for a status that is not rightful, and so his dignity is not genuinely violated when his employees deny him deference. A politician who insists that no one photograph her in public does not have her dignity violated when a journalist takes a picture at a news conference. The politician has been exposed to some degree, but she is still able to maintain *adequate* control over her self-presentation to others. "Adequate" is understood here not with reference to the individual's personal standards, but with reference to standards that apply beyond individual approaches to self-presentation.

Why not define dignity subjectively? Doing so would reduce dignity's ability to serve as a normatively compelling legal value. If legal institutions are obliged to pay attention whenever an individual subjectively senses a violation of dignity, they would be pulled in a variety of conflicting directions. Notably, they would arrive at outcomes that many would view as morally repugnant—for instance, by crediting the claims of a man who believes his

[21] For discussion of objective and subjective definitions of dignity and humiliation, see Daniel Statman, *Humiliation, Dignity and Self-Respect*, 13 Phil. Psych. 523 (2000).

dignity has been violated simply because he loses his job to a woman. Most likely, legal institutions would stop listening to people's claims about dignity, and this would diminish the capacity of dignity to play a useful role in the legal system.

Is relational dignity intersubjective or objective? In other words, do social norms determine the contents of dignity, or could social norms reflect a mistake about the nature of dignitary violations? This is a more complicated question than the issue of whether dignity is purely subjective. In response: Although explaining what it means to violate dignity requires reference to social practices, there is a truth of the matter about whether dignity has been violated, and this truth is not reducible to prevailing social norms.

To elaborate: Social norms help to fill in the content of dignitary claims. The practice of referring to medical doctors as "Dr." is a socially contingent one. But if someone refers to white doctors as "Dr." and to Black doctors by their first names, that person is denying the rightful status of Black doctors. The idea that social practices play a role in defining dignitary violations is reflected in the American legal system. Juries gauge the "reasonableness" of defendants' conduct in tort lawsuits, including for dignitary claims such as invasion of privacy or battery that involves "offensive" touching. Assigning these tasks to juries suggests a recognition that dignitary claims arise out of social life, and that juries have some function, even if imperfect, in reflecting societal sensibilities.

Despite the connection between dignitary claims and social norms, legal actors should also look beyond current societal arrangements in identifying dignitary violations. Otherwise, it is hard to see how appeals to dignity could spur legal change. In a sexist society, for example, many would take the position that confining women to domestic occupations protects rather than denigrates women. A lawyer might nonetheless argue that a law barring women from professional occupations is a violation of dignity. (In the words of a brief then-advocate Ruth Bader Ginsburg co-wrote in the 1970s, "[t]he pedestal upon which women have been placed has all too often, upon closer inspection, been revealed as a cage."[22]) A judge might hold that a law excluding women from professional occupations infringes a constitutional or statutory equality guarantee. We should not close off the possibility that lawyers and judges challenging the status quo correctly understand how to promote dignity.

[22] Brief for Appellant at 21, Reed v. Reed, 404 U.S. 71 (1971) (No. 70-4), 1971 WL 133596, at *21.

On which grounds, however, may legal actors endorse a view of dignity that extends beyond social conventions? Put differently, from which moral, social, or legal sources may the critique of existing practices emanate? One possibility is "immanent critique": drawing on normative values contained in existing societal understandings to argue for a change in social practices. For example, one might challenge the practice of not permitting nineteen-year-olds to vote by observing that society permits nineteen-year-olds to serve in the military and so treats them as responsible contributors. There might theoretically be a society in which immanent critique is impossible, because societal history and traditions contain no resources to support alteration of the status quo. Yet it is highly unlikely for such a society to exist in actuality. At any rate, the focus of this book is on American society, which has constitutional and other legal bases for appeals to equality, liberty, and other ideas that could provoke legal change.

Beyond immanent critique, another possibility is freestanding moral analysis. Relational dignity does not purport to contain a complete or foundational normative account of how people should be treated. Consequently, relational dignity does not provide ultimate answers to questions about whether a status is "rightful" or whether control over self-presentation is "adequate." Put differently, dignity does not exhaust the moral universe. A complete analysis of the status to which people are entitled or the ways they should be treated requires further philosophical material, such as a theory of egalitarianism, autonomy, or democracy. I do not aim here to provide such material; that task would require a much broader project in moral philosophy.

The fact that relational dignity does not include answers to foundational moral questions does not mean the concept lacks normative bite. Relational dignity can help explain why certain situations are detrimental from a normative point of view. Say that someone publishes intimate text messages with a romantic partner without permission. In condemning such a practice, it would be appropriate to say that the romantic partner's dignity is being violated because she is unable to maintain adequate control over her self-presentation to others.[23] A full account of the moral wrongness of the perpetrator's behavior should reference dignity. Further philosophical

[23] Of course, one could also appeal to other moral concepts, notably privacy—but privacy might itself be deemed valuable because it helps to protect dignity. *See* notes 37–44 for discussion of the relationship between dignity and involuntary exposure.

resources might be needed to explain why individuals are morally entitled to a private sphere. But the concept of dignity still helps to provide an account of why the publication of intimate messages is wrong.

More generally, the focus here is not on doing moral philosophy from the ground up, but on tackling issues of institutional role. How can legal decision-makers, especially in the judiciary, address and adjudicate dignitary claims? Relational dignity is meant to provide a working basis for reflection on that query.

Overall, then, the following conclusions can be drawn about relational dignity and subjectivity. Relational dignity is not defined according to each individual's personal view. Instead, there is a rightful status that stands outside each individual's sense of how she should be treated. The rightful status is related to, but not reducible to, prevailing social understandings. The question is then how to allocate authority across different legal and social institutions to identify and apply the normative content of dignity (for instance, the nature of "rightful" status or "adequate" control over self-presentation). Responding to this question benefits from attention to particular institutional and doctrinal contexts, which is the task of subsequent chapters.

Dignity's Normative Weight

The second overarching point about relational dignity, in addition to the subjectivity issue, concerns the normative weight that dignity should carry. Relational dignity, as earlier noted, does not carry absolute weight. Instead, the dignity that attaches to people in the course of social relations can be infringed in more and less serious ways, with dramatic differences between forms of treatment. Dignitary violations include torture and concentration camps, racial segregation, and apartheid. They also include newspaper articles defaming people or revealing private details of a person's life. The latter forms of conduct may be normatively troubling, but not on the same scale as the former. Thus, dignity can carry varying levels of normative weight.

Can dignitary violations ever be justified? It depends on the conception of dignity in question. Some might take the view, for example, that a journalist's mockery of a political figure is a "justified" violation of dignity. Others might believe that such mockery is no dignitary violation, precisely because it is justified. For the most part, the phrase "dignitary violation" has negative associations. In other words, violating a person's dignity is usually thought to create at least a debit on the moral scale. This association may not be universal, but it is common.

The relational dignity account, by building in a normative or "objective" component, suggests that disrespect for dignity is normatively bad. For instance, if treating people with dignity includes respecting their rightful status, then the denial of such status is a moral "minus." For the purpose of evaluating the ideas of *dignitary harm* and *remedies for dignitary harm*—as this book does—it makes sense to conceive of dignity in such a way that its violation is normatively bad.

Nonetheless, dignitary violations could be justified all things considered. Relational dignity does not treat dignity as the only normative value, nor does it assign to dignity overriding moral weight. Therefore, it could be proper on balance to take action that infringes dignity. In a national emergency, for example, it could be appropriate for the government to infringe on privacy in a manner that violates dignity. But the violation of dignity would not be a positive normative good, or justified "in itself."

Having identified the general outlines of relational dignity, I now turn to elaborate on the specific interests involved in protecting this form of dignity.

Dignitary Interests

Here I discuss the central forms of social interaction present in a society that instantiates relational dignity. They are, as noted earlier, *respect for status*, *absence of domination*, and *control over self-presentation*. These criteria have a substantial basis in dignity's historical roots, and they resonate with intuitive understandings of dignity. The overarching theme of these aspects of relational dignity is protection of the social self. Relational dignity centers on the way people treat one another in social and political life. To treat one another with dignity requires not an abstract commitment to recognizing one another's worth but the real-world absence of degrading social relations.

Respect for Status

There is a deep connection between dignity and status. *Dignitas* in Roman thought, as observed in Chapter 1, "rest[ed] on a particular office or status."[24] Dignity's twists and turns over the years have preserved the concept's strong association with rank or status. However, the nature of the rank has shifted: from high social position, to humanity's rank in the order of nature,[25] to the equal status of each human being in a democracy.[26] These varieties of rank differ greatly. Yet the shared language and imagery of status and rank reflect a fundamental intuition: that dignity demands a form of respect, attention, deference, regard.

Indeed, paradigm cases of dignitary violations consist in treating others as though they did not possess a certain status—equality, or even humanity itself. The Nazis dehumanized the Jews: boarding them up in cattle cars, torturing them, exterminating them, burning them, or burying them en masse. In apartheid and segregation regimes, racial minorities live amid constant reminders of their supposed inferiority, and the law facilitates brutality or fails to protect them from it. It is no surprise, therefore, that demands for "dignity" have featured prominently in movements for racial equality.[27] In patriarchal societies, women are denied the status of both equals and adults: they are treated as childlike, dependent, meant to serve. Thus, violations of dignity frequently involve the denial that the victims possess a certain status.

Sometimes, the status in question is not humanity, equal citizenship, or adulthood, but rather a status defined with reference to social position. For example, failing to treat someone with the status befitting a teacher, physician, or employer could also violate dignity. At times, these forms of disrespect could be relatively light, especially in comparison to cases of (say) genocide and apartheid. An example is a student's addressing a teacher in mocking tones. Nonetheless, disrespect for social role could overlap with disrespect for deeper attributes such as equal citizenship. For instance, a scholarly article might use the title "Professor" to refer to male academics but not female academics. That practice implies a view (conscious or subconscious) about women's equality. Whether or not disrespect is tied to a "protected" characteristic, it can have a substantial dignitary impact. Being

[24] Miriam Griffin, *Dignity in Roman and Stoic Thought*, *in* DIGNITY: A HISTORY 50 (Remy Debes ed., 2017).

[25] *See* GIOVANNI PICO DELLA MIRANDOLA, ORATION ON THE DIGNITY OF MAN (A. Robert Caponigri trans., 1996).

[26] *See* WALDRON, note 3, at 34.

[27] Christopher A. Bracey, *Dignity in Race Jurisprudence*, 7 J. CONST. L. 669, 669 (2005) ("Dignity remains the core aspirational value in the struggle for racial justice.").

treated in ways at odds with one's social role—for instance, being given more tedious assignments at work based on the supervisor's personal whims—can over time be highly demeaning and destabilizing.

Relational dignity is predicated on the notion that the social self matters in important ways. Human beings are situated in complex webs of social belonging, and threats to social belonging can have a serious effect on people's senses of identity and meaning. In this sense, relational dignity has much in common with theories of recognition, which posit that individual identity is constituted through interactions with others and can be deeply affected when these interactions are degrading.[28]

Relational dignity is not subjective, as discussed. In the context of the status criterion, it is people's *rightful* status that warrants respect. Not every claim to possess dignity based on a given status needs to be accepted. If a citizen born in the United States contends that her dignity is violated because her vote counts the same as the vote of a naturalized citizen, one can rightly argue that she is mistaken.

The idea of the rightful status raises questions about moral objectivity and relativism. If a white person in the Jim Crow South contended that his dignity would be violated if he were forced to share a drinking fountain with a Black person, would the white person's dignity actually be violated? Being "lowered" from an elevated position in a racial hierarchy is not a blow to the *rightful* status. Specific circumstances could make the episode into a violation of the rightful status—for example, if that white person were singled out to share the fountain because of his disability. But the white person would not suffer an infringement of his dignity, in the sense of a violation of the rightful status, purely by virtue of being forced to use a desegregated fountain. Support for the view that desegregation does not constitute disrespect for the rightful status can be found in the same sources that would justify a theory of egalitarianism more generally. This is an example of how relational dignity does not provide a complete moral account and must work in tandem with other normative theories.

It may be argued that legal decision-makers are not well situated to determine which status is rightful. But that is a question about institutional competency, different from the issue of whether dignity should include an

[28] *See, e.g.*, NANCY FRASER & AXEL HONNETH, REDISTRIBUTION OR RECOGNITION? A POLITICAL-PHILOSOPHICAL EXCHANGE (2003); Charles Taylor, *The Politics of Recognition*, *in* MULTICULTURALISM: EXAMINING THE POLITICS OF RECOGNITION 25 (Amy Gutmann ed., 1994).

"objective" component—as relational dignity does. As later chapters will discuss, legal decision-makers faced with morally freighted questions can draw on sources such as historical materials, precedent, and prevailing practice. They need not be guided solely by their own unfettered sense of justice. The point for now is that interactions characterized by respect for relational dignity are those in which society recognizes people's rightful status and treats them accordingly.

Absence of Domination

Another feature characteristic of respect for relational dignity is the absence of domination. The term "domination" is borrowed from "republican" political theory,[29] although I do not mean to track every nuance of this strain of political thought. The basic insight behind the idea of nondomination is that it is harmful, in Philip Pettit's words, to "hav[e] to live at the mercy of another, hav[e] to live in a manner that leaves you vulnerable to some ill that the other is in a position arbitrarily to impose."[30] Some examples that Pettit gives are "the wife who finds herself in a position where her husband can beat her at will, and without any possibility of redress"; "the employee who dare not raise a complaint against an employer, and who is vulnerable to any of a range of abuses, some petty, some serious, that the employer may choose to perpetuate"; and "the welfare dependant who finds that they are vulnerable to the caprice of a counter clerk for whether or not their children will receive meal vouchers."[31]

Notably, the dominating individual does not need to be actively interfering with the dominated party's actions at all times in order for a relationship of domination to exist.[32] The dominating person might be benevolent, or the dominated person might be sufficiently "cunning or fawning" to accomplish what he wishes.[33] Rather, the dominating party must be in a position to "interfere on an arbitrary basis with the choices of the dominated";

[29] *E.g.*, PETTIT, note 20.
[30] *Id.* at 4–5.
[31] *Id.* at 5.
[32] *Id.* at 22.
[33] *Id.*

the dominating party can act on the dominated person "at will and with impunity."[34]

The idea of nondomination has powerful dignitarian resonances. Being at the mercy of someone who can interfere in one's choices with impunity is a profoundly degrading situation. It can give rise to reactions by the dominated individual that compound humiliation: groveling, forced secrecy, Stockholm syndrome. To take an extreme example, part of the dignitary violation involved in torture—over and above the highly significant feature of physical pain—lies in the tortured individual's being utterly subject to the torturer's will, the torturer's ability to take cruelty however far he wants to go.

In keeping with the social emphasis of relational dignity, the interpersonal interactions that domination creates can be especially undermining of dignity. The harm of being at another's mercy is particularly demeaning when, in Pettit's words, the dominating party and the dominated party are each "in a position to see that [one is] dominated by the other, in a position to see that [each one] see[s] this, and so on."[35] Mutual knowledge that one is part of a relationship of domination is antithetical to respectful forms of social recognition.

As with the status component of relational dignity, the idea of nondomination is not subjective. An individual is not dominated simply because she believes herself to be. Further, there are many forms of social control that do not amount to domination, because they do not involve "arbitrary" restraints.[36] Laws requiring children to attend school, for example, plausibly do not amount to domination. The question then arises how the arbitrariness of a restraint is to be determined. May employees be required to come into the office during a pandemic, at pain of being fired? May citizens be conscripted as soldiers? May individuals convicted of a crime be imprisoned?

One response to these questions is to focus on the procedures used to impose various restraints. Provided these procedures conform to rule-of-law principles, one might contend, a restraint is not "arbitrary," and the restrained individual is not dominated. Yet people can still reasonably disagree about the adequacy of the process by which a given restraint is imposed, and

[34] *Id.*
[35] Pettit, note 20, at 5.
[36] *See* Ian Shapiro, Uncommon Sense 89–90 (2024).

they may differ on whether certain kinds of restraints, such as solitary confinement, can ever be rendered nondominating by proper procedure. These disputes, like those over the "rightful status," will be the subject of moral controversy. The relational dignity account does not itself purport to resolve such debates. The overall point is that relational dignity is not opposed to all situations in which one person has power to interfere with another person's choices—only situations in which the power is wielded arbitrarily.

Finally, the nondomination criterion is not completely distinct from the criterion of "respect for rightful status." These ideas overlap. For example, subjecting an adult to the whims of another person could amount to treating the adult as though she possessed the status of a child. This does not render the nondomination criterion redundant. One gains more purchase on the nature of dignity as a social phenomenon by considering the experience of domination in addition to the concept of status. To exist in thrall to another's whims is deeply contrary to a life lived with dignity.

Control over Self-Presentation

A third feature of relational dignity is *adequate control over one's self-presentation to others*. This criterion is rooted in the long-standing relationship between dignity and concepts such as privacy, exposure, and uncovering. The connection between shame and exposure reaches as far back as the Bible, with Adam and Eve becoming aware of their nakedness after eating the forbidden fruit and then covering themselves. The continuing cultural potency of this episode bolsters the notion that "[t]he core experience of shame is feeling exposed, subject to the gaze of another."[37] Indignity and exposure are also connected through the concept of stigma. As Erving Goffman has written, people often make substantial efforts to conceal "stigmas," from physical differences to ethnic identities, and shame can attend exposure of these stigmas.[38]

Involuntary exposure is especially likely to cause humiliation. People continually expose various aspects of themselves to selected others or to

[37] George P. Fletcher, *Punishment, Guilt, and Shame in Biblical Thought*, 18 NOTRE DAME J. L. ETHICS & PUB. POL'Y 343, 355–56 (2004).

[38] ERVING GOFFMAN, STIGMA: NOTES ON THE MANAGEMENT OF SPOILED IDENTITY 7, 83–84 (1963).

the public. But being forced to lay bare private aspects of the self to others is particularly demeaning. Thus, the interest at stake in the "exposure" aspect of relational dignity is the individual's *control* over self-presentation to others.

The idea of control over self-presentation also implicates the link between dignity and certain forms of physical bearing. As Waldron puts it, there is a "moral orthopedics" of dignity—a physical presence and sense of self-possession associated with dignity.[39] Accordingly, he writes, "the ban on degrading treatment" in human rights covenants and international humanitarian law "can be read as requiring that people must be permitted to present themselves (even in detention, even in the power of the police) with a modicum of self-control and self-possession."[40] The idea of control over self-presentation should not be interpreted to blame the victim—that is, to criticize people in oppressive circumstances for failing to retain self-control. The point is rather: Social conditions should be such that individuals, with a reasonable amount of effort, are generally able to maintain control over the way they appear before others in society.

In legal settings, the connection between dignity and involuntary exposure is evident in the relationship between dignity and privacy.[41] In the words of the Supreme Court of India, "[t]he right to privacy is an element of human dignity. . . . Privacy ensures that a human being can lead a life of dignity by securing the inner recesses of the human personality from unwanted intrusion."[42] The US Supreme Court's jurisprudence on abortion—prior to the overruling of *Roe v. Wade* in 2022—included references to the relationship between dignity and privacy.[43] Moreover, invasion of privacy is frequently numbered among the "dignitary torts."[44] Legal associations of dignity with privacy speak to the sense that a dignified life is one in which an individual is able to preserve a personal domain against intrusion.

There is overlap between the self-presentation feature of relational dignity and the other two: respect for status and nondomination. Being able

[39] *See* WALDRON, note 3, at 21–22.

[40] *Id.* at 22.

[41] *See* Daniel J. Solove, *A Taxonomy of Privacy*, 154 U. PA. L. REV. 477, 534 (2006); *see* DANIELLE KEATS CITRON, THE FIGHT FOR PRIVACY: PROTECTING DIGNITY, IDENTITY AND LOVE IN THE DIGITAL AGE (2022).

[42] Justice K. S. Puttaswamy & Anr. v. Union of India & Ors., AIR 2017 SC 4161 (India).

[43] *See, e.g.*, Planned Parenthood of Se. Pa. v. Casey, 505 U.S. 833, 851 (1992), *overruled by* Dobbs v. Jackson Women's Health Org., 597 U.S. 215 (2022).

[44] Kenneth S. Abraham & G. Edward White, *The Puzzle of the Dignitary Torts*, 104 CORNELL L. REV. 317, 338–353 (2019).

to control one's self-presentation to others is frequently the prerogative of those with high status, and the inability to exercise such control is closely correlated with domination at the hands of another. Indeed, several types of dignitary violations cut across the different aspects of relational dignity. For example, a prison guard who gratuitously strip-searches an inmate may engage in domination in addition to stripping the inmate of control over self-presentation. Accordingly, the elements of relational dignity overlap. Yet the idea of control over self-presentation furnishes an additional dimension to dignity and helps to make the concept more concrete.

Relational dignity involves *adequate* control over self-presentation to others. After all, people are often unable to control every aspect of their appearance. Older people might be unable to present the same image of strength as they could when they were younger. A person with a broken leg is temporarily unable to present dexterity. Individuals do not suffer a blow to dignity whenever they encounter some limits on their ability to control their presentation to others. Thus, the notion of "adequate" control imports a nonsubjective element into the exposure feature of relational dignity.

The question of what it means to exercise "adequate" control over self-presentation depends to some extent on social norms. This is consistent with the close connection between relational dignity and social arrangements. If society treats aging as an ordinary and unremarkable process, then an elderly person's inability to control his appearance to others as someone who moves slowly need not undermine the person's adequate grasp over self-presentation. If, by contrast, all signs of aging are viewed as pathetic and deplorable, then an elderly person's inability to control exposure of his slow movement would undermine his dignity.

The relevance of social norms in defining "adequate" control over self-presentation does not mean these norms are impervious to critique. In some societies, for example, servants or other low-status people might be denied private spaces. Even if that state of affairs were considered socially appropriate, one could criticize those social views on normative grounds—namely, that they are inegalitarian and help to cement unjustifiably hierarchical social roles. Relational dignity, as earlier discussed, does not mandate deference to prevailing social norms; it leaves open the possibility of freestanding moral analysis even though it does not itself incorporate a complete moral account. Ultimately, the idea of "adequate" control over self-presentation depends not only on social norms but also on independent moral ideas.

Relational Dignity: Summing Up

Relational dignity, then, centers on protection of the social self. To respect people's dignity is to treat them in accordance with their rightful status; to refrain from subjecting them to domination, understood as vulnerability to arbitrary interference; and to allow them to exercise adequate control over their self-presentation to others. To disrespect relational dignity is to engage in any one of the "opposite" actions: to infringe rightful status, to dominate, or to strip adequate control over self-presentation.

Defining relational dignity does not close off debate about the nature of the concept or its applications. In particular, relational dignity's rejection of subjectivity means that disputes about the proper way for people to be treated, and about the moral legitimacy of social norms, will continue.[45] At the same time, focusing on the interests in status, nondomination, and control over self-presentation helps to make the idea of dignity more precise.

Further, *expressive theories of law* illuminate relational dignity. According to these theories, legal acts can express meanings or make a statement even if they do not have a more "tangible" impact on the world.[46] For example, a legal regime that permits same-sex couples to enter into civil unions but not to marry expresses certain meanings about the nature of same-sex partnerships and their relationship to their opposite-sex counterparts. These meanings will be conveyed even if same-sex couples are entitled to all the material benefits of opposite-sex marriages.

Respecting or violating relational dignity often involves actions that express a message. These actions may not make a physical or economic difference, but they "make a statement" about a person's place in a social setting. This statement could be one of respect or one of contempt. People inhabit a web of social meanings influenced by these kinds of messages, and the experience of dignity depends importantly on the statements made, through actions and words, by fellow members of society.

[45] *See* Deborah Hellman, When Is Discrimination Wrong? 41 (2008) ("[J]udging whether a particular classification in a particular context does demean calls for a complex interpretive judgment.").

[46] For discussions of legal expressivism, see, for example, Hellman, note 45; Elizabeth S. Anderson & Richard M. Pildes, *Expressive Theories of Law: A General Restatement*, 148 U. Pa. L. Rev. 1503 (2000); Dan M. Kahan, *What Do Alternative Sanctions Mean?*, 63 U. Chi. L. Rev. 591, 597 (1996); Andrew Koppelman, *On the Moral Foundations of Legal Expressivism*, 60 Md. L. Rev. 777 (2001).

Relational dignity can be summarized with reference to the taxonomy provided in Chapter 1. That taxonomy involved the following questions: What is the object of dignity? What is the basis for dignity? What kind of treatment does dignity demand? Can dignity be lost? What is the relationship between dignity and equality?

The object of respect for dignity, on the relational dignity account, is individual persons—rather than collective bodies such as nations or ethnic groups, or institutions such as sovereign states. In that sense, relational dignity is an account of "human dignity." As to the basis for the obligation to treat people with dignity, relational dignity does not attempt to provide a complete moral justification. Relational dignity is meant to be logically compatible with multiple rationales for the obligation to respect people, including at least some versions of utilitarianism, deontology, and virtue ethics. One could take the position that relational dignity is morally valuable because it promotes utility, because it conforms to a moral duty independent of consequences, or because its advancement is grounded in (or conducive to) good character.

An approach that gives dignity absolute weight in all circumstances would not be compatible with relational dignity, which permits other moral imperatives to override the obligation to respect dignity in some contexts. This does not commit the relational dignity account to consequentialism. A nonconsequentialist can accept the existence of competing moral imperatives; the nonconsequentialist would simply deny that what gives these moral imperatives their normative force is their consequences. It may be true, however, that relational dignity fits more comfortably into a worldview in which the moral valence of an action depends meaningfully on its consequences.

The forms of treatment that relational dignity demands are those analyzed in this chapter: respect for rightful status, absence of domination, and preservation of a person's adequate control over self-presentation to others. These forms of treatment overlap, and it is possible that other interests could be described as dignitary. Yet the forms of treatment analyzed here, when taken together, encompass numerous experiences that have been connected to dignity both historically and in the present day. They provide, at a minimum, a starting point to examine the relationship between dignity and judicial institutions.

Can relational dignity be lost? Given that relational dignity is present when people interact with one another in respectful ways, relational dignity could be absent when these social conditions do not obtain. Moreover, people can be treated in ways that undermine their dignity, and one might describe the victims of such treatment as being bereft of dignity. At the same time, the obligation to treat people with respect does not disappear when people fail to honor it. Even when this obligation is overridden by another normative principle, its moral force is not erased.

When it comes to the issue of whether dignity can be lost, a critical question is why it matters how we answer. What is the difference between saying "people cannot lose dignity, but their dignity can be violated" and "people can lose their dignity when they are treated disrespectfully"? At one level, the difference appears semantic; it is a question of whether "dignity" will be used to refer to an alienable or inalienable quality. Perhaps, however, the way of talking about dignity makes a difference. Some might take the position that it is more conducive to social change, or more realistic, to acknowledge that dignity can be lost. For example, Bird urges recognition that social circumstances can "leave human lives forsaken"—that dignity is vulnerable and fragile, and in need of protection.[47] If casting dignity as inalienable breeds a lack of urgency about removing obstacles to a dignified life, then that development is troubling. Still, many might find it meaningful and fortifying to be reminded that they have dignity even in the face of degradation.

There is no clear answer to the question of whether dignity should be treated as alienable (in the sense that it can be lost) or inalienable. This book does not shy away from locutions, such as "stripping people of their dignity," that suggest dignity can be lost. However, it characterizes the obligation to treat people with respect as an enduring quality of social affairs.

The final feature of the taxonomy of dignity introduced in Chapter 1 is the relationship between dignity and equality. How does relational dignity, then, interact with equality? Relational dignity includes an objective component that calls for people to be treated in accordance with their rightful status. Relational dignity does not itself incorporate a moral account of the rightful status; a further normative theory must do that work. There are ample moral reasons to support equality, as explained in a large scholarly literature on the meaning and justification of equality.[48] Moreover, equality is an important value in contemporary American society and law, even if it is not fully instantiated. Thus, the "rightful" status should plausibly be interpreted to

[47] BIRD, note 4, at 238.

[48] *See, e.g.*, MARTHA C. NUSSBAUM, HIDING FROM HUMANITY (2004); JOHN RAWLS, A THEORY OF JUSTICE (1971); Elizabeth S. Anderson, *What Is the Point of Equality?*, 109 ETHICS 287 (1999).

encompass basic norms of equality. Yet the more precise contours of egalitarianism, and the basis for it, depend on one's particular normative theory.

The fact that relational dignity overlaps with other concepts, such as equality and autonomy, does not mean that appeals to dignity can be replaced without loss. These appeals capture a cluster of powerful intuitions, and our moral vocabulary would be less rich were dignity eliminated from it. Furthermore, as Parts II and III demonstrate, dignity possesses justificatory and explanatory power in doctrinal contexts, such as constitutional standing and the law of torts. In other words, dignity can and should do actual work in shaping legal results.

Dignitary Violations and Dignitary Harms

As a bridge to Part II, which addresses dignitary harm, it is useful to consider the relationship between a dignitary *violation* and a dignitary *harm*. This distinction might seem subtle, but clarifying the point will be helpful in teeing up Part II's discussion of legal recognition for dignitary harm.

To violate dignity—in the sense of relational dignity—is to deny a person's rightful status, to subject a person to domination (in the sense of arbitrary interference), or to strip a person of adequate control over self-presentation. In other words, "dignitary violation" refers to one person's action against another. "Dignitary harm," by contrast, refers to a state of affairs that is detrimental, adverse, or disadvantageous in particular ways.

Dignitary harm is frequently the downstream consequence of a dignitary violation. The bullying supervisor, in violating the employee's dignity, causes the employee to suffer dignitary harm. One might ask, though, whether it is possible for a dignitary violation to occur without dignitary harm, and vice versa.

How could a dignitary violation occur without dignitary harm? One possibility is that the victim does not experience a form of treatment as harmful. For example, an abused servant who is severely demoralized may not object to his mistreatment. On the account here, however, such a person may still suffer dignitary harm; the existence of dignitary harm does not depend on the victim's mental state. This approach maintains the distinctiveness of dignitary harm rather than reducing it to another form of damage, notably emotional harm. Another possibility for violation-without-harm is that the victim does not know about the violator's conduct. For example, if

Bob falsely imprisons Jenny while she is sleeping, and she never becomes aware of her mistreatment, has she suffered dignitary harm? Readers might have competing intuitions about this case. As a practical matter, however, litigation settings such as the ones addressed in this book will rarely involve this kind of scenario. If Jenny brings suit against Bob, she must have become aware of her false imprisonment at some point—and she would have suffered dignitary harm at least at that juncture.

A similar pragmatic perspective helps in addressing the question of whether there can be dignitary harm without a dignitary violation. If the wind takes off a person's clothing in a public place, leading to embarrassment, has the person suffered dignitary harm even absent a dignitary violation? Again, readers might have different intuitions on whether the person has truly incurred dignitary "harm." But in a litigation setting, it is unlikely for dignitary harm to be referenced in court without an allegation that the harm resulted from a dignitary violation. After all, the plaintiff claiming she incurred dignitary harm is presumably accusing the defendant of causing such harm. From a practical standpoint, then, dignitary violations and dignitary harms are interlinked. But it is worth keeping in mind the conceptual distinctions as the book proceeds.

To conclude, this chapter has offered an account of dignity that is rooted in concrete social relationships. Relational dignity is a feature of social relations that involves treating people in certain ways: respect for rightful status, absence of domination, and preservation of adequate control over self-presentation. The next chapters focus on the role of dignity in legal decision-making and judicial adjudication more specifically. In doing so, they further flesh out the account of dignity that this chapter has introduced.

PART II
DIGNITARY HARM

Part I elucidated the concept of dignity from a historical and conceptual perspective. It canvassed different understandings of dignity and proposed an account of "relational dignity" centered on protection of the social self. The book now turns from theoretical analysis to legal discussion. In particular, the book focuses on the relationship between dignity and courts. To what extent should judges address dignitary harm? How should dignitary considerations enter into judicial assessments of the remedies they provide? Issues of harm and remedy are central to the judicial role, and they are practically significant. Although doctrines involving legally cognizable harm and the scope of judicial relief might seem technical, they operate as gatekeepers to the courts; they determine who may sue and what litigants may obtain from a suit. Part II focuses on harm, while Part III focuses on remedy. Both Parts are trained on the American legal system, although they incorporate some comparative elements.

The basic issue in Part II is: Which dignitary harms warrant judicial action? The world is filled with harms—physical, economic, psychological; blows, insults, slights. But not all of these harms are *legal* injuries of the kind that judges can address. It is possible to have "damnum absque iniuria"—factual harm without a legally cognizable or actionable injury.[**] The feeling of chagrin resulting from light mockery is an example of damnum absque iniuria. There is a difference between the empirical phenomenon of damage and harm that justifies judicial intervention.

Chapter 3 examines the place of dignitary harm in constitutional standing doctrine. Standing doctrine works to guard the boundaries of federal courts in the United States. The doctrine requires federal judges to decide which kinds of harms are "injury in fact." Physical or economic harms usually

[*] *See* F. Andrew Hessick, *Standing, Injury in Fact, and Private Rights*, 93 Cornell L. Rev. 275, 280–81 (2008).

qualify; but what about less "tangible" types of harm, such as dignitary harm? Chapter 3 explains the challenges that dignitary harm poses for constitutional standing doctrine and proposes ways for judges to recognize dignitary harm as injury in fact without eviscerating limits on standing.

Chapter 4 explores the function of dignity in tort law, a body of doctrine through which real-world harm becomes legally actionable. Certain tort claims—such as offensive-touching battery, privacy violations, and defamation—are distinctively likely to protect dignitary interests. These torts both reveal the long-running concern with dignity in the American legal system and highlight shifting understandings of dignity over time. Chapter 4 identifies difficulties that judges face in adjudicating dignitary tort claims, such as divergent perspectives about whether dignity has been violated, and it offers ways to ameliorate these difficulties.

Both chapters in Part II demonstrate that dignity provides justification and explanation for doctrinal developments: the law of constitutional standing, in Chapter 3, and the law of torts, in Chapter 4. In other words, dignity is a generative concept from a doctrinal perspective. This helps to support the view that appeals to dignity cannot be replaced by appeals to other legal concepts. More generally, Part II probes the boundary between actual damage and legally cognizable harm. At what point does a "factual" harm become a legal injury appropriate for a claim in court? And what does that line tell us about judicial competence and authority? The legal effects of dignitary harm have broader ramifications for the nature of the judicial role.

3

Dignity and Constitutional Standing

This chapter investigates the relationship between constitutional standing doctrine and dignitary harm. First, it briefly provides background on standing doctrine, noting that the doctrine focuses both on the factual reality of the harm and on the administrability of suits involving such harms. Second, the chapter highlights a dilemma facing judges when the basis for standing is dignitary harm: Although dignitary harm is genuine and difficult to ignore, it raises the specter of unlimited standing, intractable line-drawing problems, and morally controversial judicial rulings. Third, the chapter identifies ways for judges to address this dilemma by integrating dignity more effectively into constitutional standing doctrine. Judges should rely on more representative branches of government, such as Congress, to decide when dignitary harm furnishes a basis for standing. If judges are unwilling to take that step, they should build up a body of law identifying cognizable dignitary harm. To construct this body of precedent, they can look to sources of positive law and prevailing social understandings, while maintaining independent moral judgment. Overall, the chapter uses standing doctrine to illustrate several issues involved in adjudicating allegations about dignitary harm.

Constitutional Standing Doctrine: Legal or Factual Harm?

Article III of the US Constitution restricts the federal judicial power to "Cases" and "Controversies." The US Supreme Court has interpreted this language to impose "standing" limitations on the parties who can sue in a federal court. In the 1970s and 1980s, the current doctrinal formulation of constitutional (or "Article III") standing doctrine took root: Plaintiffs must have suffered an injury "in fact" that was caused by the defendant's conduct and that could be redressed by a judicial decision in the plaintiff's favor.[1]

[1] *See, e.g.*, Allen v. Wright, 468 U.S. 737, 751 (1984).

Dignity and Judicial Authority. Rachel Bayefsky, Oxford University Press. © Rachel Bayefsky 2024.
DOI: 10.1093/oso/9780197750322.003.0003

In short: injury in fact, causation, redressability. The injury-in-fact criterion originally served to widen the circle of potential plaintiffs, to include not only those who had suffered a traditional legal injury but also those who had incurred real-world harm.[2]

Over time, however, the Supreme Court came to treat the injury-in-fact criterion as a limitation on which parties could sue. The Court's move to tighten standing rules came amid an increase in federal legislation protecting a broad array of interests and authorizing plaintiffs to sue to enforce federal law.[3] The Supreme Court required plaintiffs to possess an actual "personal stake" in order to satisfy Article III, even when, the Court held in the 1992 case *Lujan v. Defenders of Wildlife*, Congress had passed a statute authorizing "any person" to sue.[4] In other words, the Court "constitutionalized" standing doctrine. The Article III standing requirements of injury in fact, causation, and redressability became constraints on Congress's ability to create rights of action enabling private individuals to sue in federal court.

The Court's primary justification for Article III standing doctrine has been the separation of powers. According to the Court, standing confines federal courts to the limited sphere of "decid[ing] only 'the rights of individuals'" with skin in the game, rather than "publicly opin[ing] on every legal question."[5] Constitutional standing doctrine has attracted considerable criticism for decades. Scholars have charged that the doctrine tasks judges with making normatively laden and contestable judgments about whether plaintiffs have "in fact" suffered an injury.[6] Nonetheless, Article III standing doctrine remains alive and well. In recent formulations, injury in fact must be both "particularized" in the sense that it "affect[s] the plaintiff in a personal and individual way,"[7] and "concrete" in the sense of being "real"; injury must also be "actual or imminent, not conjectural or hypothetical."[8] Unpacking these descriptions can be tricky. As Richard Re put it in 2014,

[2] *See* Richard H. Fallon, Jr., *The Fragmentation of Standing*, 93 TEX. L. REV. 1061, 1065–67 (2015).

[3] RICHARD H. FALLON, JR., ET AL., HART & WECHSLER'S THE FEDERAL COURTS AND THE FEDERAL SYSTEM 116–17 (7th ed. 2015) [hereinafter HART & WECHSLER].

[4] Lujan v. Defs. of Wildlife, 504 U.S. 555, 571–73 (1992).

[5] TransUnion LLC v. Ramirez, 594 U.S. 413, 423 (2021) (quoting Marbury v. Madison, 5 U.S. (1 Cranch) 137, 170 (1803)).

[6] *See, e.g.*, William A. Fletcher, *The Structure of Standing*, 98 YALE L.J. 221 (1988); Cass R. Sunstein, *What's Standing after* Lujan? *Of Citizen Suits, "Injuries," and Article III*, 91 MICH. L. REV. 163, 188–89 (1992).

[7] Spokeo v. Robins, 578 U.S. 330, 339–40 (2016).

[8] *Id.* at 339 (internal quotation marks omitted).

"the Court has adopted a 'standard' for factual injury defined only by a list of synonymous adjectives."[9]

In particular, the doctrinal question of whether the plaintiff has "really" suffered harm is not straightforward. In practice, courts consider not merely whether the plaintiff has "actually" been harmed but also whether the plaintiff has incurred the type of harm suitable for adjudication in federal court. For example, courts may be reluctant to permit plaintiffs to assert claims of Article III injury that would result in interference with executive national security or intelligence functions.[10] Relatedly—as Richard Fallon has pointed out—the definition of injury is not hermetically sealed off from the remedial question of whether a court could redress a plaintiff's harm without unacceptably high costs.[11] Thus, the Court sometimes denies standing to plaintiffs seeking, as a remedy, a broad restructuring of government policies,[12] or an order to executive officials to change their arrest or prosecution practices.[13] In other words, injury and remedy are not wholly separate inquiries.

More broadly, courts may consider the consequences of their rulings on standing for the volume of future litigation. As the Supreme Court stated in 2000, "Standing doctrine functions to ensure, among other things, that the scarce resources of the federal courts are devoted to those disputes in which the parties have a concrete stake."[14] If a permissive ruling on standing threatens to deplete scarce judicial resources, judges might well shy away from issuing the ruling—though some judges may be unwilling to acknowledge this administrability-related motivation.

Overall, the Supreme Court, in addition to insisting on "injury in fact," considers the case's suitability for adjudication in federal court when assessing standing. As a result, an analysis of dignitary harm as cognizable injury requires attention both to the reality of dignitary harm and to the administrability of lawsuits based on this kind of harm.

[9] Richard M. Re, *Relative Standing*, 102 Geo. L.J. 1191, 1203 (2014).

[10] *See, e.g.*, Clapper v. Amnesty Int'l USA, 568 U.S. 398, 409 (2013).

[11] Richard H. Fallon, Jr., *The Linkage between Justiciability and Remedies—And Their Connections to Substantive Rights*, 92 Va. L. Rev. 633, 693–701 (2006).

[12] *Id.* at 649–51, 679.

[13] United States v. Texas, 599 U.S. 670, 677 (2023).

[14] Friends of the Earth, Inc. v. Laidlaw Env't Servs. (TOC), Inc., 528 U.S. 167, 191 (2000).

Dignitary Harm as Injury in Fact: Challenges for Judicial Authority

Judges face a dilemma when adjudicating suits in which dignitary harm is the asserted basis for standing. Dignitary harm can be a powerful injury in "fact"—that is, in actual life. Yet this kind of harm presents a challenge for judges attempting to apply standing doctrine in a manner that creates clear and ideologically neutral boundaries around federal jurisdiction. How to decide who has suffered dignitary harm? Can this decision be made without resort to the judge's normative perspective? Does the link between stigma directed at a group and stigma directed at an individual threaten the requirement that injury in fact be "particularized"? These types of questions illuminate the contours of federal judicial authority.

The Reality of Dignitary Harm

The Supreme Court has mandated that injury in fact be both "concrete" and "particularized." Dignitary harm (as understood in this book) seems to be concrete in the sense of being "de facto" or "real." Dignitary harm is generally the result of a dignitary violation, at least in litigation settings (as discussed in Chapter 2). To violate dignity is to deny a person's rightful status, to subject a person to domination, or to strip a person of adequate control over self-presentation. Each of these aspects of relational dignity has a nonsubjective element. For example, it is the *rightful* status that is violated. Being denied one's rightful status is genuinely detrimental. The same is true of the other features of relational dignity. Dominating a person, in the sense of subjecting the person to arbitrary interference, and stripping a person of adequate control over self-presentation create harmful states of affairs. Therefore, dignitary harm appears to be "concrete" in the sense of being "*de facto*" or "actually exist[ing]."[15]

Notably, dignitary harm cannot be reduced to "the psychological consequence presumably produced by observation of conduct with which one disagrees," which the Supreme Court has rejected as a basis for standing.[16] In particular, dignitary harm is different from emotional harm. A demoralized

[15] Spokeo, Inc. v. Robins, 578 U.S. 330, 340 (2016).

[16] Valley Forge Christian Coll. v. Americans United for Separation of Church & State, Inc., 454 U.S. 464, 485 (1982).

servant who has no negative emotional reaction to abuse can nevertheless suffer dignitary harm (as observed in Chapter 2). No doubt, dignitary violations frequently cause emotional harm, such as feelings of humiliation. Thus, feelings of humiliation could serve as defeasible evidence of dignitary harm. The main point is that stigma is not simply a "feeling"; it is the result of forms of status demotion, domination, and exposure that exist outside people's minds.

To be sure, there are more and less grave forms of dignitary harm. The interest in promoting dignity can be outweighed by other interests. Yet the Supreme Court has not instituted a "gravity" threshold for injury in fact. For economic harm, the Court has stated that "[f]or standing purposes, a loss of even a small amount of money is ordinarily an 'injury.'"[17] If the same principle is applied to dignitary harm, even a relatively light form would be a real harm for Article III standing purposes.

In addition to being *concrete*, dignitary harm can be *particularized* in the sense of affecting plaintiffs personally. If a person releases intimate pictures of an ex-partner on the Internet, the ex-partner has individually been harmed. The chapter later identifies certain challenges involved in particularizing dignitary harm, but in principle (and in many cases), this kind of harm can meet the particularity requirement.

Despite the logical basis for viewing dignity as concrete and often particularized, the idea of dignity as injury in fact raises difficulties, some of which are reflected in current doctrine. I now turn to the current treatment of dignitary harm in the law of standing. Certain lines of Supreme Court precedent have recognized dignitary harm as a possible form of injury in fact, albeit with caveats. In a 1984 gender discrimination case, the Court stated, in explaining why the plaintiff had standing:

> [D]iscrimination itself, by perpetuating archaic and stereotypic notions or by stigmatizing members of the disfavored group as innately inferior and therefore as less worthy participants in the political community, can cause serious non-economic injuries to those persons who are personally denied equal treatment solely because of their membership in a disfavored group.[18]

[17] Czyzewski v. Jevic Holding Corp., 580 U.S. 451, 464 (2017).

[18] Heckler v. Mathews, 465 U.S. 728, 739–40 (1984) (internal quotation marks and citations omitted).

Thus, the violation of status involved in gender discrimination can give rise to injury cognizable for standing purposes.

The Court confirmed that discrimination can cause cognizable dignitary harm in the 1984 case *Allen v. Wright*—though with important limitations. The plaintiffs in *Allen* were parents of Black schoolchildren; they argued that the Internal Revenue Service was illegally granting tax exemptions to racially discriminatory private schools.[19] The Court denied standing because the parents could not demonstrate, in the Court's view, that these tax exemptions were diminishing their children's ability to be educated in a racially integrated environment.[20] The Court also considered the argument that the parents had suffered "stigmatic injury, or denigration," because the government was discriminating against their racial group.[21]

The "stigmatizing injury often caused by racial discrimination," the Supreme Court stated, is "one of the most serious consequences of discriminatory government action and is sufficient in some circumstances to support standing."[22] The qualifying "circumstances" are those where the plaintiff was "personally denied equal treatment by the challenged discriminatory conduct."[23] The plaintiffs in *Allen*, according to the Court, had not been personally subject to discriminatory treatment because they could not show their own children's ability to receive a racially integrated education had been diminished. To accept the plaintiffs' stigmatic injury as cognizable, the Court charged, would mean that "[a] black person in Hawaii could challenge the grant of a tax exemption to a racially discriminatory school in Maine."[24]

Thus, the Supreme Court has recognized dignitary harm as a possible basis for injury in fact in the discrimination setting, but it has required plaintiffs to be "personally denied equal treatment." In other contexts, too, federal courts have both accepted and limited dignitary harm as a ground for standing. In some Establishment Clause cases, federal appellate courts have recognized plaintiffs' claims of stigma stemming from exposure to government-sponsored religious hostility. For example, the Ninth Circuit held in 2010 that Catholic plaintiffs in San Francisco had standing to bring an Establishment Clause challenge to a city resolution criticizing Catholic

[19] Allen v. Wright, 468 U.S. 737, 739–40 (1984).
[20] *Id.* at 756–57.
[21] *Id.* at 754.
[22] *Id.* at 755.
[23] *Id.* (internal quotation marks omitted).
[24] *Id.* at 755–56.

teachings on homosexuality.[25] The plaintiffs, the court observed, "allege that the stigmatizing resolution leaves them feeling like second-class citizens of the San Francisco political community, and expresses to the citizenry of San Francisco that they are."[26] Stigmatic harm as a ground for injury in fact also played a role in some Establishment Clause challenges to President Trump's "travel ban."[27] Thus, courts have sometimes credited the claim that a government-sponsored message harms plaintiffs by diminishing the status of those belonging to a certain religion—a form of dignitary harm.

At the same time, federal courts have not uniformly embraced dignitary harm as injury in fact in Establishment Clause cases. Sometimes, the court's objection is that the plaintiffs were not personally affected by the alleged message of hostility "except through their abstract offense."[28] Indeed, some justices have objected to what they call claims of "offended observer" standing emerging from plaintiffs' exposure to religious displays on government property or to religious events taking place under government auspices.[29] According to these justices, a plaintiff's feelings of offense at the state's alleged endorsement of religion do not amount to injury in fact. Overall, standing based on stigma directed at religious practices, or resulting from government-sponsored religious activity, has some support in judicial rulings; but there are also notes of skepticism.

The Supreme Court's treatment of standing grounded on reputational harm provides additional backing for dignitary harm as injury in fact. Reputational harm, the Court has held, can be a concrete injury.[30] For example, the Court in 1987 found standing for a plaintiff who claimed his reputation would suffer if the films he wished to exhibit were classified as

[25] Catholic League for Religious & Civil Rights v. San Francisco, 624 F.3d 1043, 1053 (9th Cir. 2010).

[26] *Id.* at 1052.

[27] The US Court of Appeals for the Fourth Circuit—in an opinion later vacated by the Supreme Court, though on different grounds—found standing for a Muslim plaintiff to bring an Establishment Clause challenge partly on the basis that the travel ban conveyed an "alleged message of religious condemnation," a message that "foreign-born Muslims . . . are outsiders, not full members of the political community." Int'l Refugee Assistance Project v. Trump, 857 F.3d 554, 584–85 (4th Cir.) (internal quotation marks omitted), *as amended* (May 31, 2017), *as amended* (June 15, 2017), *vacated and remanded sub nom.* Trump v. Int'l Refugee Assistance, 583 U.S. 912 (2017).

[28] In re Navy Chaplaincy, 534 F.3d 756, 764–65 (D.C. Cir. 2008).

[29] *See, e.g.*, Statement of Justice Gorsuch Respecting the Denial of Certiorari, Ocala v. Rojas, 143 S. Ct. 764, 764–65 (2023); Dissent from Denial of Certiorari, Ocala v. Rojas, 143 S. Ct. 764, 765–68 (2023) (Thomas, J.). For discussion of expressive theories of law in the setting of government-sponsored religious displays, see Richard C. Schragger, *Of Crosses and Confederate Monuments: A Theory of Unconstitutional Government Speech*, 63 Ariz. L. Rev. 45, 80–81 (2021).

[30] TransUnion LLC v. Ramirez, 594 U.S. 413, 425 (2021).

"political propaganda."[31] In a more recent court of appeals case, a nonprofit organization successfully asserted injury in fact when its website was placed on a list of "unreliable" sites that included ones denying the Holocaust.[32] Reputational harm often involves damage to status or loss of control over self-presentation to others. Thus, the cognizability of reputational harm bolsters the notion of dignitary harm as injury in fact.

Another doctrinal area involving dignitary harm and exposure involves privacy violations. Infringements of privacy expose sensitive or vulnerable parts of the self to the views of others without the person's consent. The individual is thereby stripped of control over his or her self-presentation. As the Supreme Court noted in a case involving disclosure of a rap sheet, privacy "encompass[es] the individual's control of information concerning his or her person."[33] The Court has connected privacy to dignity—for example, describing "[t]he overriding function of the Fourth Amendment" as "protect[ing] personal privacy and dignity against unwarranted intrusion by the State."[34] Therefore, standing in privacy cases reveals aspects of a court's approach toward dignitary harm as injury in fact.

Federal courts have found standing for some plaintiffs alleging violations of privacy, although plaintiffs have a better shot if they incur discernible economic harm[35] or have their information "actual[ly] misuse[d]," such as through the filing of a fraudulent tax return.[36] When such downstream harm is less clear, courts are more reluctant to rule that plaintiffs have standing.[37] That poses a problem for standing based on privacy violations, as the harm stemming from these violations is often difficult to identify or quantify in the near term. As Danielle Citron and Daniel Solove write, "[m]any privacy violations involve broken promises or thwarted expectations about how people's data will be collected, used, and disclosed. The downstream consequences of these practices are often hard to determine in the here and now."[38] Further, privacy violations may involve "small harms [that] are dispersed among millions—and sometimes billions—of people."[39] These

[31] Meese v. Keene, 481 U.S. 465, 474–75 (1987).
[32] Turkish Coal. of Am., Inc. v. Bruininks, 678 F.3d 617, 622–23 (8th Cir. 2012).
[33] U.S. Dep't of Just. v. Reps. Comm. For Freedom of Press, 489 U.S. 749, 763 (1989).
[34] Schmerber v. California, 384 U.S. 757, 767 (1966).
[35] In re Equifax Inc. Customer Data Sec. Breach Litig., 999 F.3d 1247, 1262 (11th Cir. 2021).
[36] Webb v. Injured Workers Pharmacy, LLC, 72 F.4th 365, 373 (1st Cir. 2023).
[37] *See, e.g.*, Hunstein v. Preferred Collection & Mgmt. Servs., Inc., 48 F.4th 1236, 1245 (11th Cir. 2022).
[38] Danielle Keats Citron & Daniel J. Solove, *Privacy Harms*, 102 B.U. L. Rev. 793, 796–97 (2022) (internal footnote omitted).
[39] *Id.* at 797.

features of privacy violations create tension with the strictures of Article III standing doctrine, with its requirements of concrete and particularized harm. This kind of tension is explored in the next section.

Overall, there is doctrinal support for the idea that dignitary harm qualifies as injury in fact, but under limited circumstances. The limitations reflect certain features of dignity that render it challenging to integrate into Article III standing doctrine, as is explored in what follows.

The Challenges of Dignitary Harm

Dignitary harm has aspects that may prompt skepticism about its suitability as Article III injury in fact. These challenges are surmountable, but identifying them helps to clarify the possibilities and difficulties for dignity as a legal concept.

Breadth of Dignitary Harm

Dignitary harm raises the concern that the circle of plaintiffs permitted to sue in federal courts could expand substantially. Why? First, dignitary harm is not necessarily tied to a particular physical location. If a national political party adopts a platform using derogatory language to refer to people with disabilities, the resulting dignitary harm could affect an array of geographically dispersed individuals. Second, dignitary harm may stem from membership in a collective body in a manner that magnifies the effects of a dignitary violation. Individuals may suffer dignitary harm due to denigration of their group. For example, the exclusion of members of a religious group from admission to medical school sends the message that all members of the group occupy a lower status, and so it may stigmatize even those members with little interest in medical school.

Doctrinally, the Supreme Court has permitted a "widely shared" harm to qualify as injury in fact.[40] In practice, however, concerns about the volume and reach of federal litigation often fuel skepticism regarding dignitary harm. In the 1984 discrimination case *Allen v. Wright*, the Supreme Court (as earlier noted) expressed concern that accepting the plaintiffs' claim of stigmatic harm would mean that "[a] black person in Hawaii could challenge the grant of a tax exemption to a racially discriminatory school in Maine."[41]

[40] Fed. Election Comm'n v. Akins, 524 U.S. 11, 24 (1998).
[41] Allen v. Wright, 468 U.S. 737, 755–56 (1984).

The Court feared, that is, that recognizing dignitary harm stemming from membership in a group that was the object of discrimination would lead to significant expansion of standing across geographic boundaries.

The prospect of expansive standing is of concern to courts for multiple reasons. Judges often seem wary of opening the "floodgates of litigation" and depleting judicial resources.[42] Instead of citing this worry, though, judges tend to emphasize the separation of powers and the proper scope of judicial authority. Federal courts have limited jurisdiction and, in the Supreme Court's words, "do not exercise general legal oversight of the Legislative and Executive Branches, or of private entities."[43] If many plaintiffs could assert injury in fact based on dignitary harm, the argument runs, federal courts might turn into a forum for the resolution of essentially political disputes. Later in this chapter, I argue that a restrictive approach to standing may actually undermine the separation of powers, as judges themselves assume the authority to decide which cases to hear. Nonetheless, a practical approach to dignitary harm and Article III standing must account for the concern that an expansion of federal jurisdiction would erode the distinction between judicial and political functions.

Dignitary Harm and Ideological Litigation

Standing doctrine is sometimes employed to cut back on "ideological" lawsuits brought by those pursuing public policy goals through litigation. To be sure, federal courts still adjudicate numerous cases by individuals and organizations seeking to achieve public aims—in areas such as immigration, voting rights, affirmative action, and so on. But skepticism about "ideological" plaintiffs persists and may affect courts' approaches toward dignitary harm.

Plaintiffs often experience dignitary harm as a consequence of actions that express a denigrating message, and their adverse reaction to those messages may be rooted in political or philosophical opposition. Or, at least, courts might so suspect. An example involves a Mississippi statute barring the government from taking "discriminatory action" against those who acted in accordance with the belief that marriage is between a man and a woman.[44]

[42] *See* Marin K. Levy, *Judging the Flood of Litigation*, 80 U. Chi. L. Rev. 1007 (2013); Michael T. Morley, Spokeo: *The Quasi-Hohfeldian Plaintiff and the Nonfederal Federal Question*, 25 Geo. Mason L. Rev. 583, 603 (2018).

[43] TransUnion LLC v. Ramirez, 594 U.S. 413, 423–24 (2021).

[44] Barber v. Bryant, 860 F.3d 345, 350–51 (5th Cir. 2017).

For instance, the law protected businesses that declined to provide wedding-related services (presumably, to gay couples) on the basis of the owners' belief.[45] A constitutional challenge to the Mississippi statute was filed in a federal court; the plaintiffs were individuals who did not agree with the covered beliefs, including religious leaders, and gay and transgender individuals who argued they would be negatively affected by the statute.[46] The lawsuit was based on both the Equal Protection Clause and the Establishment Clause. In particular, the plaintiffs objected to "the clear message sent by [the statute] that the 'state government disapproves of and is hostile to same-sex couples . . .' "[47]

The US Court of Appeals for the Fifth Circuit in 2017 denied standing, reasoning that the plaintiffs were not personally harmed. According to the court, the plaintiffs had not "personally confront[ed]" any Establishment Clause violation—for an individual "cannot confront statutory text."[48] As to the equal protection claim, the plaintiffs, according to the Fifth Circuit, lacked standing because they could not show with sufficient definiteness that they would be personally subject to unequal treatment through the denial of services.[49] Regardless of whether the court's conclusion was correct, the case speaks to the blurriness of the line between personal harm and ideological opposition in the realm of dignitary violations. Can a plaintiff truly be harmed by a "message"? Does a federal court properly exercise its authority when it adjudicates a suit based on this type of harm? The concern is that courts will find themselves mired in ideological grievances.[50]

Moreover, the adjudication of disputes based on dignitary harm may invite charges that judges are biased. The perception of dignitary harm (or the lack thereof) is often tied up with a person's values. In the Fifth Circuit case just mentioned, some might argue that a gay couple is not genuinely stigmatized when certain wedding vendors deny service, provided the services are available elsewhere. Others would take the view that the denial of service works dignitary harm regardless of whether the material benefits

[45] *Id.* at 351.
[46] *Id.*
[47] *Id.* at 352.
[48] *Id.* at 354.
[49] *Id.* at 354–58.
[50] *See* Schragger, note 29, at 48 ("Whether religious symbols or Confederate iconography, competing cultural and political forces are engaged in highly fraught battles over government expressive conduct."). On ideologically motivated plaintiffs and standing, see Rachel Bayefsky, *Public-Law Litigation at a Crossroads: Article III Standing and "Tester" Plaintiffs*, 99 N.Y.U. L. Rev. Online 128, 148–49 (2024).

are available elsewhere, by conveying a message of disrespect for same-sex unions. Drawing the line between unwarranted "offense" and dignitary harm may lead to the perception that judges are relying on their normative presuppositions, and that may lower public assessments of judicial legitimacy.

Evidentiary Issues with Dignitary Harm

A third reason for dignitary harm to elicit disfavor in the standing analysis involves evidence. It is relatively straightforward, one might argue, for courts to ascertain whether someone has suffered economic or physical harm. Is there a debit in the bank account? Is there a broken leg? It might seem more difficult to tell whether someone has suffered dignitary harm.[51] At the motion-to-dismiss stage of litigation, the question is whether a plaintiff has "plausibly" alleged dignitary harm; at summary judgment, the plaintiff must produce sufficient evidence (say, in the form of affidavits or testimony) that she has suffered dignitary harm; and at trial, the plaintiff's evidence of harm must satisfy the relevant burden of proof.[52] With respect to any of these stages, it could be argued that dignitary harm is especially difficult to identify or support.

Later in the chapter, I question the claim that dignitary harm is distinctively problematic from an evidentiary perspective. But to flesh out the objection: the evidentiary point bleeds into the worry about ideological influence. If dignitary harm is hard to prove from an "objective" perspective, then judges' ideological predilections may be more likely to play a role in determining when dignitary harm has occurred. The evidentiary concern also raises issues about the bounds of judicial authority. If judges cannot readily determine whether injury in fact has occurred (or has been plausibly alleged), then they are being asked to resolve cases when they cannot clearly decide whether their legal authority justifies it. Again, dignitary harm prompts unease about overshooting the proper scope of federal judicial power.

Many of the critiques of dignitary harm discussed above could be directed at any court. But some may be directed specifically toward the *federal* courts,

[51] Spokeo v. Robins, 578 U.S. 330, 340 (2016) ("[T]angible injuries are perhaps easier to recognize.").
[52] Lujan v. Defs. of Wildlife, 504 U.S. 555, 561 (1992).

which (the Supreme Court frequently emphasizes) have limited jurisdiction and are not supposed to encroach on the powers of Congress or the President.

Dignitary harm, then, seems as though it should often qualify as concrete and particularized injury in fact. But integrating dignity into constitutional standing doctrine leads to challenges; it creates the prospect of unlimited standing, intractable line-drawing problems, and controversial judicial rulings. The next step is to respond to these challenges.

Integrating Dignitary Harm into Constitutional Standing Doctrine

Courts should not exclude dignitary harm from the ambit of Article III injury in fact. As an initial matter, dignitary harm is not the only form of injury to raise questions about expansiveness, ideological influence, and proof. "Tangible" varieties of economic and physical harms also pose these problems. To reject dignitary harm would not be a neutral decision, but one that invites charges of arbitrariness or bias. At the same time, judges face the challenge of determining whether plaintiffs have plausibly alleged (or proven) dignitary harm, as well as the question of whether all dignitary harm should qualify as injury in fact.

The most appropriate way for the American legal system to react to these difficulties, I suggest in this section, is for Congress rather than the federal courts to identify proper plaintiffs. Because the Supreme Court has long eschewed reliance on congressional judgment in defining injury in fact, however, I examine other options. The Court has looked to "history and tradition" to define cognizable harm. This approach risks embroiling the federal courts in contentious decisions about which historical injuries correspond to today's dignitary harms. Yet to the extent the Court looks to history, it should take into account the pedigree of dignitary harm. More promisingly, federal courts can and should create a body of law recognizing certain assertions of dignitary harm as injury in fact. To do so, they can draw on constitutional and statutory sources, as well as judicial precedent outside the standing context. Courts can also limit the circle of plaintiffs able to assert dignitary harm by enumerating criteria to identify the parties most likely to be affected by a dignitary violation. Federal courts can hence recognize dignitary harm as injury in fact without bursting open the gates of federal jurisdiction.

The Trouble with "Tangible" Harm

Constitutional standing doctrine generally privileges "tangible" over "intangible" forms of harm. Courts seem more inclined to recognize "traditional tangible harms, such as physical and monetary harms," as injury in fact.[53] "Intangible" harms can also be cognizable injury; the Supreme Court has given the examples of "reputational harms, disclosure of private information, and intrusion upon seclusion."[54] But the Court typically subjects intangible harm to a more rigorous inquiry to determine if the harm counts as injury in fact.

To elaborate, the Court has recently turned to a "history and tradition" inquiry for constitutional standing doctrine: In the words of its 2021 *TransUnion* case, the question is whether an asserted harm bears a sufficiently close connection to a harm "traditionally recognized as providing a basis for lawsuits in American courts."[55] Physical and monetary harms appear quite likely to be deemed "traditional," while "intangible" harms warrant a more searching, case-specific inquiry into whether the harm is concrete.[56]

Dignitary harm is prone to be viewed as intangible and therefore subject to the more probing constitutional standing analysis. The world is not divided neatly, however, into categories of tangible and intangible harms.[57] For example, monetary loss is viewed as tangible for standing purposes but can be seen as "intangible" in the context of property insurance—for, unlike "tangible property," money cannot be "touched, seen, and smelled."[58]

[53] TransUnion v. Ramirez, 594 U.S. 413, 425 (2021).

[54] *Id.*

[55] *Id.*

[56] Physical and monetary harms may not *always* be cognizable. The Supreme Court in 2023, for example, held that state plaintiffs Texas and Louisiana lacked Article III standing in a suit against the federal government for failing to arrest and prosecute more noncitizens. United States v. Texas, 599 U.S. 670, 676 (2023). The states alleged that they had incurred monetary costs due to the absence of more arrests and prosecutions. Although "[m]onetary costs are of course an injury," the Court stated, the states' injury was not "traditionally redressable in federal court" because courts did not traditionally order executive officials to change their arrest or prosecution policies. *Id.* at 676–77. The Court appeared to be importing a "traditionally redressable" requirement into the injury analysis even in a case involving monetary harm. The *Texas* case, however, may have reflected specific concerns about preserving executive discretion with respect to arrests and prosecutions. Moreover, the Court has not overruled its case law providing that "traditional tangible harms, such as physical harms and monetary harms," "readily qualify as concrete injuries," and that "[i]f a defendant has caused physical or monetary injury to the plaintiff, the plaintiff has suffered a concrete injury in fact under Article III." *TransUnion*, 594 U.S. at 425.

[57] *See* Rachel Bayefsky, *Constitutional Injury and Tangibility*, 59 Wm. & Mary L. Rev. 2285, 2330–35 (2018) [hereinafter Bayefsky, *Tangibility*]. The discussion that follows draws partially on points in this article. *See also* Rachel Bayefsky, *Tangibility and Tainted Reliance in* Dobbs, 136 Harv. L. Rev. F. 384, 394–95 (2023).

[58] Kazi v. State Farm Fire & Cas. Co., 15 P.3d 223, 229 (Cal. 2001).

Economic loss is sometimes deemed "intangible" for purposes of the economic loss doctrine in negligence law, which generally blocks parties from recovering in tort when negligence causes purely economic loss as opposed to physical damage.[59]

In legal settings, then, the terms "tangible" and "intangible" are not solely descriptive; they reflect normative judgments about the kinds of harms that warrant legal redress or judicial adjudication. It is no coincidence that economic harm is viewed as "intangible" when courts are skeptical about permitting recovery. To say that dignitary harm is "intangible" is to express concern about judicial capacity to resolve cases involving dignity or the legitimacy of courts' doing so. Such skepticism may emanate from the kind of difficulties discussed in the previous section.

Do these difficulties, however, warrant a more searching approach to the concreteness of dignitary harm? Take the problem of breadth. Dignitary harm can, as noted, affect a wide swath of people. But economic harm can affect many individuals as well. A data breach resulting in financial loss to millions of people is an example. In a mass tort situation, numerous individuals suffer harm, but the harm (according to the Supreme Court) is still cognizable injury in fact.[60] Dignitary harm might have a special propensity to affect many people, perhaps because it could result from expressive activity or actions directed at members of a collective. Yet courts could adopt doctrines that prevent the unlimited assertion of dignitary harm, as discussed below. In other words, they could acknowledge that dignitary harm is real—even when widespread—and nevertheless restrict its capacity to ground standing. Large-scale dignitary harm is no more illusory than large-scale physical or economic harm.

The concern about ideological litigation may affect lawsuits based on "tangible" harm as well. Litigants who wish to achieve ideological goals may assert economic harm; for example, a data-privacy activist may allege that she suffered monetary harm due to a data breach. The Supreme Court has not rebuffed lawsuits simply because plaintiffs are ideologically motivated or because they care more about "principle" than about monetary loss.[61]

Indeed, excluding lawsuits based on dignitary harm would compound the very problems that underlie skepticism regarding "ideological" litigation. It

[59] *See, e.g.*, Floor Craft Floor Covering, Inc. v. Parma Cmty. Gen. Hosp. Ass'n, 560 N.E.2d 206, 208 (Ohio 1990).

[60] Fed. Election Comm'n v. Akins, 524 U.S. 11, 24 (1998).

[61] *See* Bayefsky, note 50, at 137, 148–49.

is not "neutral" to treat litigation seeking to advance public aims as less suited to the federal courts than traditional private-law litigation. Judges taking this approach would be making a normative determination that itself risks producing judicial overreach and courting political controversy.

One might argue that dignitary harm warrants exclusion for a reason that is actually neutral—the evidentiary challenges of identifying dignitary violations. It is not clear, however, that the presence of dignitary harm is so difficult to ascertain. The fact that dignitary harm takes effect primarily on plaintiffs' psyches does not render it impervious to evidentiary proof. By way of comparison, parties seeking to prove emotional distress damages often introduce medical witnesses. To be sure, an emotional reaction is not essential to dignitary harm. But plaintiffs in many cases could offer proof that they have undergone a mental experience characteristic of a response to stigma.

Moreover, for numerous instances of dignitary harm, the facts underlying the allegation that the plaintiff suffered harm are not difficult to prove. If members of an atheist group assert that they are stigmatized through contact with a religious monument on public land, they can demonstrate fairly readily that the monument exists and that they regularly encounter it. The facts are not obscure; the challenging issues are whether these facts amount to genuine *harm* and whether such harm properly serves as an impetus for judicial action. Those issues do not depend on a factual evidentiary determination.

There are reasons to question, therefore, the view that dignitary harm is categorically more problematic for federal courts to address than "tangible" harm. In fact, claims involving monetary harm may call on courts to exercise considerable judicial superintendence of executive or legislative functions, such as healthcare or retirement programs.[62] The risks attending broader standing for cases concerning dignitary harm are not *sui generis*. Thus, judges should be hesitant to downgrade dignitary harm in the injury-in-fact analysis.

Congressional Judgment and Dignitary Harm

Excluding dignitary harm from the ambit of injury in fact, the chapter has argued, would be unwarranted and would inflate judges' power in a way that

[62] *See* United States v. Texas, 599 U.S. 670, 676 (2023).

those committed to bounds on judicial authority generally strive to avoid. Surely, however, judges are not required to find standing anytime a party alleges dignitary harm. The question, then, is how to undertake the standing analysis in cases where the plaintiff claims to have incurred dignitary harm.

As a first-cut response, federal judges should leave this determination to a body that is more clearly authorized to make contentious moral and political choices—namely, Congress. Relational dignity includes a normative component. For example, a student does not ordinarily incur dignitary harm when denied the opportunity to speak from the professor's lectern during class, because her *rightful* status was not infringed. A politician does not suffer dignitary harm from routine media coverage of his transgression, because he has not been denied *adequate* control over self-presentation. These views require normative judgments about "rightful" status and "adequate" control.

Accordingly, decisions about whether to treat asserted dignitary harm as cognizable for standing purposes require contestable normative judgments. Has a store owner properly alleged dignitary harm when state antidiscrimination law requires her to provide a service that she finds morally objectionable? To avoid entanglement in such disputes, judges could rely on Congress to identify cognizable dignitary harm. Specifically, courts could hold that standing depends on the existence of a cause of action—including a congressional statute authorizing suit—rather than on judicially determined injury in fact. Contrary to the Supreme Court's 1992 holding in *Lujan*, standing would become a matter of legal injury rather than of factual harm. Hence, congressional authorization to sue would suffice for standing.

A common rejoinder is that Congress could then green light types of lawsuits that are wholly inappropriate for adjudication in federal court, such as a lawsuit seeking an advisory opinion.[63] But federal courts could reserve the right to hold that certain clearly problematic lawsuits fall outside the bounds of an Article III case or controversy. For example, courts could continue to rule out requests from executive officials for legal advice from the Supreme Court,[64] as well as suits brought under a statutory scheme subjecting federal judges' rulings to executive revision.[65] In reaching these holdings, courts could note that Founding-era evidence prohibits such suits. Requiring "concrete" and "particularized" harm across the board, by

[63] *See* TransUnion LLC v. Ramirez, 594 U.S. 413, 424, 430 n.3 (2021).
[64] *See* Letter from Thomas Jefferson, Sec'y of State, to Chief Justice Jay and Associate Justices (July 18, 1793), *in* HART & WECHSLER, note 3, at 50–52.
[65] *E.g.*, Hayburn's Case, 2 U.S. (2 Dall.) 409 (1792).

contrast, is an overbroad response to the possibility that Congress could authorize these kinds of problematic suits.

The argument that Article III standing ought to depend on causes of action rather than injury in fact has been made many times,[66] and it has not secured much support at the Supreme Court. Many justices, with varying jurisprudential views, seem to prefer to preserve federal courts' gatekeeping function in the standing analysis. In order to speak to current legal realities, the rest of the chapter will proceed on the assumption that the federal courts will maintain injury in fact as a judicially enforced Article III check on Congress's ability to authorize plaintiffs to sue.

It is still worth keeping in mind that the challenge of identifying cognizable dignitary harm is compounded by the Supreme Court's decision to assign to federal judges the task of gauging particularized and concrete harm. This challenge is not impossible to meet, as discussed below. Yet to the extent one finds any given line-drawing solution to be unsatisfying, one ought to question the use of injury in fact as a basis for standing.

History and Tradition

If federal courts are not to follow Congress in deciding which harms are cognizable, then how should they make these determinations? One response the Supreme Court has furnished is "history and tradition." According to the Court, "history and tradition offer a meaningful guide to the types of cases that Article III empowers federal courts to consider."[67] In the 2021 *TransUnion* case, the Supreme Court directed courts to ascertain, in assessing the concreteness of harm, "whether plaintiffs have identified a close historical or common-law analogue for their asserted injury."[68] The turn to "history and tradition" may reflect the search for a more "objective" analysis than judges' individual examinations of asserted harm.

How does dignitary harm fit into "history and tradition"? Legal concern for certain varieties of dignitary harm has a meaningful historical pedigree. As Chapter 4 will explain, causes of action with a strong dignitary dimension, such as offensive-touching battery and defamation, have deep roots. Newer privacy torts that developed in the late nineteenth and early twentieth

[66] *E.g.*, Fletcher, note 6, at 229; Sunstein, note 6, at 222–23.
[67] Sprint Commc'ns Co., L.P. v. APCC Servs., Inc., 554 U.S. 269, 274 (2008).
[68] *TransUnion*, 594 U.S. at 424.

centuries also protect dignitary interests. Therefore, a "history and tradition" approach can treat certain types of dignitary harm as injury in fact.

A focus on "history and tradition" is not straightforward to apply. At the outset, which historical period is relevant? One possibility is the Founding era. An originalist might argue that in identifying justiciable "cases" or "controversies," courts should be guided by the kinds of disputes that courts in England or the American colonies adjudicated at the time of the Founding.[69] In that event, causes of action that developed after the Founding, such as the privacy torts, would not function as suitable analogues for today's dignitary harm. Yet the Supreme Court has not (thus far) insisted on a Founding-era analogue for a justiciable suit. In *TransUnion*, the Court left open the possibility that emotional harm could suffice for injury in fact "by analogy to the tort of intentional infliction of emotional distress"[70]—a tort that arose only after the Founding.[71] Perhaps, then, post-Founding torts such as intentional infliction of emotional distress or the privacy torts could serve as adequate analogies to dignitary harms. But if "history and tradition" is untethered from the Founding, the question becomes which traditions, from which historical period(s), are to be credited. If a nineteenth-century tort is an acceptable analogue, why not a twenty-first-century one? These issues introduce an element of judicial discretion into the standing calculus.

Further, it is far from simple to connect harms reflected in common-law causes of action to modern-day injuries, which often stem from statutory violations. Is an "unauthorized inquiry into a consumer's propensity-to-pay score"[72]—an alleged infringement of the federal Fair Credit Reporting Act—analogous to the tort of intrusion upon seclusion, which occurs when someone intrudes in a "highly offensive" way "upon the solitude or seclusion of another or his private affairs or concerns"?[73] What about an unwanted phone call and voicemail?[74] Or unwanted text messages?[75] Or a debt collector's failure to reveal its full name in voice messages?[76] Courts have

[69] *See Sprint*, 554 U.S. at 275–76; Vermont Agency of Nat. Res. v. U.S. ex rel. Stevens, 529 U.S. 765, 774 (2000).
[70] *TransUnion*, 594 U.S. at 436 n.7.
[71] John J. Kircher, *The Four Faces of Tort Law: Liability for Emotional Harm*, 90 MARQUETTE L. REV. 789, 795 (2007).
[72] Persinger v. Sw. Credit Sys., L.P., 20 F.4th 1184, 1192 (7th Cir. 2021).
[73] Restatement (Second) of Torts § 652B (AM. LAW. INST. 1977).
[74] Lupia v. Medicredit, Inc., 8 F.4th 1184, 1191 (10th Cir. 2021).
[75] Gadelhak v. AT&T Servs., Inc., 950 F.3d 458, 462–63 (7th Cir. 2020); Salcedo v. Hanna, 936 F.3d 1162, 1172 (11th Cir. 2019).
[76] Ward v. Nat'l Patient Acct. Servs. Sols., Inc., 9 F.4th 357, 362 (6th Cir. 2021).

come to different conclusions regarding the cognizability of these kinds of harms. The task of pairing common-law torts with statutory violations is not a mechanical exercise, and it can be influenced by normative perspectives.

The "history and tradition" approach, therefore, does not solve the separation-of-powers issue created by entrusting judges with authority to determine injury in fact. When judges draw analogies between dignitary harm and historical legal wrongs, they face methodological challenges and the possibility of ideological influence. But to the extent judges undertake the historical inquiry, it is worth pointing out that dignitary harm has meaningful historical roots.

The Common Law of Standing

If the Supreme Court is to retain injury in fact as a judicially determined criterion for Article III standing, then federal courts ought to develop a body of doctrine, in common-law fashion, to identify cognizable dignitary harm. Judges should look to plaintiffs' allegations or evidence to see whether plaintiffs have adequately asserted that they are subject to wrongful status demotion, domination, or exposure. Examples that would make the cut are: a prisoner's claim to have been abused by guards (even absent physical harm); an employee's claim that his employer mocked his disability in front of coworkers; or an individual's claim that she was filmed unclothed without her permission.

Significantly, courts would not need to work entirely from scratch in each case; they could build up and draw on a body of precedent indicating that various types of asserted dignitary harm are cognizable. This precedent would accumulate in the common-law fashion, as judges encounter new scenarios and consider their similarities and differences with standing determinations made in the past. The workability of various doctrinal results could be tested against the experience in the jurisdictions that reach them, with the Supreme Court intervening when necessary, after a period of percolation, to institute a nationwide rule.

On which bases should judges decide that asserted dignitary harms are cognizable? One resource is positive law, such as constitutional provisions, legislative enactments, and judicial precedent. In *Allen v. Wright*, for instance, the Supreme Court explained that the absence of racial integration in education was "one of the most serious injuries recognized in our legal system" and was therefore sufficient to "support standing in some circumstances."[77] The Court supported this claim by referring to its prior cases, notably *Brown v. Board of Education*. In other words, the injury-in-fact analysis was influenced by previous judicial rulings outside the standing context and presumably by the constitutional provisions underlying those rulings. (In *Allen*, the Court ultimately concluded that the plaintiffs' claimed racial-integration injury did not support standing because it failed the "causation" prong of standing doctrine.[78]) Judicial precedent and constitutional provisions therefore provide legal sources to bolster a court's identification of injury in fact.

Congressional legislation is another potential source of guidance on standing. To be sure, the Supreme Court has emphasized the distinction between the presence of a statutory cause of action and the existence of injury in fact.[79] In other words, it has rejected the view that a congressionally created cause of action should suffice for Article III standing. Nonetheless, the Court has called for "due respect to Congress's decision" to prohibit conduct and to create a cause of action,[80] and courts making standing determinations could refer to statutory material even if they do not treat congressional judgment as dispositive.

There are limits to reliance on positive law in the injury-in-fact analysis, especially because some plaintiffs may sue with the goal of changing existing legal arrangements. For example, the Supreme Court held in the 1872 case *Bradwell v. Illinois* that the Fourteenth Amendment did not require states to admit married women to the bar as lawyers.[81] If a married woman wishing to become a lawyer in Illinois had brought suit in 1900 asking for *Bradwell* to be overruled, could she have asserted injury in fact based on dignitary harm?[82]

One way for courts to answer in the affirmative—and, more generally, to permit standing for plaintiffs urging a change in existing law—is for courts to be receptive to claims of Article III injury that rest on a "good faith argument for an extension, modification or reversal of existing law" (to borrow a phrase from the context of legal ethics rules).[83] Thus, a female plaintiff

[77] Allen v. Wright, 468 U.S. 737, 756 (1984).
[78] *Id.* at 756–57.
[79] TransUnion LLC v. Ramirez, 594 U.S. 413, 426–27 (2021).
[80] *Id.* at 425.
[81] 83 U.S. 130 (1872).
[82] Assume she would not have been able to demonstrate any economic harm, perhaps because of the structure of family finances.
[83] *See* Model R. Prof. Conduct 3.1 (ABA 2021). A district court is bound to follow the Supreme Court's precedent. But a district court could still recognize a good-faith argument that the Supreme Court, at a later stage of the proceedings, should reverse its precedent.

challenging a restriction on admission to the Illinois bar as a violation of the Fourteenth Amendment could have argued that the amendment provided a basis for her claim of cognizable dignitary harm despite the Supreme Court's prior constitutional interpretation. For a court to agree, it would not have needed to hold that the plaintiff *had suffered* a Fourteenth Amendment violation; that is a merits question. But the Fourteenth Amendment's language would have furnished some support for a claim that she had incurred a status harm—sufficient support to afford the plaintiff standing to challenge precedent. Thus, dignitary harm as a basis for standing need not be tethered to existing legal arrangements.

What happens when plaintiffs assert claims of injury in fact that are based on morally repugnant ideas about status? For example, what if a white plaintiff during desegregation argued that he was subject to dignitary harm when he was forced to share public parks with Black individuals, and urged the reversal of *Brown v. Board* and its progeny? Today, one could respond that the plaintiff is not making even a good faith argument for a reversal of existing law. But that response might have been more difficult in an earlier era, when some social mores supported racial segregation.

The challenge posed by morally repugnant views about status hearkens back to the discussion in Chapter 2 of intersubjective understandings of dignity—those based on prevailing social perspectives—versus objective understandings of dignity, which are grounded in moral truths that extend beyond social views. Relational dignity as understood in this book is not grounded solely in social perspectives. In other words, a claim about dignitary violations that seems socially plausible can still fail to justify standing. This would happen, for example, if the plaintiff does not adequately assert that the *rightful* status was infringed. In evaluating dignitary claims, judges should consider social understandings but should not entirely relinquish their independent judgment. Therefore, a judge would have been justified in rejecting, on moral grounds, an assertion of dignitary harm stemming from desegregation. A plaintiff asserting such harm would not be alleging a violation of the *rightful* status. To be sure, this position requires judges to wield their own moral authority. Yet that is the consequence of the Supreme Court's assignment of responsibility to judges to rule on the existence of injury in fact.

Another option is for judges to be relatively open to assertions of dignitary harm in the threshold standing inquiry. This suggestion applies particularly strongly when claims of dignitary harm are more borderline, from a normative perspective, than in the desegregation example. After all, standing is a threshold inquiry that leaves the merits to be determined. Plaintiffs who successfully assert standing based on dignitary harm may still lose on the merits if the court decides they have not proven the elements of their claim. For example, a plaintiff might allege that her employer negligently released compromising personal information and assert that she incurred dignitary harm. On the standing front, the employer might counter that the relevant information was insufficiently significant to deprive the plaintiff of adequate control over her self-presentation. Even if the court decides at the outset of the litigation that the plaintiff has borne her burden to plausibly allege dignitary harm,[84] the plaintiff might later be unable to prove that her employer was negligent. That would doom her claim on the merits. In other words, the standing analysis is not the end of a lawsuit.

In sum, judges are not bereft of tools to identify cognizable dignitary harm even if today's standing inquiry is taken on its own terms, namely, if one accepts the requirement of concrete and particularized injury. Judges can look to positive law and recognize good-faith attempts to change existing law. Value choices may enter the picture, especially when the claim of dignitary harm is problematic from a normative point of view. But the involvement of value choices is a feature of judicial inquiries into injury in fact more generally.

If a court decides that a plaintiff has plausibly alleged (or proven) dignitary harm, must the court hold that the plaintiff has satisfied the "injury" prong of Article III standing? The idea of injury "in fact" might suggest that a plaintiff has met the injury requirement as soon as she plausibly alleges real harm to herself—that is, concrete and particularized harm. Dignitary harm is real, and it can affect plaintiffs personally. That might suggest that all dignitary harms incurred by the plaintiff must be the basis for Article III standing.

In actuality, however, courts do not rely merely on the existence of real-world harm to identify injury in fact. As earlier discussed, courts consider the broader implications of allowing a particular type of lawsuit into federal court, such as the impact on administrability and remedies. Even when these inquiries are cast as part of the doctrinal analysis of injury in fact,

[84] *See* TransUnion v. Ramirez, 594 U.S. 413, 430–31 (2021) ("As the party invoking federal jurisdiction, the plaintiffs bear the burden of demonstrating that they have standing.").

they implicate more general issues about cases' suitability for federal-court adjudication.

As part of the wider inquiry, courts could address concerns about unfettered expansion of standing for plaintiffs asserting dignitary harm. If judges are worried about opening the floodgates of litigation, for instance, they could enumerate criteria to restrict the circle of potential plaintiffs.[85] In Establishment Clause challenges to religious displays, for example, courts have pursued this goal by requiring plaintiffs to come in "direct and unwelcome contact" with the offending display.[86] Other criteria that courts could employ are the longevity and frequency of the plaintiff's encounter with the source of dignitary harm.

These criteria might be understood as rough proxies for the circle of potential plaintiffs who are especially likely to have a serious stake in a lawsuit. They are, to be sure, imperfect proxies. In the Establishment Clause example, one might ask who has the greater stake in the outcome of a challenge to a religious display: the activist who leads an atheist organization and has spent her life fighting for the separation of religion and state, or the local resident she recruits to challenge the display because he walks past it every day? One might accept that proxies will be imperfect, or one might seek to change the criteria for identifying individuals with a serious stake in the outcome of a lawsuit. For instance, a long history of advocating on behalf of a cause could help to ground a claim of dignitary harm.

Over time, courts' determinations about the circle of potential plaintiffs could form part of the "common law" of standing; they would become more regularized and predictable. Nonetheless, this approach would leave open the possibility that some plaintiffs who genuinely incurred dignitary harm would be unable to assert Article III standing. That result might be especially likely if the form of dignitary harm is relatively light. Denying standing to some plaintiffs with dignitary harm, however, may be an acceptable trade-off if it encourages courts to be generally less wary about recognizing dignitary harm as cognizable.

As a whole, this chapter has aimed to demonstrate that dignity can be productively integrated into a practical doctrinal structure—here, the law of

[85] *See* Rachel Bayefsky, *Psychological Harm and Constitutional Standing*, 81 Brook. L. Rev. 1555, 1602–14 (2016).

[86] *See, e.g.*, Freedom From Religion Foundation, Inc. v. Lehigh, 933 F.3d 275, 279–80 (3d Cir. 2019).

constitutional standing. It is not the case that "anything goes" when dignitary harm becomes injury in fact. Dignitary harm is frequently a proper basis for Article III standing, even though it raises concerns about expansiveness and line-drawing. The task of identifying cognizable dignitary harm requires judges to employ normative judgment. The goal, therefore, ought to be to guide and discipline the employment of such judgment.

4
Dignity and Tort Law

In tort law, as in the law of constitutional standing, courts confront the question of whether to treat dignity as a legally recognized harm. Tort law, and the civil justice system that permits private individuals to sue for tort violations, protect certain human interests. Among them are bodily integrity, economic security, and emotional tranquility. To what extent are dignitary interests safeguarded by tort law? To what extent should they be? Tort law, after all, is one vehicle through which society expresses its views as to the range of human needs and wants that warrant legal protection. By analyzing the ways that dignitary considerations have been incorporated—and not incorporated—into tort law, we can gain further insight into the promise and risks of legal solicitude for dignity. Tort law is its own legal domain with its own logic. But it opens a window onto the relationship between dignitary harm and judicial redress.

The role of dignity in tort law sheds light on the question of how dignitary interests interact with judicial authority. Judges, usually state judges, are often at the forefront of defining and applying common-law tort claims. Judges face the challenge of legitimating their decisions to treat dignitary interests as worthy (or not) of legal protection, as well as their determinations on the scope of such protection. Dignity can be understood in multiple ways, and people with different worldviews may come to different conclusions on whether dignity has been violated. How can judges adjudicate among competing visions of dignity and its violation? If judges are perceived as "partisan" in their treatment of dignity, they risk forfeiting some of their legitimacy.

These difficulties are compounded by free expression issues that have long attended tort claims associated with dignity. Dignitary harm is often the result of words or actions that express a message. Attempts to attach liability to these sources of dignitary harm run into objections based on the First Amendment or freedom of expression values more generally.

Courts and legislatures have instituted mechanisms to discipline the adjudication of dignity-related tort claims and to spread responsibility for

Dignity and Judicial Authority. Rachel Bayefsky, Oxford University Press. © Rachel Bayefsky 2024.
DOI: 10.1093/oso/9780197750322.003.0004

determining whether dignitary harm is legally cognizable. These mechanisms include "reasonableness" requirements, such as the doctrine that intrusion upon seclusion is actionable only "if the intrusion would be highly offensive to a reasonable person,"[1] and the assignment of certain contentious decisions about liability to juries instead of judges. Nonetheless, courts determining whether dignitary harm is actionable in tort are delineating the bounds of their own authority. They are taking a position on the power of courts to recognize and respond to dignitary violations. In so doing, they are speaking to the appropriate role of courts.

The current chapter analyzes the approaches that judges do and should take to dignitary harm in tort law, as well as the ramifications for issues of judicial power. It focuses on the idea of "dignitary torts": common-law torts, sometimes supplemented by statutes, that centrally embody a concern for dignitary interests and their infringement. As the chapter explains, there is no generally accepted list of "dignitary torts" or a clear way to distinguish dignitary from nondignitary torts. It is most fruitful to recognize that several tort causes of action have dignitary features, and that these features are especially prominent in a subset of tort claims.

After highlighting various tort claims that are particularly related to dignitary interests, the chapter identifies implications of the "dignitary torts" for inquiries into the historical pedigree of dignity. As the Supreme Court turns toward "history and tradition" in a variety of areas, the historical roots of concepts like dignity take on greater importance. The idea that American tort law properly protects dignity is not a new phenomenon. At the same time, tort law's concern with dignity has grown in the past hundred years, and older causes of action have morphed in accordance with changing social values.

The chapter then turns to the intersection between dignity in tort law and questions of judicial authority. Courts are faced with the challenging task of sifting cognizable from noncognizable dignitary claims. In undertaking this task, judges risk being perceived as ideologically motivated or arbitrary decision-makers, and they must also contend with concerns about opening the "floodgates of litigation" and proving dignitary claims (some of which also applied in the standing context considered in Chapter 3). This chapter examines and endorses certain strategies that courts and legislatures have deployed to alleviate these difficulties. It then tackles the vexed relationship

[1] Restatement (Second) of Torts § 652B (Am. L. Inst. 1977).

between dignity in tort law and the First Amendment, arguing for greater weight to be assigned to dignitary values when they conflict with First Amendment principles.

Overall, the chapter investigates the reception of dignity in tort law and its implications for the broader question of how courts can recognize dignity as a legally significant value.

The Dignitary Torts?

Scholars and courts refer to a category of tort claims called "dignitary torts."[2] The boundaries of this category are fuzzy and shifting, but some torts that tend to be included are: invasion of privacy torts (such as intrusion into seclusion and public disclosure of private facts), defamation, intentional infliction of emotional distress (IIED), offensive-touching battery, assault, and false imprisonment. These torts appear to have in common that they do not primarily safeguard economic or physical interests. Instead, they safeguard some other kind of interest—one that is sometimes associated with emotional tranquility, but that may also be understood as a dignitary interest.

The notion of "dignitary torts" has been difficult to pin down. Indeed, some scholars have argued that dignitary torts are not a unified legal category, or at least not one that can be operationalized. Kenneth Abraham and G.E. White have contended, for example, that dignitary torts protect "three distinct core interests": protections against "interferences with liberty and personal autonomy"; "protections against speech or conduct that embarrasses, humiliates, or shows blatant disrespect"; and "protections against communications that diminish the regard that others have for the plaintiff."[3] Various torts protect different interests in a complex and sometimes overlapping manner, and the result is a "whole messy picture" that courts have not satisfactorily sorted out.[4] Abraham and White also point to certain historical trends that have complicated the effort to operationalize dignity in tort law, including the Supreme Court's use of the First Amendment to cut back on

[2] *E.g.*, Kenneth S. Abraham & G. Edward White, *The Puzzle of the Dignitary Torts*, 104 Cornell L. Rev. 317, 338–53 (2019); Stephen D. Sugarman & Caitlin Boucher, *Re-imagining the Dignitary Torts*, 14 J. Tort L. 101 (2021); Fantasia v. Montefiore New Rochelle, No. 19 CV 11054 (VB), 2022 WL 20540940, at *4 (S.D.N.Y. June 16, 2022) ("Torts of this type, that is, invasions or deprivations of a person's dignity, are sometimes called 'dignitary torts.'").

[3] Abraham & White, note 2, at 354.

[4] *Id.* at 360.

defamation and privacy claims.[5] Further, Abraham and White suggest, the nature of the common law is that each apparently "dignitary" tort develops doctrinally on its own, without substantial cross-pollination.[6]

The end result, Abraham and White argue, is that American tort law has not developed a unified tort for violation of dignity; indeed, judges and scholars have engaged in little systematic analysis of the nature of dignity and its implications for tort law.[7] As a descriptive matter, Abraham and White are surely correct that the category of dignitary torts has not been defined or explicated in a comprehensive manner. Many divergent interests can be captured under the label of dignity. The question remains, however, whether the challenge of rendering meaningful the category of dignitary torts can be met.

One effort to meet this challenge can be found in an article by Stephen Sugarman and Caitlin Boucher, who argue for the recognition of a unitary dignitary tort characterized by the following principle: "[T]ortfeasors should be liable when they wrongfully harm another person's dignity in a highly offensive way and cause more-than-trivial emotional injury."[8] Sugarman and Boucher draw on an understanding of dignity as "center[ing] on respect for a person's *intrinsic worth*," so that "dignitary torts" are "those in which a defendant's wrong lies in failing to respect a person's worth."[9] Sugarman and Boucher catalog a range of torts that "fi[t] within the framework of wrongful affronts to dignity."[10] These torts include assault, negligent infliction of emotional distress, offensive battery, false imprisonment, intrusion, public disclosure of private facts, defamation, nuisances that cause emotional distress, malicious prosecution, and IIED. These torts appear to have in common, most conspicuously, that they do not necessarily cause physical or economic harm. Even if they do cause physical or economic harm, those kinds of harm are secondary considerations.

Sugarman and Boucher properly seek to draw connections between tort claims in which the central wrong stands at a remove from physical or economic harm. But there are difficulties with the notion of a unified dignitary tort based on the obligation to respect other people's intrinsic worth. Failure

[5] *Id.* at 364–68.
[6] *Id.* at 378–79.
[7] *Id.* at 379–80.
[8] Sugarman & Boucher, note 2, at 103.
[9] *Id.* at 105.
[10] *Id.* For further discussion of "dignitary invasions" in tort law, see Dan B. Dobbs & Caprice L. Roberts, Law of Remedies: Damages-Equity-Restitution 639 (3d ed. 2018).

to respect intrinsic worth is a fairly abstract criterion, and it could embrace a wide swath of tortious conduct, from "ordinary" negligence to malicious wrongdoing.[11] This criterion seems not to be sufficiently well defined to serve as the basis for a unified form of tort liability. Hearkening back to the different understandings of dignity discussed in Chapter 2, the conception of dignity in Sugarman and Boucher's account is an "inherent worth" view, according to which a violation of dignity consists of the failure to respect each person's intrinsic value. Such accounts risk significantly expanding the category of dignitary violations and weakening the analytic utility of the "dignitary" appellation.

So how to proceed in characterizing the relationship between dignity and tort law? There is no objectively correct way to define "dignitary tort," just as there is no correct way to define "dignity." A fruitful path is to focus on dignitary features of a variety of tort claims. Thus, I do not attempt to identify a fixed category of tort causes of action that are essentially dignitary in nature, or to create a unified tort to address dignitary harm.

Rather, numerous tort claims involve the violation of dignity. For some tort causes of action, however, the violation of dignity is often a prominent aspect of the legal wrong. Put differently, certain tort claims are distinctively likely to protect dignitary interests. For these tort claims, the legal violation is especially prone to cause dignitary harm. (As noted in Chapter 2, dignitary *violation* and dignitary *harm* may conceptually diverge, but in the practical setting of lawsuits they usually appear together.)

The next section identifies several ways in which tort law safeguards dignitary interests, highlighting such claims as battery, privacy torts, and defamation. I connect these tort claims to the components of relational dignity as outlined in Chapter 2: respect for status, the absence of domination, and the ability to exercise control over one's self-presentation to others.

Torts and Dignitary Interests

Here I highlight the link between dignitary interests and various tort claims. A couple of preliminary points: First, there are multiple theories regarding

[11] *See* Kenneth W. Simons, *Justifying and Categorizing Tort Doctrines: What Is the Optimal Level of Generality*? 14 J. Tort L. 551, 570 (2021) (concept of dignitary harm would do little justificatory work if defined so capaciously as to cover "any nonphysical injury from any conduct for which tort law should provide a remedy.").

the nature of tort liability. They include theories focused on economic efficiency and the role of tort law in creating incentives;[12] "corrective justice" accounts according to which "liability rectifies the injustice inflicted by one person on another";[13] and "civil recourse" theory, which posits that tort claims "empowe[r] [victims] to act against others who have wronged them."[14] The notion that tort law protects dignitary interests may seem most naturally consonant with noneconomic theories of tort law. These accounts recognize explicitly that tort plaintiffs seek to vindicate interests other than economic compensation or welfare, and that the tort system advances aims other than deterrence. At the same time, economic theories of tort law should not be oversimplified. They may be able to accommodate the view that individuals have dignitary preferences, the satisfaction of which ought to be part of tort law's calculus.

The goal in this chapter is not to delve deeply into tort theory, but to analyze the implications of tort law's treatment of dignity for the relationship between dignity and courts more generally. The chapter therefore does not endorse a particular theory of tort law. But its conclusions may be more compatible with tort theories that foreground individuals' noneconomic interests.[15]

Second, the focus here is on the connection between the substantive components of tort claims and the violation of dignity. Tort law could also serve dignitary interests in the sense that the processes of tort litigation are conducive to dignitary aims.[16] For example, tort plaintiffs publicly identify the alleged perpetrator, and they can seek answers and accountability in court. These features of tort litigation may apply to civil process more generally, and they are raised in Chapter 5 on remedies for dignitary harm. The emphasis here is on the dignitary goals served by the substantive elements of tort claims, rather than the processes by which these claims are brought.

[12] *See, e.g.*, STEVEN SHAVELL, ECONOMIC ANALYSIS OF ACCIDENT LAW (1987).

[13] Ernest J. Weinrib, *Corrective Justice in a Nutshell*, 52 U. TORONTO L.J. 349, 349 (2002).

[14] John C.P. Goldberg & Benjamin C. Zipursky, *Torts as Wrongs*, 88 TEX. L. REV. 917, 974 (2010).

[15] Because this chapter identifies ways that tort law protects dignitary interests, it is worth making another point about the nature of tort law: Tort law does not generally protect people's interests by directly preventing the infringement of these interests. The existence of a cause of action for negligence does not, for example, "force" people not to be negligent. For the most part, tort law instead acts by threatening liability, creating incentives, and offering compensation and redress. Tort law is also plausibly understood to express societal values. Different theories of tort law emphasize these functions to different degrees. The point here is that tort law does not "make" people accommodate the interests of others (dignitary or otherwise). I thank Ken Abraham for discussion of this point.

[16] I thank Steve Schaus for encouraging me to raise this point.

The following sections explain how various tort claims implicate the dignitary interests in respect for status, nondomination, and control over self-presentation. The tort claims referenced below are meant to illustrate the manifestations of dignity in tort law, rather than to be an exhaustive enumeration of tort claims that protect dignitary interests. Moreover, individual tort causes of action may safeguard multiple dignitary interests; for example, battery may protect against both disrespect for status and domination. The point is to highlight areas in which tort law embodies a concern with dignitary violations.

Respect for Status

A tort claim that strongly implicates respect for status is battery. To intentionally cause harmful or offensive contact with other people is to treat those others as though they lacked a status they are due. The infliction of physical harm has long been used as a tool to reinforce status distinctions. For instance, corporal punishment is a well-known mechanism of establishing and policing status differences between (depending on the society in question) parent and child, teacher and student, master and servant, guard and prisoner. When harmful or offensive contact is inflicted on people in violation of their rightful status, those people's dignity is infringed. To be sure, battery frequently causes physical harm in addition to dignitary harm. But the knowledge that physical harm stems from the intentional act of another person adds a "sting" to the physical injury. As Oliver Wendell Holmes once remarked, "even a dog distinguishes between being stumbled over and being kicked."[17]

In the case of "offensive battery" or "offensive-touching battery," the dignitary element of battery comes to the fore. Offensive-touching battery involves "making bodily contact with another person that does not cause physical harm but that is objectionable nevertheless."[18] Scott Hershovitz gives the example of an 1872 Illinois Supreme Court case, *Alcorn v. Mitchell*, in which a jury awarded a large "vindictive damages" sum in a battery case against a defendant who spit in the plaintiff's face in front of others.[19] The spit itself

[17] O.W. Holmes, Jr., The Common Law 3 (1881).

[18] Kenneth S. Abraham & G. Edward White, *The Offensiveness Torts*, 17 J. Tort Law 1, 4 (2024).

[19] Scott Hershovitz, *Treating Wrongs as Wrongs: An Expressive Argument for Tort Law*, 10 J. Tort L. 1, 5–6 (2017); *see* Alcorn v. Mitchell, 63 Ill. 553 (1872).

did not cause serious physical harm. In spitting on the plaintiff, though, the defendant expressed contempt for the plaintiff and signaled that the plaintiff was in some way "lower" or "inferior"—not a member of the community in good standing. The defendant thereby imposed a status-based dignitary harm on the plaintiff, and that harm served as the basis for a significant civil penalty.

A stark example of a case in which the dignitary elements of battery stand out comes from the 1967 Texas Supreme Court case *Fisher v. Carrousel Motor Hotel.*[20] There, a hotel employee grabbed a plate from a Black visitor to the hotel restaurant, shouting that the visitor (later the plaintiff) could not be served due to his race. The plaintiff suffered great embarrassment but no physical injury. The Texas Supreme Court upheld a jury verdict in the plaintiff's favor on a battery claim, reasoning that the grabbing of the plate was an "offensive invasion of [the plaintiff's] person."[21] Further, the plaintiff could recover damages for mental suffering absent physical injury, because "[p]ersonal indignity is the essence of an action for battery; and consequently the defendant is liable not only for contacts which do actual physical harm, but also for those which are offensive and insulting."[22] The dignitary harm in *Fisher* consisted of publicly humiliating the Black restaurant patron as part of an effort to uphold a system of racial subordination that consigned him to a lower status. The "hook" for the battery claim was the contact with the plate, but the gravamen of the tort lay in the status-based meanings that grabbing the plate conveyed.

Battery is by no means alone in expressing disrespect for status. Negligence could also be understood as a failure to care enough about the plaintiff's status to take reasonable precautions. In other words, negligence could send the message that—as Hershovitz puts it—"I don't have to watch out for you."[23] The dignitary harm involved in disrespect for status should not be viewed as attaching to some tort causes of action rather than others in a binary way. Instead, there is a continuum between tortious conduct that clearly involves disrespect for status and tortious conduct that is less intuitively described that way. Certain forms of negligence are more likely to fall into the former category—for instance, if a driver is negligent specifically toward people from low-status groups or is egregiously negligent in a way

[20] 424 S.W.2d 627 (Tex. 1967).
[21] *Id.* at 629.
[22] *Id.* at 630.
[23] Hershovitz, note 19, at 22.

that edges toward recklessness. Other negligence cases, however, are less naturally described as disrespect for status. An example is per se negligence resulting from failing to pay attention to traffic signs.

The aim here is to link tort law to the distinctive experience of dignitary harm and to avoid treating all wrongful conduct as an infringement of dignity. Certain instances of negligence could properly be characterized in terms of a violation of the rightful status. But that characterization will be apt more frequently in cases of offensive-touching battery than in cases of negligence. Overall, the interest in maintaining the rightful status finds expression in tort law, and offensive-touching battery is a notable example.

Absence of Domination

The absence of domination—another feature of relational dignity—also figures in certain torts. To dominate people is to subject them to arbitrary interference. False imprisonment is an example of domination in tort law. False imprisonment consists of intentionally confining a victim to an area without the victim's consent or authority of law, where the victim is aware of his or her confinement.[24] False imprisonment is a form of domination, as the defendant exercises control over the victim's ability to occupy physical space. The defendant might not touch the victim; physical contact is not an element of false imprisonment. Yet the victim has been placed at the defendant's mercy, vulnerable to a damaging exercise of the defendant's arbitrary power. For example, a wealthy hotel guest in Texas in 1990 pointed a gun at a hotel employee's head, demanding that the employee kneel and kiss his feet, and holding the employee hostage for over half an hour.[25] A Texas court of appeals upheld a punitive damages award against the guest for false imprisonment and other legal violations.[26] The guest's treatment of the employee was a disturbing instance of domination.

Assault, too, calls to mind the theme of domination. Assault consists of intentionally putting another person in reasonable apprehension of imminent harmful or offensive contact. Even without actually touching the victim, the

[24] Restatement (Second) of Torts § 35 (Am. L. Inst. 1965).

[25] Haryanto v. Saeed, 860 S.W.2d 913, 917 (Tex. App. 1993), *writ denied* (Feb. 9, 1994). For discussion of this case, see Erik Encarnacion, *Resilience, Retribution, and Punitive Damages*, 100 Tex. L. Rev. 1025, 1026–27 (2022).

[26] *Haryanto*, 860 S.W.2d at 917.

defendant wields his or her power to harm in a manner that tort law treats as worthy of redress. Assault creates an immediate concern about physical contact, and so the victim's emotional response to assault may sound more in fear than in resentment of domination. Nonetheless, assault places the victim in a position of subjugation to the other's will. There would be physical harm were the defendant more inclined to strike the victim, or more successful in the attempt to land a blow. The tort of assault thus reflects legal protection against a form of domination.

A third example of a tort that implicates domination is fraud, although this tort may appear less intuitively dignitary. Fraud might seem like a tort centered on financial concerns, and of course, people bring fraud claims when they have lost money. In fact, damages for fraud are often limited to pecuniary injuries.[27] Given the centrality of economic damage in the tort law of fraud, it may seem puzzling to refer to fraud as a dignitary tort.

Fraud, however, affects social relationships in addition to pocketbooks. In defrauding another person, the defendant takes advantage of the victim, exploiting the victim's trust for personal gain. The victim is "played," used as a tool for the defrauder's pursuit of financial benefit. That position of subjugation points to the harm of domination. In fact, Andrew Merritt has argued that fraud should be conceptualized as "a dignitary tort that justifies the awarding of emotional distress damages."[28] Recognizing the dignitary component of fraud would suggest that the line between economic and dignitary harm is not a strict one, and that economic injuries can be entwined with disrespect.

It may be argued that the interest in avoiding domination could support a characterization of many legal violations as dignitary, even ones that initially appear to have little to do with dignity. For example, breach of contract might seem to be a quintessentially nondignitary matter: Parties are legally obliged to fulfill the representations they have made in commercial society. Yet, as Tess Wilkinson-Ryan and David Hoffman have demonstrated in an experimental survey, "people often consider breach of contract to be a form of exploitation and a violation of the norm of reciprocity."[29] In particular, people who believe that the breacher is acting intentionally and profiting from the

[27] *See* Restatement (Second) of Torts § 525 (Am. L. Inst. 1977).

[28] Andrew L. Merritt, *Damages for Emotional Distress in Fraud Litigation: Dignitary Torts in a Commercial Society*, 42 Vand. L. Rev. 1, 3 (1989).

[29] Tess Wilkinson-Ryan & David A. Hoffman, *Breach Is for Suckers*, 63 Vand. L. Rev. 1003, 1004 (2010); *see also id.* at 1033.

nonbreacher's loss are more likely to feel like "suckers." The experience of being "suckered" bears some resemblance to the phenomenon of domination. The nonbreaching party has been subjected to the breacher's control, to be wielded in accordance with the breacher's pursuit of personal gain or the breacher's whims.

Certain types of contractual breaches, then, may indeed violate dignity. But the manipulation in which fraudsters engage seems especially likely to infringe dignitary interests. And there are many contractual breaches in which dignitary harm looms less large, such as breach of a standard commercial contract between large companies. In fact, dignitary interests might provide one reason why some legal violations occurring in the setting of contractual relationships—such as fraud or intentional interference with contract—are actionable in *tort*.[30] The goal here (as earlier noted) is not to draw a strict line between dignitary and nondignitary legal claims, but to highlight dignitary aspects of a variety of torts, including fraud. The broader point is that several torts protect dignity by advancing the interest in nondomination.

Control over Self-Presentation

Control over one's self-presentation to others appears especially prominently in certain torts that are frequently deemed "dignitary." The first is defamation. The second consists of invasion of privacy torts (the latter encompassing intrusion upon seclusion, public disclosure of private facts, false light, and commercial appropriation).

Defamation, for its part, could well cause economic harm; but it might additionally cause noneconomic harm, including dignitary harm. Defamation, by causing the target's reputation to be falsely tarnished, strips the defamed of control over her appearance in front of others. In another example of tort claims' capacity to protect multiple dignitary interests, defamation could also impose a status harm on the plaintiff if other people's regard for the plaintiff is diminished.

The privacy torts—such as "intrusion upon seclusion" and "public disclosure of private facts"—raise issues too about control over self-presentation. Examples of actionable privacy violations include a landlord's placement of

[30] I thank Steve Schaus for raising this point.

a recording device inside a couple's bedroom[31] and a magazine's publication of an article about a woman's eating disorder with a picture of her in a hospital room.[32] The privacy torts reflect a concern that one's self-presentation has been taken out of one's hands. People carefully guard the information that they are willing to reveal about themselves to the outside world. When these guardrails are breached, part of the harm that people suffer is dignitary. As Edward Bloustein wrote in 1968, in describing privacy torts, there is "a blow to human dignity[] in having the world intrude as an unwanted witness to private tragedy. The wrong is to be found in the fact that a private life has been transformed into a public spectacle."[33]

The dignitary interest in control over self-presentation, as noted in Chapter 2, is a dignitary interest in *adequate* control over self-presentation to others. There are limits to the power that individuals should possess over their appearance before the public. One might argue, in fact, that a robust sphere of democratic participation requires us to accept a fair amount of public scrutiny and criticism, especially when it comes to public figures. It is typical of an authoritarian regime, after all, to permit certain powerful individuals to control tightly the information disclosed about them.

One response to the concern about preserving robust debate is found in First Amendment doctrines restricting liability for defamation and invasion of privacy. These doctrines are discussed later in the chapter. For now, the aim is to flag the potential tension between protecting the ability to maintain one's self-presentation, on the one hand, and preserving the flow of information that is important to the operations of a democratic society, on the other.

In sum, several tort claims are distinctively likely to protect dignitary interests in status, nondomination, and control over self-presentation.

Dignity and Infliction of Emotional Distress

Torts involving IIED and the negligent infliction of emotional distress (NIED) are sometimes treated as dignitary. Dignitary harm and emotional distress are not identical, as discussed in Chapter 3. A tortfeasor can impose

[31] Hamberger v. Eastman, 206 A.2d 239, 240 (N.H. 1964). For this and other examples, see Danielle Keats Citron, *Mainstreaming Privacy Torts*, 98 Calif. L. Rev. 1805, 1807–08 (2010).

[32] Barber v. Time, Inc., 159 S.W.2d 291, 293 (Mo. 1942).

[33] Edward J. Bloustein, *Privacy, Tort Law, and the Constitution: Is Warren and Brandeis' Tort Petty and Unconstitutional As Well?* 46 Tex. L. Rev. 611, 619 (1968).

dignitary harm without inflicting emotional distress—if, for example, the victim's psyche is impervious to the tortfeasor's emotional blows. One might argue that lawsuits involving such victims will be rare because, practically speaking, such a victim is less likely to sue. But she may be motivated to litigate out of a sense of justice even if she does not personally feel an emotional blow.

Despite the distinction between dignitary and emotional harm, there is considerable overlap between protection for dignitary interests and at least IIED. Many forms of conduct actionable as IIED also cause dignitary harm. An example is sexual harassment, which implicates the dignitary interests in nondomination and control over self-presentation, as well as (in many cases) respect for the status of women. Further, IIED claims are often brought to challenge conduct that is also alleged to constitute discrimination, defamation, or violation of privacy. Each of these forms of conduct frequently imposes dignitary harm. To be sure, IIED need not involve a dignitary violation; IIED does not infringe dignity interests purely because it causes emotional distress. But there is substantial overlap between IIED liability and dignitary violations, particularly because an IIED claim generally lies only in cases of "extreme and outrageous conduct" that causes "severe emotional distress."[34]

The connection between *negligent* infliction of emotional distress and dignitary interests is less clear. The nature of conduct actionable as NIED varies in different jurisdictions, and some cases of NIED are not closely associated with dignitary harm. Driving negligently so that one hits a child in front of the child's mother may cause extreme emotional distress to the mother,[35] but it seems counterintuitive to describe the situation as centrally involving dignitary harm to the mother. The reduced valence of dignitary harm in this type of "bystander" case may be due to the distinction between intentional and negligent conduct, or to the fact that the plaintiff herself is not placed in fear of imminent wrongful contact with her body. The latter point would not apply in some other NIED cases, such as those in which the defendant's negligence nearly causes physical harm to the plaintiff herself.[36] Nonetheless, the disjunction between NIED and dignitary harm underscores that "emotional distress" torts do not necessarily safeguard dignitary interests. Courts and

[34] Restatement (Second) of Torts § 46 (Am. L. Inst. 1965).
[35] *See* Dillon v. Legg, 441 P.2d 912, 914 (Cal. 1968).
[36] *See* Consol. Rail Corp. v. Gottshall, 512 U.S. 532, 547–48 (1994) (discussing the "zone of danger" test for NIED liability).

commentators should not treat solicitude for emotional distress in tort law as a proxy or substitute for concern with dignitary harm.

Tort Law, History, and Tradition

Tort law sheds light on the historical pedigree of legal protection for dignitary interests. Why does historical pedigree matter? One reason is conceptual: Understanding dignity's roots helps us to grasp the role that dignity has played in the American legal tradition. Other reasons are doctrinal. Many judges, including on state common-law courts, are concerned with the longevity of precedent supporting their rulings. Highlighting dignity's historical pedigree could help shape their decisions in a dignity-protective direction.

Moreover, federal judges, particularly on the US Supreme Court, have shown increasing interest in "history and tradition." Originalist legal philosophy tasks courts with determining the meaning of constitutional provisions at the time of their enactment. More generally, the Supreme Court has underscored the relevance of "tradition" to legality—asking, for example, whether government-sponsored activities alleged to violate the Establishment Clause are supported by "historical practices and understandings";[37] whether a restriction on firearms "is consistent with this Nation's historical tradition of firearm regulation";[38] and whether the rights guaranteed by the Due Process Clause are "deeply rooted in this Nation's history and tradition."[39]

To be sure, the adjudication of tort claims based on dignitary harm is usually subject to state law, and state common-law courts may interpret these claims in an evolving manner. But common-law tort claims affect federal jurisprudence as well. In constitutional standing doctrine (as noted in Chapter 3), the Supreme Court has instructed courts to look for "a close historical or common-law analogue" for plaintiffs' asserted injury.[40] Another relevant doctrinal setting involves conflicts between the First Amendment and liability for torts like defamation (a matter discussed later in this chapter). There, historical recognition for tort claims based on dignitary harm might

[37] Kennedy v. Bremerton Sch. Dist., 597 U.S. 507, 535 (2022) (internal quotation marks omitted).
[38] New York State Rifle & Pistol Ass'n, Inc. v. Bruen, 597 U.S. 1, 34 (2022).
[39] Dobbs v. Jackson Women's Health Org., 597 U.S. 215, 231 (2022) (internal quotation marks omitted).
[40] TransUnion LLC v. Ramirez, 594 U.S. 413, 424 (2021).

affect the original understanding of the First Amendment. The historical pedigree of tort claims based on dignitary harm could thus influence the Supreme Court's approach to doctrinal questions, especially for justices who heavily weigh "history and tradition."

The treatment of dignity in tort law reveals both dignity's genuine roots in the law and the changing shape of legal protection for dignitary interests over time. With respect to dignity's roots, legal safeguards for dignitary interests in American law are not a new phenomenon. Offensive-touching battery is "an ancient tort."[41] Blackstone explained that a minor offensive touch could constitute battery because "every man's person [is] sacred, and no other ha[s] a right to meddle with it, in any the slightest manner."[42] The tort of defamation has also existed since the American Founding. As Justice White noted in dissent in a Supreme Court case endorsing a First Amendment hurdle to defamation liability, "[u]nder typical state defamation law, the defamed private citizen had to prove only a false publication that would subject him to hatred, contempt, or ridicule."[43] Long-standing causes of action like battery and defamation reflect "traditional" or "historical" regard for dignitary interests.

Yet other tort claims that are especially likely to safeguard dignitary interests have a more recent provenance. The privacy torts are often linked to an 1890 article by Samuel Warren and Louis Brandeis (which itself references older streams of American law),[44] but these torts gained steam in legal practice in the mid-twentieth century.[45] Claims for IIED not tied to unwelcome physical contact were explicitly recognized only in the 1930s.[46] Thus, the twentieth century witnessed broader legal recognition of individual interests in avoiding status-based harm and unwarranted exposure, even when those forms of treatment did not cause physical or economic damage.

Further, the nature of the dignitary interests protected by tort law may change over time, and tort claims with a strong dignitary valence may become connected to different social goals. A possible story to tell about the development of dignity in tort law is that a historical interest in honor has been supplemented over time by an interest in personal autonomy. Concerns about "every man's person being sacred" (in Blackstone's terms) or about

[41] Abraham & White, note 18, at 4.

[42] 3 William Blackstone, Commentaries on the Laws of England *120.

[43] Gertz v. Robert Welch, Inc., 418 U.S. 323, 370 (1974) (White, J., dissenting).

[44] Samuel D. Warren & Louis D. Brandeis, *The Right to Privacy*, 4 Harv. L. Rev. 193, 220 (1890).

[45] *See* Neil M. Richards & Daniel J. Solove, *Prosser's Privacy Law: A Mixed Legacy*, 98 Calif. L. Rev. 1887, 1894–1901 (2010).

[46] Abraham & White, note 2, at 337.

people's good names may have been more characteristic of the "older" dignitary torts. These concerns sound in the language of affront and insult that is often associated with older, honor-based regimes. The "newer" dignitary torts feature greater regard for individual autonomy; for example, the privacy torts protect an interest in maintaining personal space free from external interference.

The "honor to autonomy" story should not be understood as a simple binary. The concern for honor and the concern for autonomy are not mutually exclusive, and we have scarcely abandoned our interest in affronts and insults in the current day. But dignitary interests are indeed reshaped over time in accordance with shifting social mores.

For example, there is evidence that the centuries-old tort of offensive-touching battery has been invoked much more frequently in recent decades, partly due to a rising number of suits alleging sexual harassment—a wrong to which legal decision-makers have become more attuned over time.[47] Further, claims of offensive-touching battery are often joined to other common-law or statutory claims such as those alleging civil rights violations, excessive force by the police, employment discrimination, physically harmful battery, and IIED.[48] Offensive-touching battery and civil rights violations share the common element of causing dignitary harm by infringing upon the victim's rightful status. As John Goldberg and Benjamin Zipursky have suggested, "[i]t takes but a short step to move from the vindication of individuals' dignitary interests via battery, assault, and false imprisonment claims (among others) to the recognition as torts of workplace sexual harassment, civil rights violations, and human rights violations."[49] Offensive-touching battery has thus developed in a way that bolsters liability for sexual harassment and other civil rights violations, even though this tort did not fulfill that function centuries ago.

Tort liability can also be reduced as a consequence of shifting social mores. An example is the eclipse (though not total) of torts involving a third party's interference with the marital relationship, notably through adultery.[50]

[47] Kenneth S. Abraham & G. Edward White, *How an Old Tort Became New: The Case of Offensive Battery*, 73 DEPAUL L. REV. 185, 200–01 (2024).

[48] *Id.* at 189.

[49] Goldberg & Zipursky, note 14, at 939; *see also* Curtis v. Loether, 415 U.S. 189, 195 n.10 (1974) (Marshall, J.) ("[I]t has been suggested that 'under the logic of the common law development of a law of insult and indignity, racial discrimination might be treated as a dignitary tort.'") (quoting CHARLES O. GREGORY & HARRY KALVEN, JR., CASES AND MATERIALS ON TORTS 961 (2d ed. 1969)).

[50] I thank Steve Schaus for suggesting this point.

A primary reason for the judicial or legislative abolishment of these torts in several states is their association with outdated views of the wife as the husband's property stolen through adultery.[51] A husband's claim against a third party for seducing his wife sounds in a conception of honor that many modern-day courts and legislatures would not wish to endorse. Though actions related to interference with the marital relationship have not been wholly eliminated, their diminishment speaks to the impact of changing conceptions of spousal honor and the dignity of women.

Legal concern for dignity, therefore, is both historically rooted and subject to temporal change. The historical protection for dignitary interests in tort law means that dignitary harm cannot be categorically dismissed as an extralegal form of damage. At the same time, historical protection for dignity does not translate straightforwardly into contemporary doctrinal results. Because dignity is a multifaceted concept, a historical dignitary interest may not match a contemporary one simply because the term "dignity" or a similar one is invoked in both settings.

Relatedly, there is a question about the level of generality at which to characterize dignitary interests. For example, is the stigma suffered by a plaintiff with disabilities similar in relevant respects to offensive-touching battery? At some level, both cases involve the violation of the rightful status. But at the time the common-law tort of offensive-touching battery developed, discrimination against people with disabilities may have been more accepted than it is today. The level-of-generality issue complicates the project of turning to history to draw conclusions about which legal protections would today be appropriate, though this issue is by no means unique to dignitary claims.

In sum, dignitary harm cannot be dismissed as ahistorical. But the turn to "history and tradition" to evaluate dignitary harm does not produce fixed results.

Dignitary Torts and Judicial Authority

The relationship between dignity and tort law both reflects and sheds light on questions of judicial power and role. A concern that frequently arises in the adjudication of tort claims involving dignitary harm is the competence and authority of courts to make decisions about whose dignity has been

[51] *See, e.g.*, Hoye v. Hoye, 824 S.W.2d 422, 423 (Ky. 1992).

violated and how. The current section unpacks this concern and then turns to a particular source of tension, namely, the interplay between dignitary torts and the First Amendment.

Dignity and Tort Law: Problems and Solutions

In 1939, William Prosser remarked of tort claims for "intentional infliction of mental suffering": "The most valid objection to the protection of 'mental' interests lies in the 'wide door' which might be opened, not only to fictitious and fraudulent claims, but to litigation in the field of trivialities and mere bad manners."[52] In other words, "[i]f the plaintiff is to recover every time that her feelings are hurt, we should all be in court twice a week."[53] Although dignitary harm is not equivalent to emotional harm, similar concerns could be raised about legal recognition of dignitary harm. Does such recognition lead down a slippery slope toward unlimited liability for trivial acts?

More specifically, dignitary claims raise multiple issues for courts. First, courts may be concerned about the evidentiary problems with proving dignitary harm.[54] When plaintiffs assert that their dignity has been harmed, how can courts ascertain whether this is indeed the case? Second, judges may find it difficult to draw lines between actionable and nonactionable claims that a person's dignity has been violated.[55] What is the difference between the types of exposure that people should accept as a corollary of living among others, and the types of exposure that cause actionable dignitary harm? Third, judges may worry that treating dignitary harm as actionable will open the "floodgates of litigation"—that, if dignitary claims are recognized, liability may extend too far.[56] Fourth, judges may question whether dignitary harm

[52] William L. Prosser, *Intentional Infliction of Mental Suffering: A New Tort*, 37 Mich. L. Rev. 874, 877 (1939).

[53] *Id.* Prosser nevertheless went on to argue that "the elimination of trivialities" calls simply for "common sense," *id.* at 878, and to support recognition of "intentional infliction of extreme mental suffering by outrageous conduct" as a "separate and independent tort," *id.* at 892.

[54] *See* Restatement (Third) of Torts: Remedies § 22 cmt. d (Tentative Draft 2, 2023) (dignitary harms "are difficult to value because they are never traded in any market," and for dignitary torts, "proof and quantification of damages is especially difficult"). The final Third Restatement on this topic has not yet been published.

[55] *See id.* at Reporters' Notes b (citing "objection that the concept of dignity lacks philosophical integrity"); *cf.* Restatement (Second) of Torts § 46 cmt. d (Am. L. Inst. 1965) ("There is no occasion for the law to intervene in every case where some one's feelings are hurt.").

[56] For discussion of this objection in the context of dignitary torts in the workplace, see Rosa Ehrenreich Brooks, *Dignity and Discrimination: Toward a Pluralistic Understanding of Workplace Harassment*, 88 Geo. L.J. 1, 57–60(1999).

is really the sort of serious or important damage that ought to prompt legal liability.[57]

Many of these issues mirror the challenges facing courts deciding whether plaintiffs have properly asserted dignitary harm for constitutional standing purposes, as discussed in Chapter 3. But the doctrinal areas of constitutional standing and tort law also have differences. In the constitutional standing context, the question is whether the doors to federal court will be opened; in the tort law context, the question is the "merits" one of whether liability will lie. This might make judges in tort cases especially cautious about crediting dignitary claims. At the same time, tort cases are often common-law cases brought in state courts, while Article III standing arises in federal courts (though state courts may also have standing rules). The common-law setting might give state judges more latitude to recognize dignitary harm, as federal judges do not generally engage in common lawmaking. Still, state judges in tort suits do not exercise freewheeling discretion to deem certain kinds of harm actionable. They are constrained by precedent and sometimes by legislative direction.

As with constitutional standing doctrine, the challenges facing courts adjudicating dignitary claims speak to the role of judges and the bounds of their authority. To the extent judges have difficulty ascertaining the existence of dignitary harm or determining when dignitary harm should be actionable without opening the floodgates, judges' treatment of dignitary harm may seem "subjective." One person's dignitary harm may be another's harmless remark. Judges may then face the charge that they are making decisions about dignity in a manner influenced by their ideological views. As noted in Chapter 1, people with divergent social and political opinions may come to different views about when someone has incurred dignitary harm.

If judges are perceived to be drawing conclusions about dignity based on their social and political opinions, they risk losing some of their legitimacy. "Legitimacy" here is understood in terms of public perception that courts are sites for the fair adjudication of legal claims.[58] Even beyond the issue of

[57] *See, e.g.*, Restatement (Second) of Torts § 42 cmt. a (Am. L. Inst. 1965) (in cases of false imprisonment, the "mere dignitary interest in being free from an interference with his personal liberty which he has only discovered later is not of sufficient importance to justify the recovery of the nominal damages involved").

[58] Thus, "legitimacy" is understood here in terms of what Richard Fallon has called "sociological legitimacy," which depends on the public's acceptance of a "claim of legal authority . . . as deserving of respect or obedience." Richard H. Fallon, Jr., *Legitimacy and the Constitution*, 118 Harv. L. Rev. 1787, 1790–91, 1849 (2005).

public perception, there is the normative task of justifying judicial authority to adjudicate dignitary claims that implicate contested social matters of status, power, and privacy.

A possible response would be simply to exclude dignitary harm from consideration in tort law. Dignitary harm, however, is already a component of otherwise actionable forms of injury. Part of what separates battery from negligence, for example, is the "sting" involved in intentionally causing harm. That sting plausibly has a dignitary component. To the extent one finds it valuable for tort law to respond in a distinctive way to legal violations with a stronger dignitary valence, one ought to take the view that dignitary interests have a worthwhile role to play in tort law. Further, given that torts responding centrally to dignitary concerns—such as offensive-touching battery and intrusion upon seclusion—are now established parts of tort law, it seems more practically useful to consider how to define their contours than to try to eliminate legal protection for dignitary harm.

Perhaps most fundamentally, excluding dignitary harm would leave out of the tort-law calculus an important human interest that has a serious impact on people's ability to participate in society. Dignitary violations fall along a spectrum of gravity, but some are very significant and socially destructive occurrences.

Notably, dignitary harm is not uniquely vulnerable to challenges related to subjectivity, unlimited liability, and so on. For many tort claims, questions about foreseeability and the reasonableness of a defendant's conduct require legal decision-makers to make contested calls. To the extent that dignitary harm elicits an increased amount of skepticism, however, there are ways to account for dignity in tort law while addressing concerns about proof, line-drawing, and floodgates.

In particular, the existence of actionable dignitary harm can frequently be indexed to a community standard. For example, the definition of "offensive" contact in the Restatement (Third) of Torts section on battery states that a contact qualifies if it "is offensive to a reasonable sense of personal dignity."[59] The definition of intrusion upon seclusion in the Restatement (Second) of Torts explains that "[o]ne who intentionally intrudes, physically

[59] Restatement (Third) of Torts: Inten. Torts to Persons § 3 (Tentative Draft 4, 2019). The final Third Restatement on this topic has not yet been published. The cited portion of the draft Restatement states that a contact may also be offensive if "the actor knows that the contact is highly offensive to the other's sense of personal dignity, and the actor contacts the other with the primary purpose that the contact will be highly offensive."

or otherwise, upon the solitude or seclusion of another or his private affairs or concerns, is subject to liability to the other for invasion of his privacy, if the intrusion would be highly offensive to a reasonable person."[60] For defamation, the Restatement (Second) of Torts, in commenting on the "standard by which defamation is determined," indicates that "it is not enough that the communication would be derogatory in the view of a single individual or a very small group of persons, if the group is not large enough to constitute a substantial minority."[61]

All of these standards—"a reasonable sense of personal dignity," "highly offensive to a reasonable person," or derogatory in the eyes of a "substantial minority"—serve to tie dignitary harm to a social peg. These community standards are meant to extend beyond the idiosyncratic views of individuals. They introduce an "intersubjective" element into the determination of tort liability for dignitary harm. An individual with an unusual or heightened sense of personal dignity is generally not entitled to impose legal liability on another.

Community standards help to alleviate concerns about dignity in tort law. Concepts of reasonableness and great offensiveness create evidentiary benchmarks that address qualms about proving dignitary harm. Instead of inquiring into the contents of the plaintiff's or the defendant's inner mind, a legal decision-maker can look to prevailing social standards to evaluate offensive contact, or invasion of privacy, or defamation. Social standards are not self-evident, but they are usually easier to discern than individual sensibilities. Social standards also cannot readily be faked, so reliance on them diminishes the lingering suspicion that claims of dignitary harm are invented. Moreover, community standards lessen (though they do not eliminate) variability in the determination of when dignitary harm is the basis for a tort claim. This can help to create workable boundaries around actionable dignitary harm.

The turn to community standards should not be accepted uncritically. These standards may encode a certain degree of "small-c" conservativism, in the sense that defendants are held liable when they transgress existing understandings of unreasonable or highly offensive conduct. Further, societies may contain multiple communities. Reasonableness and "highly offensive" standards lead to the question of who counts as the reasonable

[60] Restatement (Second) of Torts § 652B (Am. L. Inst. 1977).
[61] Restatement (Second) of Torts § 559 cmt. e (Am. L. Inst. 1977).

person, and how that person is characterized along the lens of gender, race, and other characteristics. These concerns are valid, but they do not mean that community standards must be jettisoned in favor of individualized views. In response to concerns about conservatism and prejudice, one can try to shift community standards by changing social norms, and one can urge legal actors to be attentive to changes in social norms. In response to the challenge of defining reasonableness norms in a pluralistic society, one could work to make legal decision-makers—judges and juries—more representative.

Community standards for liability, then, offer one way to address concerns about adjudicating dignitary claims. Another mechanism consists of heightened thresholds for liability. For example, a claim for intrusion upon seclusion lies (according to the Restatement (Second) of Torts) if "the intrusion would be *highly* offensive to a reasonable person."[62] Liability for IIED—which overlaps to some extent with liability for dignitary harm even though the two are conceptually separate—generally applies only to "extreme and outrageous conduct" that causes "severe emotional distress."[63] Raised thresholds for liability make it less likely for the "floodgates of litigation" to open for dignitary claims, and they counteract the concern that "insignificant" dignitary harms will prompt judicial action. Heightened thresholds come at a cost in terms of the tort system's capacity to address all dignitary harms. But they help to address frequent worries about dignitary claims.

Institutional design choices furnish another response to these worries. Judges can and should share power with juries to adjudicate dignitary tort claims. In fact, the jury is often the primary decision-maker on issues of what counts as "reasonable" or "highly offensive." As the draft Restatement (Third) of Torts states regarding offensive-touching battery, "[w]hether a contact offends a reasonable sense of dignity is ordinarily a question for the jury, applying its judgment about contemporary social norms."[64] The jury is assigned the task of channeling complex social norms about offensiveness into legal results.

The involvement of juries raises the specter of subjectivity and variability, as juries differ in makeup and outlook. But even if the jury is an imperfect mechanism, it allows for the views of multiple members of the community to be channeled into the decision-making process. It also permits normative determinations about reasonableness and offensiveness to be made with

62 Restatement (Second) of Torts § 652B (Am. L. Inst. 1977) (emphasis added).
63 Restatement (Second) of Torts § 46 (Am. L. Inst. 1965).
64 Restatement (Third) of Torts: Intentional Torts to Persons § 3 cmt. a (Tentative Draft 2, 2017).

regard to lay opinions, instead of relying on the viewpoints of judges who have undergone a distinctive socialization process. Moreover, juries and judges can complement each other; judges must still guard the boundaries of reasonableness and offensiveness determinations, such as through motions for judgment as a matter of law and evidentiary rulings. The involvement of juries in identifying actionable dignitary harm renders judges less vulnerable to charges of arbitrariness or favoritism.

Another institutional design choice involves legislative decision-making as a complement to judicial proceedings. Legislatures can create causes of action that respond to dignitary harm. For instance, some states have enacted statutory protections for privacy.[65] Insofar as legislators are deemed to be more directly accountable to the people than judges—even those who are elected—judges adjudicating statutory causes of action act on behalf of a more representative body in applying tort claims to factual situations.

Codification is not a complete solution to the challenges associated with the dignitary torts. Judges with general common-law authority may be called on to shape tort law in response to real-world harm, and judges should not be disabled from exercising this authority when it comes to dignitary harm. Indeed, declining to exercise judicial authority to develop the common law to address dignitary harm would be a contestable choice on the part of judges, one that is itself vulnerable to critiques about ideological influence. Moreover, judges adjudicating statutory causes of action must still interpret and apply the law, and these are often not mechanical exercises. Nonetheless, judges need not bear complete responsibility for treating or not treating dignitary harm as actionable in tort. The work of legislatures, like the participation of juries, disperses authority for decision-making about dignity.

In sum, dignitary claims in tort law give rise to concerns about subjectivity and line-drawing that put pressure on trust in judges to separate meritorious from nonmeritorious claims. This pressure can be considerably alleviated, however, by community standards for liability, increased liability thresholds for certain forms of dignitary harm, the assignment of responsibility to juries to apply liability standards in many cases, and the function of legislatures in codifying protections for dignitary harm.

The treatment of dignity in tort law has broader ramifications for the exploration of dignity and judicial authority. Dignity in tort law provides an

[65] *See* Danielle Keats Citron & Daniel J. Solove, *Privacy Harms*, 102 B.U. L. Rev. 793, 810–11 (2022).

example of how dignitary harm may be deemed actionable and also of the risks attending such legal recognition—that is, the challenge that dignitary harm poses to judges' capacity to adjudicate claims fairly and legitimately. Dignity in tort law demonstrates that judges and other legal actors (such as legislatures) need not throw up their hands when they are faced with claims implicating dignitary harm. Dignitary harm can be recognized without an "anything-goes" approach.

Nevertheless, the interaction between dignity and tort law forces legal actors to confront the boundaries of judicial power in ordering private conduct. When should individuals' spheres of action be limited to avoid infringing on the dignity of others? This question comes to the fore in considering the relationship between dignity in tort law and freedom of expression—the topic to which I now turn.

Dignitary Torts and Freedom of Expression

A persistent challenge for the incorporation of dignitary interests into tort law involves the relationship between legal protection for dignity and respect for freedom of expression. Dignitary wounds may be caused by physical contact, but they are frequently inflicted through language or expressive conduct. The sting of a defamatory insult, the revelation of private facts, the humiliation caused by a racial epithet—we encounter all these phenomena via words. Should tort law impose liability for the dignitary harm caused by forms of expression?

Two sets of values are in conflict here. On the one hand, dignitary harm is real and socially pernicious; actions such as highly offensive touching, invasions of privacy, and defamation cause actual damage to individuals and society. On the other hand, it is worthwhile to live in a society where people can tell one another disturbing truths, or even lies, without fearing legal consequences.[66]

The common law of torts recognized the trade-off between protecting dignity and not chilling freedom of expression.[67] For example, common-law defamation contained privileges, such as the "fair comment" privilege protecting some expressions on matters of public interest,[68] that helped

[66] *Cf.* Restatement (Second) of Torts § 46, cmt. d (Am. L. Inst. 1965) ("There must still be freedom to express an unflattering opinion.").
[67] Abraham & White, note 2, at 362–63.
[68] *E.g.*, Magnusson v. New York Times Co., 98 P.3d 1070, 1075 (OK 2004).

to lessen the risk that defamation would curb freedom of expression. Heightened standards for liability, of the kind discussed earlier, are also built into the common law. These internal limitations on tort claims alleviate part of the tension between legal protection for dignity and the value of freedom of expression.

In the past several decades, the First Amendment has become an important player in curbing tort liability for dignitary harm. The Supreme Court has cut back on common-law defamation, for example, on First Amendment grounds. A well-known instance is the Court's holding, in the 1964 case *New York Times v. Sullivan*, that to hold someone liable for defamation, a public official must prove that the defendant acted with "'actual malice,'—that is, with knowledge that [the statement] was false or with reckless disregard of whether it was false or not."[69] This federal constitutional rule overrode any state common-law rule to the contrary. The Supreme Court subsequently employed the First Amendment to invalidate certain state-law protections for privacy[70] and IIED.[71]

According to some commentators, American law has now tilted decidedly in favor of the First Amendment and against tort liability for dignitary harm. For instance, Cristina Carmody Tilley describes the dignitary torts—a category in which she includes defamation, invasion of privacy, and IIED—as "besieged."[72] She critiques the threat to "a tort forum . . . for injuries to personality" that is "posed by the Supreme Court's imposition of a tort-diminishing theory of the First Amendment."[73] Tilley therefore urges legal actors to "[r]escu[e] dignitary torts from the Constitution."[74] Abraham and White explain that the Supreme Court's constitutional decisions beginning in the 1960s "cut[] deeply into actions for defamation, false light and disclosure privacy, and IIED."[75] The result was to significantly curtail the development of the dignitary torts, to discourage systematic analysis of the concept of dignity, and to decrease the possibility that the dignitary torts "might merge into a generic action imposing liability for dignitary invasions or mental suffering."[76]

69 New York Times Co. v. Sullivan, 376 U.S. 254, 280 (1964).

70 *E.g.*, Cox Broadcasting Corp. v. Cohn, 420 U.S. 469, 491 (1975); Time, Inc. v. Hill, 385 U.S. 374, 397 (1967).

71 *E.g.*, Hustler Mag., Inc. v. Falwell, 485 U.S. 46, 56 (1988).

72 Cristina Carmody Tilley, *Rescuing Dignitary Torts from the Constitution*, 78 BROOK. L. REV. 65, 65 (2012).

73 *Id.*

74 *Id.*

75 Abraham & White, note 2, at 367.

76 *Id.*

Are First Amendment restrictions on tort liability for dignitary harm justified? Tort liability for the infringement of dignitary interests has drawbacks from a free speech perspective. Penalizing actions or words that diminish the status of others may well stifle people's ability to express themselves. Partially for that reason, torts that protect dignitary interests should not be structured in a broad and open-ended manner. The law should not simply impose civil liability for any action that lowers the status of others, including (say) an employer's dismissive comment about an employee's competence. Speech-based restrictions on tort liability for dignitary harm reflect in part an interest in preventing the overextension of judicial authority—in preventing tort liability from intruding too deeply into individuals' personal domains.

Thus, the doctrine and theory surrounding dignity in tort law correctly contain resources to address worries about judges' entry into areas closely tied to individual expression. First, there are legal safeguards. Higher thresholds of liability for dignitary harm, in reducing the scope of actionable dignitary claims, make it less likely for these claims to impinge on First Amendment freedoms. The same is true of common-law privileges for defamation causes of action.

Second, the idea of dignity (as characterized in this book) has conceptual resources to restrict liability. Violations of dignity infringe on *rightful* status, or subject people to *arbitrary* restraints, or strip people of *adequate* control over self-presentation. These nonsubjective components of dignity enable normative concerns to be incorporated into an account of dignity. In asking whether a person's control over self-presentation is adequate, for example, one could ask whether giving that person more control would wrongfully curb other people's expression.

In that way, freedom of expression values can help to shape the contents of dignity itself. Yet First Amendment concerns should not swallow the definition of dignity. To do justice to both dignitary values and First Amendment principles, it is best to allow for the possibility that these normative considerations could genuinely clash. For instance, the goal of respecting the rightful status could conflict with the goal of safeguarding freedom of speech.

In the event of a clash, First Amendment principles can properly lose. At the outset, judicial interpretation of the First Amendment has frequently been criticized for inconsistency, if not incoherence.[77] Elevating the First

[77] *E.g.*, David S. Han, *Compelled Speech and Doctrinal Fluidity*, 97 Ind. L.J. 841 (2022); Robert Post, *Recuperating First Amendment Doctrine*, 47 Stan. L. Rev. 1249 (1995).

Amendment over dignity, therefore, may reduce rather than raise the level of legal coherence. The question remains, however, how far the First Amendment ought to restrict tort liability for violations of dignity.

That question raises the issue of what First Amendment free speech protections are *for*. A commonly cited justification for these protections is the maintenance of a public sphere in which citizens can contribute to democratic life by airing their political opinions.[78] On this rationale, the case for protecting dignity in tort law is weakest when liability would curb politically relevant speech. Another possible justification for First Amendment speech protections is the promotion of individual autonomy.[79] This justification might support greater limitations on liability for dignitary torts than the political rationale, as a defendant's autonomy interests are at stake even when the defendant is not attempting to influence the political sphere. For example, a defendant may have an autonomy interest in publicly disclosing private details about an ordinary citizen, even if such disclosure has no bearing on political affairs.

It is not my aim to provide a full theory of the First Amendment, but here are some preliminary remarks about the relationship between dignitary torts and freedom of speech. As an initial matter, there are good reasons for tort law to protect dignitary interests. The interests in rightful status, nondomination, and adequate control over self-presentation are socially valuable, and their infringement is socially detrimental. Further, the historical discussion above demonstrates that dignitary interests have meaningful roots in American law.

Nonetheless, these interests can be overridden by other values. In the First Amendment arena, restrictions on dignitary torts are more likely to be justified when they are aimed at safeguarding speech directed at political figures. The task of sustaining a political arena open to public discussion should carry a fair amount of weight. As to defendants' autonomy interests, legal decision-makers assessing the value of these interests need not ignore the uses to which defendants' autonomy is put.[80] When the result of defendants'

[78] For analysis, see Frederick Schauer, *Free Speech and the Argument from Democracy*, 25 Nomos 241 (1983).

[79] For discussion of the autonomy interest in free speech protections, see David S. Han, *Autobiographical Lies and the First Amendment's Protection of Self-Defining Speech*, 87 N.Y.U. L. Rev. 70, 92–93 (2012).

[80] *See* Christopher McCrudden, *Human Dignity and Judicial Interpretation of Human Rights*, 19 Eur. J. Int'l L. 655, 718–19 (2008) (describing a related approach to speech that undermines dignity in the Canadian Supreme Court).

exercise of autonomy is to violate dignity—to diminish rightful status, dominate others, and strip others of adequate control over self-presentation—these autonomy interests carry less normative weight. After all, the law penalizes numerous exercises of autonomy through the criminal and civil law. The suggestion here is that the First Amendment has a particular role in facilitating wide-ranging political debate that it does not have in safeguarding autonomy interests independent of the uses to which they are put.

This view suggests that restrictions on dignitary torts are most justified when dignitary violations target a recognized political figure. First, such violations often come in the form of contributions to political debates. Second, political figures, in taking on positions of power, have assumed some risk of dignitary harm. The political arena in a democracy—in which politicians compete and the public demands answers—is fertile ground for forms of disrespect and exposure that we might not wish to eliminate. After all, there is good reason to preserve the competition among politicians and the clamor from the public for information. When political figures enter this arena, the normative force of their requests for respectful treatment is reduced, though not erased.

Thus, the First Amendment properly blocks tort liability for individuals who expose sensitive matters regarding political figures in circumstances where the exposure of sensitive matters regarding private individuals would not prompt the same result. There may be limits to First Amendment protection for certain facts about political figures, such as intrusive information about their family members. These limits, however, ought to be less restrictive in the case of political figures than for private individuals.[81]

One might seek to deny that exposing politicians, when justified, inflicts dignitary harm at all. In those cases, one might argue, the politician is not entitled to control certain aspects of her presentation to others. Yet it is more realistic to acknowledge that there could be genuine tension between dignity and the First Amendment, and that the First Amendment can win out when the victim of dignitary harm is a political figure.

Matters are more complex when the speech is on a matter of social and political relevance and yet is not directed at a political figure. An example is the 2011 case *Snyder v. Phelps*, in which members of the Westboro Baptist

[81] The case for restricting dignitary torts directed at political figures applies to some degree to the broader category of "public figures" as well. Dignitary torts targeting public figures may not contribute as directly to political debates, but many public figures have assumed some risk of dignitary harm by choosing to live in the public eye.

Church picketed near a service member's funeral with signs including "Thank God for Dead Soldiers" and homophobic slogans.[82] The Supreme Court held that the First Amendment precluded church members' liability for state-law tort claims of intrusion upon seclusion and IIED.[83] The service member and his family were not political figures (or other public figures), although the subjects covered by the picketing—the American military and homosexuality—are arguably topics of social and political interest (in the Supreme Court's parlance, matters "of public concern").[84]

In my view, the fact that the service member and his family were not public figures means that the dignitary harm imposed on the family as a result of the picketing should have carried greater weight than the Court assigned to it. When a dignitary violation is directed at an individual who is not ordinarily the subject of public discussion, the speech is less likely to contribute materially to political debate, and the victim has not assumed the risk of dignitary harm. To be sure, these are generalizations; lines involving public figures and matters of public concern are difficult to draw, and there will be intermediate cases. But it is important to consider which particular First Amendment values are at stake and not to permit the First Amendment to swallow concern for dignitary harm. Focusing First Amendment restrictions on torts committed against political figures is one step.

Some might seek to resolve the First Amendment issue through a historical inquiry into speech restrictions at the Founding.[85] The Supreme Court has not yet adopted this approach, and a historical inquiry is likely to require analogical reasoning to draw connections between the Founding and the modern day.[86] The analogical process would itself be conducted against the background of views about the role of the First Amendment in American constitutional democracy. To the extent a historical inquiry is carried out, it should take account of the deep roots of legal protection for dignitary interests (as earlier noted). These roots suggest that the original meaning of the First Amendment is compatible with legally actionable dignitary harm. At the same time, it will not be straightforward to extrapolate from historical causes of action to the dignitary claims made today.

[82] Snyder v. Phelps, 562 U.S. 443, 448 (2011).

[83] *Id.* at 459–60.

[84] *Id.* at 458 (internal quotation marks omitted).

[85] Blankenship v. NBCUniversal, LLC, 144 S. Ct. 5 (2023) (Thomas, J., concurring in the denial of certiorari).

[86] For discussion of analogical reasoning in the Second Amendment context, see New York State Rifle & Pistol Ass'n, Inc. v. Bruen, 597 U.S. 1, 28–29 (2022).

The First Amendment issue is a subset of a broader question about the extent to which dignitary harm ought to spark a legal response, especially when legal determinations are made by judges with their own understandings of insulting or offensive conduct. First Amendment issues will continue to come up in the book's discussion of dignity and judicial authority, notably in the analysis of court-ordered apologies in Chapter 6. Overall, the First Amendment gives rise to genuine tension with the concern for dignity, but it should not eclipse that concern.

To conclude, this chapter has examined the legal recognition of dignitary harm by focusing on the role of dignity in tort law. Although torts cannot be neatly divided into "dignitary" and "nondignitary" claims, numerous tort suits protect dignitary interests, and some tort causes of action are especially likely to safeguard these interests. The place of dignity in tort law suggests that dignity is not a newfangled addition to the American legal tradition, even if tort law's responses to dignity have developed and changed over time. Protection for dignitary harm in tort law poses distinctive challenges for judicial authority, as it appears to invite courts to make value-laden decisions about what counts as dignitary harm. Many of these challenges can be addressed through the adjustment of standards for liability and the institutional allocation of certain normative determinations to juries and legislatures. These resources also help to alleviate First Amendment problems with tort liability for dignitary violations. Yet there remains the possibility of clashes between the First Amendment and tort liability based on dignity. In such cases, First Amendment fire should be directed particularly at claims related to the dignity of political figures.

The role of dignity in tort law opens a window onto the legal cognizability of harms that disrespect status, block people's ability to live free from domination, and strip people of control over self-presentation. American tort law has accepted that certain claims to be treated with dignity are actionable. Yet limits on the legal recognition of dignity in tort law reflect the risks posed by dignitary claims and their capacity to expand judges' spheres of action. Thus, dignity in tort law illuminates the more general topic of dignitary harm and judicial power.

PART III
DIGNITY AND REMEDIES

The previous Parts have outlined the nature of dignity and the challenges posed by courts' decisions to recognize (or not recognize) dignitary harm as an actionable injury. In particular, the question of whether dignitary harm is legally cognizable speaks to the bounds of judicial authority. Are stigma, disrespect, humiliation, and so on among the types of harms that plaintiffs can bring to court? Or are courts institutionally ill equipped to address cases in which plaintiffs have incurred these forms of injury? Part II argued that dignitary violations properly serve as the basis for lawsuits in American courts, both from the perspective of Article III injury and from the vantage point of tort law.

Part III tackles the remedial side of the harm–remedy equation: To what extent can courts "fix" dignitary problems? To what extent should they try to do so? These questions, like the issues surrounding recognition of dignitary harm, draw attention to judicial authority and its limitations. It may be contended, for example, that courts lack authority to provide respect, esteem, or other goods that contribute to people's dignity. To take a stylized example, if a judge writes "Litigant A is worthy of respect," is the judge acting in a judicial role? Or should judges stick to allocating material resources and preventing material harm?

Part III argues that judges in American courts may and should grant remedies aimed at restoring or maintaining the dignity of the party whose rights were violated. This Part contributes to scholarship on the law of remedies, which is the subject of a burgeoning legal literature. Part III consists of two chapters. Chapter 5, "Dignity and Judicial Relief," examines the ways in which judicial remedies can redress dignitary harm. The chapter explains why courts should provide relief for dignitary harm and considers the forms that such remedies can take, ranging from compensatory damages for dignitary harm to punitive damages, nominal damages, and declaratory judgments. The chapter also takes up the counterarguments that remedies for dignitary harm license unlimited relief and that they permit illicit advisory opinions.

Chapter 6, "Dignity and Apology," focuses on a specific type of remedy that casts the relationship between dignity and judicial redress into sharp relief. This is the judicially mandated apology—an apology that a court compels a defendant to provide. Although court-ordered apologies may rehabilitate the dignity of the plaintiff, they may also threaten the dignity of the defendant and raise First Amendment concerns about compelled speech. Chapter 6 analyzes the advisability and legality of court-ordered apologies, concluding that they carry risks but should not be wholly rejected. Moreover, court-ordered apologies shed light on other societal practices, including courts' treatment of expressions of remorse as factors in criminal sentencing.

In sum, Part III explores the question of what courts can do to alleviate dignitary harm, as well as this question's impact on the bounds of judicial power.

5
Dignity and Judicial Relief

This chapter examines the potential of judicial remedies to ameliorate dignitary harm. A remedy is a critical part of a lawsuit. The remedy is the point where the rubber hits the road, where the parties find out which changes in the world the court is prepared to make. A judicial remedy can be defined as "what the court can do *for* you if you win, and what the court can do *to* you if you lose."[1]

Remedies matter not only because they determine what happens to the parties, but also because they speak to what a court can legitimately do. If a plaintiff inserted into the "prayer for relief" of a negligence complaint a request for a judge to order public flogging, that remedy would exceed the bounds of the court's remedial authority. A defamation plaintiff could not ask a judge to order the defendant to be friends with the plaintiff, because friendship is not the type of good that properly constitutes part of judicial relief. To take more prosaic examples, a federal court may not grant as a remedy an advisory opinion responding to theoretical questions from a member of the Executive Branch;[2] nor may a federal court award attorneys' fees absent statutory authorization simply because the judge believes that public policy so demands.[3]

The range of acceptable remedies, in other words, helps to delineate the court's powers. This chapter considers whether and how courts can provide relief that has an impact on dignity. Dignity thus offers a lens through which to probe the capacities and limitations of judicial institutions.

The chapter proceeds as follows. First, I identify justifications for courts to grant remedies for dignitary harm. Second, I analyze specific types of remedies that could redress dignitary harm, such as compensatory damages for dignitary harm, punitive damages, nominal damages, declaratory judgments, and even dicta in judicial opinions. Third, I address objections to

[1] Douglas Laycock, *How Remedies Became a Field: A History*, 27 Rev. Litig. 161, 165 (2008).
[2] *See Correspondence of the Justices*, *in* Richard H. Fallon, Jr. et al., Hart & Wechsler's The Federal Courts and the Federal System 52 (7th ed. 2015) [hereinafter Hart & Wechsler].
[3] Alyeska Pipeline Serv. Co. v. Wilderness Soc'y, 421 U.S. 240, 263 (1975).

Dignity and Judicial Authority. Rachel Bayefsky, Oxford University Press. © Rachel Bayefsky 2024.
DOI: 10.1093/oso/9780197750322.003.0005

the idea that courts should grant relief for dignitary harm, grounded in both practical problems and constitutional concerns.

The current chapter concentrates on remedies in civil litigation, rather than criminal cases. This focus is meant to narrow the set of cases at issue and to explore the distinctive considerations involved in civil cases, such as the relationship between the "rightful position" standard and relief for dignitary harm. Chapter 6, on court-ordered apologies, contains more discussion of criminal cases.

Dignity and Remedies

Why should courts offer remedies for dignitary harm? Here are two responses: one rooted in the conceptual structure of the law of remedies, and one based on empirical features of litigation.

The Rightful Position

A key aim of remedies is to preserve or restore the plaintiff's rightful position,[4] understood as "the position plaintiff would have been in but for the wrong"[5] or the position the plaintiff occupies in advance of an anticipated wrong.[6] The "rightful position standard," in Richard Hasen's words, "says to choose the remedy that puts the plaintiff back (or keeps the plaintiff) in the position that she would have been in but for the defendant's wrong."[7] "Puts the plaintiff back" brings to mind backward-looking remedies such as compensatory damages; "keeps the plaintiff" brings to mind forward-looking remedies such as injunctions.

The rightful position is not the only remedial standard. For example, punitive damages are often thought to punish the defendant or to deter

[4] For further discussion of the rightful position and remedies that express respect, see Rachel Bayefsky, *Remedies and Respect: Rethinking the Role of Federal Judicial Relief*, 109 Geo. L.J. 1263, 1306–08 (2021). Portions of the current chapter draw on this article.

[5] Douglas Laycock & Richard L. Hasen, Modern American Remedies: Cases and Materials 14 (5th ed. 2019).

[6] David S. Schoenbrod, *The Measure of an Injunction: A Principle to Replace Balancing the Equities and Tailoring the Remedy*, 72 Minn. L. Rev. 627, 628 (1988).

[7] Richard Hasen, Examples & Explanations for Remedies 6 (5th ed. 2024) (emphasis omitted).

misconduct rather than restoring the plaintiff's rightful position.[8] Further, the goal of restoring or maintaining the rightful position is often elusive. When A defrauds B out of $100, A may set off a chain of events and emotional responses in B's life that cannot simply be reversed. Nonetheless, the rightful position functions as a "benchmark for judging various remedies."[9]

The rightful position standard provides some support for judicial relief for dignitary harm. To restore the victim to the position she occupied prior to a dignitary violation, the court should provide a remedy for the dignitary harm caused by the violation. For example, if a prison abuses a prisoner by imposing arbitrary restraints on his movement—a form of domination—the prison inflicts dignitary harm on the prisoner. If a court issues a declaratory judgment stating that the prisoner was treated illegally and imposes an injunction against the practice, the court ends the domination to which the prisoner was subject and thereby redresses the prisoner's dignitary harm.

Yet the rightful position standard may not suffice to justify remedies for dignitary harm, because not every negative effect of a legal violation is subject to judicial redress. For example, as noted in Chapter 3, the "economic loss" doctrine in negligence law (generally) prohibits parties from recovering in tort when negligence causes purely economic loss, as distinct from personal injury or property damage.[10] Rationales for the economic loss rule include preventing plaintiffs from recovering more in tort than they would in contract, and denying recovery for economic losses that are remote and unforeseeable.[11] When the economic loss rule applies, the plaintiff in a tort suit is not restored to the economic position she occupied prior to the legal violation. In other words, complete restoration to the pre-violation position is not viewed as a necessary element of the tort remedy. The bounds of an appropriate remedy are influenced by legal decision-makers' views about *which* effects of a legal violation ought to be rectified.

To further illustrate the point, courts often say that if damages are an adequate remedy, they will not grant injunctive relief.[12] Douglas Laycock has challenged the accuracy of this principle, suggesting that courts find damages adequate "only when there is some identifiable reason to deny specific relief

[8] *See* Restatement (Second) of Torts § 908 (Am. L. Inst. 1979).
[9] Hasen, note 7, at 6.
[10] *See* Jeffrey L. Goodman, Daniel R. Peacock & Kevin J. Rutan, *A Guide to Understanding the Economic Loss Doctrine*, 67 Drake L. Rev. 1, 2–3 (2019). The economic loss rule is subject to various qualifications and exceptions, depending on the jurisdiction.
[11] *Id.* at 18–19.
[12] Douglas Laycock, *The Death of the Irreparable Injury Rule*, 103 Harv. L. Rev. 687, 689 (1990).

[such as an injunction] in a particular case."[13] These reasons include the practicability of supervising the litigants, as well as the ripeness or mootness of the case.[14] That is, courts' judgments about remedial adequacy reflect various factors bearing on the advisability of injunctive relief. Remedies do not simply target all effects of the legal violation.

The question, then, is whether dignitary harm *ought* to be a remediable consequence of a legal violation. I will argue "yes," in the following steps. First, imposing dignitary harm is morally troubling. Second, dignitary harm is legally relevant. Third, dignitary harm is the type of harm that *courts* can remedy. Notably, the argument here is not that judicial relief must address dignitary harm in all cases. It is (a) that courts and other legal decision-makers should not rule out the use of judicial relief to redress dignitary harm, and (b) more strongly, that there is substantial reason for courts to provide relief for dignitary harm, even if this reason can be outweighed by other factors.

First, then, imposing dignitary harm is morally wrong in a way that matters. As defined in this book, violations of dignity involve disrespecting people's rightful status, subjecting people to domination, and stripping people of adequate control over their self-presentation. Because this understanding of dignity has a normative component, violating people's dignity is normatively unjustified. Intuitively, actions that violate dignity are the type that most people would morally condemn. Of course, some dignitary violations (for instance, an unprovoked rude comment) are morally more benign than others, such as forcing prisoners of war to drink out of troughs. But dignity possesses moral heft, and in many cases, an infringement of dignity is a significant moral violation.

Second, dignitary harm should carry legal weight. There is a basis in positive law for this view. Dignitary harm is legally cognizable in a range of settings, as Part II of this book demonstrated, and some dignitary violations have a substantial historical pedigree. Further, as explained below, it is worth taking seriously the argument that legal redress for dignitary harm can function as a substitute for self-help or violent revenge, and so a legal response to dignitary harm is socially beneficial. This does not mean every dignitary harm should receive a legal response. Legal decision-makers face trade-offs about whether the benefits of providing relief for dignitary harm outweigh

[13] *Id.* at 691.
[14] *Id.* at 692.

the costs, which include administrative and financial burdens, as well as harms to defendants or third parties. But dignitary violations, in addition to being moral wrongs, are legally significant.

Third, judicial remedies are an appropriate tool to redress dignitary harm. In justifying this view, an important starting point is Blackstone's statement, quoted in *Marbury v. Madison*, that "it is a general and indisputable rule that where there is a legal right, there is also a legal remedy by suit or action at law, whenever that right is invaded."[15] The principle of "where there is a right, there is a remedy" suggests that courts should not turn a blind eye to morally and socially corrosive consequences of legal violations. One of these consequences is dignitary harm.

Crediting the principle that "where there is a right, there is a remedy" means there should be at least a presumption in favor of judicial remedies for the detrimental effects of dignitary violations. But not all legal wrongs warrant judicial remediation. Doctrines such as standing, mootness, harmless error, and qualified immunity suggest that there can be a gap between right and remedy. Plaintiffs may correctly assert violations of their legal rights and yet be unable to recover. In fact, according to Richard Fallon and Daniel Meltzer, "where there is a right, there is a remedy" ought not be the sole principle behind constitutional remedies.[16] Another goal is "to ensure that government generally respects constitutional values," which may not require a full remedy in every individual case.[17] John Jeffries has suggested that a gap between rights and judicial remedies can actually foster the development of constitutional law, because courts can recognize rights for future application without granting extensive remedies for past harm.[18]

Despite the possibility of a justifiable gap between right and remedy, there is good reason for judges to take dignity into account when issuing remedies. The judiciary is a significant societal institution with substantial power to affect the dignity of litigants and other members of society. Judicial decisions should not ignore the moral and legal weight attached to dignity. Indeed, judicial remedies have implications for dignity regardless of whether judges so intend. If a jury awards a small compensatory damages award when a

[15] Marbury v. Madison, 5 U.S. 137, 163 (1803) (internal quotation marks omitted).

[16] Richard H. Fallon, Jr. & Daniel J. Meltzer, *New Law, Non-Retroactivity, and Constitutional Remedies*, 104 Harv. L. Rev. 1731, 1787–89 (1991).

[17] *Id.*

[18] John C. Jeffries, Jr., *The Right-Remedy Gap in Constitutional Law*, 109 Yale L.J. 87, 90 (1999). Jeffries notes, however, that he does not view "the right-remedy gap in constitutional law" as "in itself a good thing." *Id.* at 91.

plaintiff seeks a large sum in punitive damages, the judgment will "make a statement" regardless of the jury members' or judges' intentions. If a judge enjoins a restaurant owner to serve all comers despite the owner's religiously based objection to antidiscrimination law, the injunction will send messages of respect or disrespect to various parties and to broader social groups. Thus, courts cannot extricate themselves from the dignitary thicket. Given that their rulings will have an impact on dignity—a morally and legally significant value—judges ought to consider the dignitary effects of their decisions and try to make the dignitary impact productive.

Again, this does not mean courts need to grant the remedy that expresses respect for dignity to the greatest degree possible. Later in the chapter, I examine examples of relief for dignitary harm and consider more specifically the question of when such remedies should be employed. The overall point is that a judicial remedy may appropriately target dignitary harm as part of the aim of restoring or maintaining the rightful position.

Plaintiffs' Empirical Aims

In addition to the idea of restoring the rightful status, observations regarding plaintiffs' empirical goals provide reason for courts to grant relief for dignitary harm. In particular, the interest in securing recognition, respect, or vindication plays a role in fueling litigation, and (I will argue) the remedial apparatus of the judiciary should be responsive.

The interest in securing dignitary relief helps to drive litigation in a meaningful set of cases,[19] though I do not aim here to present a comprehensive empirical study of the reasons why litigants sue. Evidence that the goal of redressing perceived disrespect spurs lawsuits comes from studies covering a range of topics: medical malpractice litigation,[20] consumer class actions,[21]

[19] Part of this discussion of plaintiffs' empirical aims is based on Bayefsky, note 4, at 1300–05. For another exploration of plaintiffs' empirical aims, see Frank B. Cross, *In Praise of Irrational Plaintiffs*, 86 Cornell L. Rev. 1, 19–23 (2000).

[20] Tamara Relis, *"It's Not about the Money!": A Theory on Misconceptions of Plaintiffs' Litigation Aims*, 68 U. Pitt. L. Rev. 701, 730, 737 (2007); Elizabeth Chamblee Burch & Margaret S. Williams, *Perceptions of Justice in Multidistrict Litigation: Voices from the Crowd*, 107 Cornell L. Rev. 1835, 1864–65 (2022).

[21] Stephen Meili, *Collective Justice or Personal Gain? An Empirical Analysis of Consumer Class Action Lawyers and Named Plaintiffs*, 44 Akron L. Rev. 67, 93–97 (2011).

defamation suits,[22] sexual assault actions,[23] landlord–tenant disputes,[24] lawsuits arising from neighborhood conflicts,[25] and victim compensation proceedings following incidents of mass violence.[26]

To provide a flavor of the sentiment: In a study on consumer class actions, a plaintiff suing an insurance company explained to researchers that "we're real people here and we're not worth dirt."[27] An individual suing a debt collector said his "main goal [was] to prove that you can't mistreat people and basically think that you can get away with it."[28] Plaintiffs in a study on medical malpractice lawsuits stated that they had sued "mostly because of the lack of concern";[29] because of the defendant's "arrogance" and "the respect and dignity of [the plaintiff's] father";[30] and because "[p]eople should have dignity in their lives."[31] Summing up studies of sexual assault survivors, Merle Weiner explains that "[s]urvivors want accountability, revenge, deterrence, empowerment, voice, healing, and respect."[32]

These statements have strong dignitary resonances. Plaintiffs are seeking to redress treatment that they view as out of step with their rightful status ("we're not worth dirt"). They are pushing back against forms of treatment that rendered them vulnerable to the whims of others or deprived them of control over their self-presentation (the company should not be able to "get away with it," and the perpetrator of sexual assault should be held accountable). Plaintiffs aim to demonstrate publicly that the defendant wronged them and to secure acknowledgment of the harm the wrong imposed.

[22] *See* David Pritchard, *The Social Foundations of Defamation in Trial Court: Why Cases Begin and How They End*, 27 COMM. L. & POL'Y 128, 158 (2022); Randall P. Bezanson, *Libel Law and the Realities of Litigation: Setting the Record Straight*, 71 IOWA L. REV. 226, 227 (1985).

[23] *See* Merle H. Weiner, *Civil Recourse Insurance: Increasing Access to the Tort System for Survivors of Domestic and Sexual Violence*, 62 ARIZ. L. REV. 957, 985, 988–91 (2020); Francis X. Shen, *How We Still Fail Rape Victims: Reflecting on Responsibility and Legal Reform*, 22 COLUM. J. GENDER & L. 1, 37–39 (2011).

[24] *See* Russell Korobkin & Chris Guthrie, *Psychological Barriers to Litigation Settlement: An Experimental Approach*, 93 MICH. L. REV. 107, 144–47 (1994).

[25] *See* Sally Engle Merry & Susan S. Silbey, *What Do Plaintiffs Want? Reexamining the Concept of Dispute*, 9 JUST. SYS. J. 151, 153–54 (1984).

[26] *See* Gillian K. Hadfield, *Framing the Choice between Cash and the Courthouse: Experiences with the 9/11 Victim Compensation Fund*, 42 LAW & SOC'Y REV. 645, 661–62 (2008); Paul Heaton, Ivan Waggoner & Jamie Morikawa, *Victim Compensation Funds and Tort Litigation Following Incidents of Mass Violence*, 63 BUFF. L. REV. 1263, 1290 (2015).

[27] Meili, note 21, at 93.

[28] *Id.* at 91 (alteration in the original).

[29] Relis, note 20, at 729.

[30] *Id.* at 730.

[31] *Id.* at 737.

[32] Weiner, note 23, at 991.

Further, they seek to effectuate change beyond the confines of their specific case, so that other individuals will not be subject to similar treatment.

Often the idea of dignitary redress is contrasted with purely financial concerns, as reflected in the title of a medical malpractice study: "It's Not about the Money!"[33] Yet plaintiffs spurred to sue by dignitary considerations still frequently seek monetary damages. This is not necessarily inconsistent, for money can also send a message. As Margaret Radin has written, the "weightiness" of a wrong "is signified by using something of great importance in our society—money."[34] Moreover, plaintiffs may have multiple and overlapping motivations. In a study of participants in multidistrict litigation focusing on products that injured women's health, Elizabeth Chamblee Burch and Margaret S. Williams found that many plaintiffs sought monetary compensation, but many also sought "protecting others," "accountability," and acknowledgment of the harm caused by the defendants' actions.[35] Financial and vindication-oriented motives may go hand in hand. One plaintiff in Burch and Williams's study stated, for example, that "[t]he only way to punish them for damaging us is to take money from these greedy criminals."[36]

Literature on "procedural justice" provides further support for the view that litigants are concerned with dignitary harm. As several scholars have suggested, litigants—both plaintiffs and defendants—have an interest in being treated with respect through the procedures followed in litigation.[37] For example, procedural rules promote dignity by allowing people to make their case and receive reasons for a decision. Although procedural fairness is conceptually distinct from dignity-affirming case outcomes, litigants' interest in procedural dignity bolsters the view that plaintiffs have a stake in redress for dignitary harm.

Not all procedural features of litigation, however, advance dignity. Matthew Shapiro has argued, for instance, that litigation may cause humiliation, as when parties are forced to reveal private information.[38] Nonetheless,

[33] Relis, note 20.

[34] Margaret Jane Radin, *Compensation and Commensurability*, 43 Duke L.J. 56, 74 (1993).

[35] Burch & Williams, note 20, at 1864–70.

[36] *Id.* at 1868.

[37] *See, e.g.*, Alexandra D. Lahav, In Praise of Litigation 146 (2017); Judith Resnik, *Tiers*, 57 S. Cal. L. Rev. 837, 847–48 (1984); Lawrence B. Solum, *Procedural Justice*, 78 S. Cal. L. Rev. 181, 273–305 (2004); Tom R. Tyler & Justin Sevier, *How do the Courts Create Popular Legitimacy? The Role of Establishing the Truth, Punishing Justly, and/or Acting through Just Procedures*, 77 Alb. L. Rev. 1095, 1105–07 (2014).

[38] Matthew A. Shapiro, *The Indignities of Civil Litigation*, 100 B.U. L. Rev. 501, 532–41 (2020).

some plaintiffs are apparently willing to bear these dignitary costs to vindicate other dignitary interests in redress.

All in all, there is substantial evidence that dignitary considerations fuel litigation. To be sure, methodological constraints restrict the conclusions that can be drawn from empirical studies of litigants' motivations. Sample sizes may be limited; the individuals who agree to be interviewed may be especially likely to be motivated by dignitary considerations; and parties may ascribe to themselves motivations that appear "purer" than a desire to make money. Yet it is still plausible that the concern for redressing perceived blows to status plays a role in driving litigation. Moreover, dignity may be especially salient in certain contexts, such as those involving the emotionally sensitive topics of medical malpractice and sexual abuse. Context sensitivity is a feature, rather than a bug, of the dignitary relief model. Because the dignitary stakes of lawsuits vary, some types of lawsuits are more likely to warrant relief for dignitary harm than others.

Still, the empirical question of why plaintiffs sue does not answer the normative one of whether their motivations should be validated. Indeed, one might contend that dignitary interests are precisely the kind that courts should not validate.[39] Perhaps the judicial system should tamp down the quest for vindication, which may come too close to the desire for revenge. In other words, there is a difference between the "is" of what plaintiffs want and the "ought" of what they should receive.

Nonetheless, if the judicial system is systematically unresponsive to the concerns that drive plaintiffs to sue, there will be a normative problem. Courts rely for the authoritativeness of their judgments on public acceptance and perceived legitimacy.[40] If judges rule out the dignitary redress that plaintiffs seek, then a gap may develop between the people and the courts. The perception that courts ignore plaintiffs' interests in certain types of relief is not one that judges in a democratic system should encourage.

Further, judicial responsiveness is productive because it provides a substitute for self-help and revenge. The idea that lawsuits can replace revenge may seem outdated, but it should be taken seriously. In fact, some courts have mentioned the link between lawsuits and revenge. As noted in Chapter 4, the Illinois Supreme Court in 1872 upheld a punitive damages

[39] *See* Relis, note 20, at 741 ("[L]awyers condition plaintiffs on legal system realities, preparing them to expect only money as 'that is all the system can provide.'").

[40] *See* Williams-Yulee v. Fla. Bar, 575 U.S. 433, 445–46 (2015) ("The judiciary's authority . . . depends in large measure on the public's willingness to respect and follow its decisions.").

award against a defendant who spat in the plaintiff's face in public.[41] The court reasoned: "The act in question was one of the greatest indignity, highly provocative of retaliation by force, and the law, as far as it may, should afford substantial protection against such outrages, in the way of liberal damages, that the public tranquillity may be preserved by saving the necessity of resort to personal violence as the only means of redress."[42]

It might be argued that times have changed since 1872, but the lawsuit as a substitute for revenge is not a thing of the past. In the 1997 case *Jacque v. Steenberg Homes*, the Wisconsin Supreme Court upheld a punitive damages award added to a nominal damages award against a mobile home company that trespassed across the Jacques' land.[43] One reason to uphold the award, the court explained, was that "[w]hen landowners have confidence in the legal system, they are less likely to resort to 'self-help' remedies. . . . Although dueling is rarely a modern form of self-help, one can easily imagine a frustrated landowner taking the law into his or her own hands when faced with a brazen trespasser . . . who refuses to heed no trespass warnings."[44]

It is difficult to prove empirically that violent self-help would increase if judicial relief for dignitary harm decreased. But the drive for vindication or satisfaction has not dissipated with the modern age. As political violence in the United States in recent years has underscored,[45] the constitution and maintenance of a community in which disputes are resolved by law rather than by brute force remains a fragile achievement. Moreover, courts are needed to provide this dispute resolution function, as they (unlike legislatures) can tackle disagreements in a case-specific fashion.

The argument that courts should provide a channel for parties' interest in relief for dignitary harm is not absolute. The desire for a remedy need not always be satisfied. A court should not offer a remedy that expresses a racist message simply because a party deprived of such relief would otherwise retaliate out of court. Racist messages, however, are morally wrong in a way that redress for dignitary harm ordinarily is not. The desire to see

[41] Alcorn v. Mitchell, 63 Ill. 553, 554 (1872).
[42] *Id.*
[43] Jacque v. Steenberg Homes, Inc., 563 N.W.2d 154, 166 (Wis. 1997).
[44] *Id.* at 160–61.
[45] *See, e.g.*, Sheryl Gay Stolberg & Brian M. Rosenthal, *Man Charged after White Nationalist Rally in Charlottesville Ends in Deadly Violence*, N.Y. Times (Aug. 12, 2017), https://www.nytimes.com/2017/08/12/us/charlottesville-protest-white-nationalist.html.

the defendant publicly rebuked could reflect an interest in having the legal system broadcast that justice was done, as well as an interest in preventing future injustices.[46] Even if one takes the view that the desire for vindication comes too close to an unsavory thirst for revenge, motivations may be mixed and complex. For instance, a person subjected to a humiliating arrest may pursue a declaratory judgment stating that the police officers acted illegally. The plaintiff may also wish to see the officers "brought low," but that does not mean his interest in redress for dignitary harm should be excluded on moral grounds. Thus, one reason for courts to remedy dignitary harm is to provide a peaceful channel for plaintiffs' interests in vindication.

Courts are justified in issuing relief for dignitary harm, then, for the following reasons. First, dignitary harm is properly rectified by judges: It is morally troubling, legally actionable, and redressable in court. Second, plaintiffs' interest in redress for dignitary harm is an empirical phenomenon that the judicial system should not ignore.

Forms of Relief for Dignitary Harm

This section considers more specifically how courts can provide relief for dignitary harm. In particular, it addresses the following forms of remediation: compensatory damages for dignitary harm, punitive damages, nominal damages, and declaratory judgments. It also suggests that dicta in judicial opinions could constitute a remedy for dignitary harm. The list of remedies here is illustrative rather than exclusive. The remedies discussed here are not the only ones with dignitary impact; for example, Chapter 6 deals with court-mandated apologies. This section is meant to explore various forms of relief for dignitary harm and to show that such relief is feasible. Indeed, in several instances, the American legal system is already providing relief for dignitary harm. In these cases, the account here justifies and urges systematization of these practices.

[46] *See, e.g.*, Maureen Balleza, *Many Rape Victims Finding Justice through Civil Courts*, N.Y. Times (Sept. 20, 1991), https://www.nytimes.com/1991/09/20/health/many-rape-victims-finding-justice-through-civil-courts.html (a rape victim who sued her residential management company for security failures stating: "It's not so much that I got revenge, but I got justice having a judge and my lawyers and a jury of my peers saying, 'We believe in you, we believe in your cause.'").

Compensatory Damages for Dignitary Harm

Compensatory damages refer to "[a]n amount awarded to a complainant to compensate for a proven injury or loss."[47] One might ask how money can compensate for dignitary harm, when dignity is not bought or sold on markets, and lacks a readily discernable market value. But other types of compensable harm—notably, emotional distress, and pain and suffering—are also not readily susceptible to market valuation. In these cases, the factfinder may assign a "reasonable" value to these harms, subject to review for gross excessiveness or gross inadequacy.[48] Compensatory damages for dignitary harm could follow suit.

The idea of the rightful position helps to illuminate compensatory damages for dignitary harm. For instance, the defendant's legal violation "lowers" the plaintiff beneath his or her rightful status. The damages remedy then returns the plaintiff to the rightful status by sending the message that the plaintiff was treated improperly. The phrase "sending the message" hearkens back to "expressive" theories of law discussed in Chapter 2. In conveying that the plaintiff should have been treated more respectfully, the damages award restores—or, at least, makes headway toward restoring—the status that the plaintiff occupied prior to the dignitary violation.

In fact, compensatory damages for dignitary harm are slated for inclusion in the Third Restatement of the Law on Torts Remedies.[49] The relevant section of the Third Restatement, currently in draft form, provides that "[a] plaintiff who establishes a defendant's liability for a tort that causes dignitary harm may recover reasonable compensation for: (1) dignitary harm if the factfinder infers significant dignitary harm and its value from the facts and circumstances of the tort itself . . . (2) emotional harm . . . (3) harm to reputation or loss of privacy . . . and (4) any other harms caused by the tort, such as lost earnings or earning capacity, lost profits, or medical expenses."[50] Thus, a court following the Third Restatement may award compensatory damages for dignitary harm arising from a tort.

Because dignitary harm is not identical to emotional harm, compensation for emotional distress does not render superfluous compensation for

[47] *Damages*, Black's Law Dictionary (12th ed. 2024).
[48] Robert L. Rabin, *Pain and Suffering and Beyond: Some Thoughts on Recovery for Intangible Loss*, 55 DePaul L. Rev. 359, 374 (2006).
[49] Restatement (Third) of Torts: Remedies § 22 cmt. a (Tentative Draft 2, 2023) [hereinafter Third Restatement of Torts Remedies] (citations omitted).
[50] *Id.* § 22 (citations omitted).

dignitary harm. Here is a case from the Third Restatement that highlights the distinction:

> Pam was riding the subway, fast asleep. Marcus fondled and squeezed her breasts without waking her up. When Pam awakened, a friend told her what had happened. Marcus is liable for battery. Even though Pam was unaware of the incident as it happened, the factfinder can infer reasonable damages for dignitary harm from the facts and circumstances.[51]

Even if Pam has difficulty proving emotional distress, she could still recover damages for dignitary harm.

Nonetheless, compensation for dignitary harm often overlaps with compensation for emotional distress (and for pain and suffering).[52] The Third Restatement recommends that factfinders generally make a single award for dignitary and emotional harm, as "[s]eparate damage awards for such closely related and overlapping categories of harm would present a serious risk of duplicative awards and overcompensation."[53] Although the possibility of duplicative awards is a reasonable concern, damages for dignitary harm risk being sidelined if they are joined with damages for emotional distress. Another approach would be to permit juries to make separate awards for dignitary and emotional harm but to include an instruction about the potential for overlap.

The Third Restatement restricts compensatory damages for dignitary harm to "significant" dignitary harm (though it allows for nominal damages for dignitary harm that does not meet the significance threshold). This decision may help to alleviate concerns about exorbitant damages and could aid in securing public acceptance of compensatory damages for dignitary harm. Yet compensation for dignitary harm is subject to a "significance" threshold that does not apply to economic and emotional harms. And the "significant" limitation would be more suitable in the setting of punitive damages, which could be awarded for particularly serious dignitary violations (as discussed below). Another way to address concerns about runaway liability in the setting of compensatory damages would be to caution juries that the amount of the recovery for dignitary harm should be commensurate with its gravity.

51 *Id.* § 22 cmt. d.
52 *See id.* § 22 cmt. e.
53 *Id.*

Judges could provide a check on jury verdicts that do not reflect that warning, in the form of judgments as a matter of law and appellate review.

Compensatory damages for dignitary harm might seem similar to punitive damages. Douglas Laycock and Richard L. Hasen have questioned whether certain awards of compensatory damages for dignitary harms are "[p]unitive damages in disguise."[54] The relationship between compensatory damages for dignitary harm and punitive damages is more of a continuum than a sharp divide. Yet redress for dignitary harm is not exclusively a role for punitive damages. Dignitary harm is a predictable result of several legal violations. Excluding dignitary harm from the circle of compensable results of legal wrongs would unjustifiably downgrade dignity from an expressive perspective. Put differently, attempts to restore the rightful position through compensatory damages should not overlook that position's dignitary dimensions. Therefore, redress for dignitary harm does not belong solely in the domain of punitive damages—although, as is argued next, punitive damages can serve an important function in expressing outrage about especially grievous dignitary violations.

Punitive Damages

Punitive damages are an appropriate way for courts to provide relief for dignitary harm in egregious cases. In the Illinois Supreme Court case upholding punitive damages for spitting in a person's face in public (referenced above), the court reasoned:

> It is customary to instruct juries that they may give vindictive damages where there are circumstances of malice, wilfulness, wantonness, outrage and indignity attending the wrong complained of. The act in question was wholly made up of such qualities. It was one of pure malignity, done for the mere purpose of insult and indignity.[55]

Here, dignitary logic explains the punitive damages award. The defendant's action—spitting in the plaintiff's face in public—inflicted dignitary harm. The jury in assessing punitive damages, and the court in upholding the

[54] Laycock & Hasen, note 5, at 211.
[55] Alcorn v. Mitchell, 63 Ill. 553, 554 (1872).

award, expressed outrage at the defendant's behavior and thereby reaffirmed the plaintiff's dignity.[56]

Theoretically, the dignitary logic might also be described in compensatory terms: The court's verdict compensated for the dignitary harm that the defendant's action imposed. Indeed, when the harm is dignitary, it may not be possible to draw a bright line between compensatory and punitive damages.

Nonetheless, punitive damages provide redress for dignitary harm in particular ways. The most commonly cited rationales for punitive damages are to punish the defendant and to deter harmful conduct.[57] Punitive damages reaffirm the plaintiff's dignity through the mechanisms of punishment and deterrence. Punitive damages are perceived as a penalty, and they carry a societal message of condemnation; accordingly, they offer vindication to the plaintiff. As to deterrence, punitive damages, by disincentivizing wrongdoing, help to satisfy victims' interest in preventing the wrong from happening again. This interest is, at least in part, a dignitary one, as empirical studies of plaintiffs' motivations suggest: Plaintiffs often want their experiences of harm to matter, in the sense that they serve as the basis for judicial action that contributes to the prevention of similar violations.[58] In other words, plaintiffs may seek "responsive policy change—making sure that lessons were learned and heeded in the future."[59] Thus, punitive damages advance dignitary aims through their punishment and deterrence functions.

An illustration of punitive damages' dignitary role comes from the 1997 Wisconsin Supreme Court trespass case, *Jacque v. Steenberg Homes* (mentioned earlier in the discussion of lawsuits as a substitute for revenge).[60] There, a mobile home company trespassed across the plaintiffs' land despite the plaintiffs' adamant refusal to allow the company to cross over. In addition, the company had falsely given the plaintiffs reason to believe it would not trespass.[61] Although the trespass caused no measurable physical

56 For discussion of connections between punitive damages and dignity or expression of a message, see, for example, Thomas B. Colby, *Clearing the Smoke from* Philip Morris v. Williams: *The Past, Present, and Future of Punitive Damages*, 118 YALE L.J. 392, 434 (2008); Anthony J. Sebok, *Punitive Damages: From Myth to Theory*, 92 IOWA L. REV. 957, 1008 (2007).

57 *See, e.g.*, Exxon Shipping Co. v. Baker, 554 U.S. 471, 492 (2008).

58 *See* Meili, note 21, at 88–92; *see also* Burch & Williams, note 20, at 1865.

59 Hadfield, note 26, at 648.

60 Jacque v. Steenberg Homes, Inc., 563 N.W.2d 154 (Wis. 1997).

61 *Id.* at 164.

damage, the jury awarded $1 in nominal damages and $100,000 in punitive damages.[62]

The Wisconsin Supreme Court upheld the punitive damages award. A ruling to the contrary, the court reasoned, would "send[] the wrong message to [the mobile home company] and any others who contemplate trespassing on the land of another. It [would] implicitly tell[] them that they are free to go where they please, regardless of the landowner's wishes."[63] The court further rejected the argument that the punitive damages award was excessive, explaining that the mobile home company had engaged in "egregious" conduct that displayed "utter disregard for the rights of" the plaintiffs.[64]

In *Jacque*, the punitive damages award served to redress the dignitary harm to which the plaintiffs had been subject—notably, the harm of domination, or being subject to the trespassers' desire to "go where they please." The penalization of the mobile home company for "egregious" conduct reaffirmed the status of the plaintiffs and (ideally) helped to deter similar conduct in the future. One might proffer alternative rationales for punitive damages, such as the argument that they respond to the low probability that the legal violation will be detected and thereby help to maintain optimal deterrence.[65] Different rationales may support punitive damages in different cases. But punitive damages have a meaningful role in redressing dignitary harm through the mechanisms of punishment and deterrence. To the extent one argues that punitive damages for dignitary harm are unnecessary because compensatory damages for dignitary harm also have the effect of punishing and deterring, this argument could render punitive damages superfluous for many types of harm, not just dignitary.

Nonetheless, punitive damages could be differentiated from compensatory damages if they are imposed only in especially egregious instances of dignitary violations. For example, a district court in Maine upheld a punitive damages award in a case involving an uncle's sexual abuse of his nephew on the ground that "[t]he harm at issue here results from a particularly egregious act that took place in secret and abused a relationship of trust. It generated relatively small economic damages, but produced noneconomic damages

62 *Id.* at 158.
63 *Id.* at 161.
64 *Id.* at 164.
65 A. Mitchell Polinsky & Steven Shavell, *Punitive Damages: An Economic Analysis*, 111 Harv. L. Rev. 869, 874–75 (1998).

from psychological trauma likely to persist for years to come, and such damages are difficult to determine."[66]

The boundaries of "particularly egregious" acts warranting punitive damages will be difficult to draw. Courts face the challenge of distinguishing these acts from those warranting compensatory damages for dignitary harm, especially if the latter are granted just for "significant" dignitary harm, as the Third Restatement on tort remedies currently proposes.[67] The focus with punitive damages is more on the reprehensibility of the act rather than the magnitude of the harm, but the two categories could overlap. Jury instructions could therefore emphasize that punitive damages are warranted only in cases involving egregious conduct that extends above and beyond acts causing "significant" dignitary harm. The combination of jury participation and judicial review should help to prevent both unfettered judicial discretion and "runaway" jury punitive damages awards.

Punitive damages have been subject to substantial criticism. It may be argued, for example, that they are inefficient[68] or that they are imposed arbitrarily and are hence unfair.[69] The goal here is not to resolve those debates. The remedial model endorsed in this chapter supports punitive damages to punish and deter egregious dignitary violations, while also allowing considerations other than dignity to take precedence. If a punitive damages award would be gravely inefficient or unfair, it may justifiably be restricted.

Restrictions need not take the form of numerical ceilings. Many states have instituted caps on punitive damages,[70] and the Supreme Court has indicated that there are constitutional limits rooted in the Due Process Clause on the ratio of punitive to compensatory damages.[71] The interest in providing redress for dignitary harm provides reason to be skeptical of a rigid cap or ratio. The magnitude of dignitary harm and the reprehensibility of the defendant's conduct are difficult to measure precisely. Yet numerical restrictions are not the only way to regulate punitive damages awards. Judges and appellate courts can steer, and act as a backstop for, juries' decisions

66 Shannon v. Sasseville, 684 F. Supp. 2d 169, 178 (D. Me. 2010).

67 Third Restatement of Torts Remedies, note 49, § 22.

68 *See, e.g.*, E. Donald Elliott, *Why Punitive Damages Don't Deter Corporate Misconduct Effectively*, 40 Ala. L. Rev. 1053, 1056 (1989).

69 *See, e.g.*, State Farm Mut. Auto. Ins. Co. v. Campbell, 538 U.S. 408, 417–18 (2003).

70 W. McDonald Plosser, *Sky's the Limit? A 50-State Survey of Damages Caps and the Collateral Source Rule*, Mondaq.com (Dec. 11, 2018), https://www.mondaq.com/unitedstates/insurance-laws-and-products/762574/skys-the-limit-a-50-state-survey-of-damages-caps-and-the-collateral-source-rule.

71 Exxon Shipping Co. v. Baker, 554 U.S. 471, 501 (2008).

about the magnitude of harm and the reprehensibility of the defendant's conduct. In identifying problematic awards, judges and appellate courts can be guided by past punitive damage remedies, so that a "common law" of punitive damages develops.

Regardless of how legal decision-makers impose limitations on punitive damages, they need not pursue the goal of redressing dignitary violations to the exclusion of other aims of the legal system, including efficiency and fairness. Nonetheless, punitive damages furnish a way to remedy dignitary harm by punishing the defendant and deterring future misconduct.

Nominal Damages

At the opposite end of the monetary spectrum from punitive damages stand nominal damages, that is, "damages in name only, usually $1 or six cents."[72] To take a couple of recent examples from the news, the singer Taylor Swift, facing a defamation suit from a radio personality who she said groped her, countersued for assault and battery; she won $1 in damages in 2017.[73] At trial, Swift's counsel indicated that Swift was suing for only $1 because she wanted to send a message: "It means 'no means no' and it tells every woman they will decide what will be tolerated with their body."[74] Actress Gwyneth Paltrow was sued for hundreds of thousands of dollars after a ski collision; she counterclaimed for $1 and won the nominal amount in 2023.[75] These awards dramatize the question of why plaintiffs sue for nominal damages and what they can achieve.

Nominal damages are a long-standing phenomenon, and historically they have played multiple roles. One is to be a "peg to hang costs on."[76] Court costs were typically borne by the losing party; if a plaintiff established a cause of action but proved no "actual" damages, nominal damages could be awarded

[72] Dan B. Dobbs, Paul T. Hayden & Ellen M. Bublick, The Law of Torts § 56 n.5 (2d ed.), Westlaw (database updated April 2024).

[73] Keith Coffman & Jann Tracey, *Taylor Swift Wins Groping Trial against DJ, Awarded Symbolic $1*, Reuters (Aug. 14, 2017), https://www.reuters.com/article/world/uk/taylor-swift-wins-groping-trial-against-dj-awarded-symbolic-1-idUSKCN1AU109/.

[74] *Id.*

[75] Sonia Rao & Maham Javaid, *Gwyneth Paltrow Not Liable for Utah Ski Collision and Awarded $1, Jury Rules*, Wash. Post (Mar. 30, 2023), https://www.washingtonpost.com/arts-entertainment/2023/03/30/gwyneth-paltrow-lawsuit-verdict.

[76] Theodore Sedgwick, A Treatise on the Measure of Damages 164 (9th ed. 1912) (quoting Stanton v. N.Y. & E. Ry., 22 Atl. 300 (Conn. 1890)); Dan B. Dobbs & Caprice L. Roberts, Law of Remedies: Damages-Equity-Restitution 226 (3d. ed. 2018).

to prevent the plaintiff from bearing the costs of the suit.[77] Today the "peg to hang costs on" rationale has a parallel in attorney's fee determinations.[78] Several federal statutes, including civil rights laws, provide for the "prevailing party" to secure attorney's fees. A plaintiff may be considered the prevailing party through an award of nominal damages, although the magnitude of the attorney's fee may be reduced as a result.[79] Thus, an award of nominal damages can pave the way for attorney's fees. Another role for nominal damages is to function as a peg for punitive damages. As in the *Jacque* trespass case discussed earlier, a nominal damages award could provide a basis for a punitive damages award if the defendant's conduct is sufficiently egregious.

In addition to the role of nominal damages as a "peg" for various other remedies, nominal damages have enabled courts to declare rights. As the Supreme Court explained in its most comprehensive discussion of nominal damages, in the 2021 case *Uzuegbunam v. Preczewski*:

> The award of nominal damages was one way for plaintiffs at common law to obtain a form of declaratory relief in a legal system with no general declaratory judgment act. For example, a trespass to land or water rights might raise a prospective threat to a property right by creating the foundation for a future claim of adverse possession or prescriptive easement. By obtaining a declaration of trespass, a property owner could vindicate his right by action and protect against those future threats. Courts at common law would not declare property boundaries in the abstract, but the suit for nominal damages allowed them to do so indirectly.[80]

In other words, nominal damages allowed courts to settle claims of right and thereby to forestall future disputes. If a property owner saw that someone else was using his property in a manner he deemed to be trespass, the property owner could bring suit for nominal damages to assert ownership even if the other person was not causing physical damage to the property. The property owner would not need to wait and risk losing the land to adverse possession in the future.

[77] Sadie Blanchard, *Nominal Damages as Vindication*, 30 Geo. Mason L. Rev. 227, 235–36 (2022).
[78] Moore v. Liszewski, 838 F.3d 877, 879 (7th Cir. 2016).
[79] Farrar v. Hobby, 506 U.S. 103, 112–14 (1992).
[80] Uzuegbunam v. Preczewski, 141 S. Ct. 792, 798 (2021) (internal quotation marks and citations omitted).

The declaratory function of nominal damages raises the question of whether nominal damages are needed now that Congress (in 1934) and several states have passed declaratory judgment acts. Are nominal damages simply a relic of a pre-declaratory judgment past?

The answer is "no," because nominal damages have not been awarded solely to determine rights prospectively. Nominal damages also redress past legal violations, as the Court confirmed in *Uzuegbunam*. The plaintiff in that case was a student who had been prevented by his college from sharing his faith on an outdoor plaza and who alleged that his First Amendment rights were violated.[81] After a suit was filed, the university changed its policy on campus speech, so the student could no longer seek injunctive relief. But the student continued to pursue a suit for nominal damages to redress the past violation of his rights. University officials argued that the suit was moot. The Supreme Court, however, rebuffed the mootness objection and permitted the student to sustain his suit because he was still seeking nominal damages. Citing historical sources, the Court stated that an "award of nominal damages by itself can redress a past injury."[82] "A contrary rule," the Court explained, "would have meant, in many cases, that there was no remedy at all for those rights, such as due process or voting rights, that were not readily reducible to monetary valuation."[83]

The *Uzuegbunam* Court's reference to nominal damages as a remedy for the violation of rights "not readily reducible to monetary valuation" is related to the idea that nominal damages offer "vindication." As the Supreme Court stated in the 1978 case *Carey v. Piphus*, "[c]ommon law courts traditionally have vindicated deprivations of certain 'absolute' rights that are not shown to have caused actual injury through the award of a nominal sum of money."[84] What does it mean for nominal damages to provide "vindication"? Sadie Blanchard suggests that nominal damages offer vindication by "empower[ing] the judiciary to provide reliable information about the plaintiff's or the defendant's behavior to assess that behavior against legal norms."[85] In turn, "[t]he availability of a forum in which to produce that information might deter violations of legal rights or aid the plaintiff in receiving

81 *Id.* at 796–97.
82 *Id.* at 796, 799–800.
83 *Id.* at 800.
84 Carey v. Piphus, 435 U.S. 247, 266 (1978).
85 Blanchard, note 77, at 250.

redress through a negotiated settlement."[86] Nominal damages may indeed enable courts to provide information about adherence to legal norms.

The notion of "vindication," however, also hearkens back to plaintiffs' dignitary aims—the kind of interest in satisfaction or honor described in the empirical studies cited earlier. For nominal damages can be a form of dignitary redress. A defendant's illegal conduct, such as denying the right to vote or thwarting procedural due process, may violate the plaintiff's dignity but cause no economic or physical harm. Nominal damages can send the message that the defendant's conduct was nonetheless unacceptable. The plaintiff, in being publicly vindicated through a nominal damages award, secures relief for dignitary injury. On this account, the "symbolic" nature of nominal damages is not a problematic aspect of the remedy; it is a constituent and valuable feature.[87]

The role of nominal damages in redressing dignitary harm helps to resolve a paradox involving nominal damages and Article III standing. The Supreme Court held in *Uzuegbunam* that a nominal damages award can redress a past injury, and so a suit for nominal damages can satisfy the "redressability" prong of the Article III standing test[88]—the requirement that the plaintiff's injury in fact "is likely to be redressed by a favorable judicial decision."[89] But the Court also requires plaintiffs to demonstrate "concrete" injury in fact.[90] What kind of concrete injury do nominal damages redress? If nominal damages do not provide relief for actual harm, then there is tension between *Uzuegbunam* and the Court's concrete harm requirement.

The tension is alleviated once nominal damages are recognized as a potential form of dignitary relief. Nominal damages, by sending a message that vindicates the plaintiff, can redress dignitary harm caused by the legal violation. This is not to say that nominal damages *always* serve the function of redressing dignitary harm. They can also declare a right or provide a basis for attorney's fees or costs. Yet the dignitary explanation of nominal damages is an integral part of the story.

One might question whether nominal damages provide redress for dignitary harm. Judge Richard Posner of the Court of Appeals for the Seventh Circuit, for instance, suggested that "[i]f the plaintiff goes around bragging

[86] *Id.*
[87] For discussion of dignity and nominal damages, see Bayefsky, note 4, at 1325–28.
[88] Uzuegbunam v. Preczewski, 141 S. Ct. 792, 801–02 (2021).
[89] Spokeo, Inc. v. Robins, 578 U.S. 330, 338 (2016).
[90] TransUnion LLC v. Ramirez, 594 U.S. 413, 424 (2021).

that he won his suit, and is asked what exactly he won, and replies '$1 dollar,' he'll be laughed at."[91] On this view, a nominal damages award signifies that the court is not taking the plaintiff's claim especially seriously. But the meaning of a remedy depends on social context. A nominal award might be inadequate relief for dignitary harm in a particular case. Yet it is implausible that across the board, the winner of a nominal-damages award will be a laughingstock. The plaintiff in *Uzuegbunam*, for example, is not likely to be the subject of laughter; instead, he is probably viewed as someone who successfully made a point on a matter of principle.

Another issue is the relationship between nominal damages and other forms of dignitary relief. If the defendant injured the plaintiff's dignity, why should the court not award compensatory or punitive damages for dignitary harm, instead of merely nominal damages? In response, multiple remedies can provide redress for dignitary harm. There is no requirement that each type of harm be targeted through one specific type of remedy. Still, courts seeking to provide relief for dignitary harm could more clearly distinguish between the role of different remedies. Nominal damages may be most fitting when the plaintiff wishes to show that she is suing solely "on principle" and is pursuing no substantial financial recovery, or that she is willing to continue with the litigation even though no substantial financial recovery is possible any longer. Celebrities like Taylor Swift may be in a better position than others to forgo a meaningful monetary award, but it is not only celebrities who pursue nominal damages, as *Uzuegbunam* shows.

Nominal damages could also serve a distinctive function when other doctrines limit the plaintiff's ability to recover compensatory or punitive damages. The law of qualified immunity provides an example. This doctrine bars financial recovery against government officers unless the plaintiff establishes a violation of a clearly established right of which a reasonable person would have known.[92] The rationale is to protect government officials from "potentially disabling threats of liability" that would chill vigorous performance of official duties.[93] Qualified immunity, however, makes it harder to hold government officers accountable for rights violations and may hinder the development of constitutional law. James Pfander has suggested that plaintiffs suing government officers for violating their constitutional rights

[91] Moore v. Liszewski, 838 F.3d 877, 879 (7th Cir. 2016).
[92] Rivas-Villegas v. Cortesluna, 595 U.S. 1, 5 (2021) (per curiam).
[93] Harlow v. Fitzgerald, 457 U.S. 800, 806 (1982); *see also* Pearson v. Callahan, 555 U.S. 223, 231 (2009).

should be able to avoid the application of qualified immunity by pursuing nominal damages alone.[94] That way, plaintiffs can secure a measure of vindication, and constitutional rights can be clarified, without officers' incurring substantial liability.[95] To be sure, a verdict for nominal damages could be viewed as shameful for the defendant, and so its availability could still have a chilling effect on officers. Nonetheless, nominal damages are useful as an alternative to a larger monetary award when the larger award is impracticable, doctrinally foreclosed, or politically unacceptable.

Overall, nominal damages can redress dignitary harm. Although they will serve this function to differing degrees in different cases, courts should harness the dignitary benefits of this remedy.

Declaratory Judgments

A declaratory judgment is another vehicle to provide relief for dignitary harm. Like nominal damages, declaratory judgments have multiple functions. One is to clarify uncertainty regarding legal rights. In a patent case, for example, an inventor might sue a patent owner for a declaratory judgment of non-infringement. The inventor can then avoid wasting time and money developing a new product that might later be deemed to infringe.

Another effect of declaratory judgments is to announce publicly that the court has deemed the plaintiff's view of the law to be correct. To the extent the plaintiff suffered dignitary harm, the public announcement could redress that harm. A female employee at a company that systematically engages in pay discrimination in favor of male employees could secure redress for dignitary harm if a court issues a declaratory judgment stating that the employer's practices are illegal.

In these cases, a declaratory judgment provides relief for dignitary harm because of the message the court expresses. True, declaratory judgments often have physical or economic effects as well. As Samuel Bray has pointed

[94] James E. Pfander, *Resolving the Qualified Immunity Dilemma: Constitutional Tort Claims for Nominal Damages*, 111 Colum. L. Rev. 1601, 1606–07 (2011).

[95] Joanna C. Schwartz has challenged the view that qualified immunity protects officers from financial liability, observing that individual officers rarely pay from their own pockets and may be indemnified by state authorities. *The Case against Qualified Immunity*, 93 Notre Dame L. Rev. 1797, 1804–08 (2018). If so, then Pfander's nominal damages proposal would alleviate concerns about a drain on the public fisc, rather than about the monetary liability of individual officers. *See* Pfander, note 94, at 1615, 1629.

out, in challenging the view that the declaratory judgment is a "milder" remedy than the injunction, courts frequently do not need to issue further commands after rendering a declaratory judgment, for "everyone knows what to do."[96] Declaratory judgments can therefore result in physical or economic changes in the world. Whether or not a declaratory judgment gives rise to physical or economic changes, however, it can reaffirm plaintiffs' status in the aftermath of a legal violation.

Recognizing declaratory judgments as vehicles for dignitary redress has implications for the permissible scope of declaratory relief. The federal Declaratory Judgment Act authorizes federal courts to issue declaratory judgments in cases of "actual controversy."[97] The Supreme Court has interpreted the Act to permit declaratory judgments only when the dispute is sufficiently immediate to satisfy the Article III requirement of a "case or controversy."[98] That way, the Declaratory Judgment Act does not exceed the bounds of Article III.

The question whether the prospect of dignitary harm creates an "actual controversy" thus overlaps with the question whether dignitary harm constitutes injury in fact. For the reasons discussed in Chapter 3, judges should be willing to treat dignitary harm as a cognizable Article III injury. For example, if an agency is preparing to implement a policy that would result in the release of sensitive personal information, there could be an "actual controversy" even if the release of information is unlikely to cause economic damage. On this account, federal courts would retain discretion to deny a declaratory judgment if the negative consequences would be too grave, consistent with the Declaratory Judgment Act's permissive language (federal courts "may" declare rights).[99] But judges should not deny the existence of an "actual controversy" simply because dignitary harm is the only form of projected damage.

In sum, declaratory judgments can redress dignitary harm, and the "actual controversy" requirement should be interpreted in a manner that recognizes the reality of dignitary harm.

[96] Samuel L. Bray, *The Myth of the Mild Declaratory Judgment*, 63 Duke L.J. 1091, 1108–09 (2014); *see also* Richard H. Fallon, Jr., *The Ideologies of Federal Courts Law*, 74 Va. L. Rev. 1141, 1239 (1988).
[97] 28 U.S.C. § 2201(a).
[98] Aetna Life Ins. Co. v. Haworth, 300 U.S. 227, 240–41 (1937).
[99] 28 U.S.C. § 2201(a).

Dicta in Judicial Opinions

The chapter has discussed various remedies for dignitary harm: compensatory damages, punitive damages, nominal damages, and declaratory judgments. A less traditional "remedy" for dignitary harm is dicta in judicial opinions. The idea of dicta as judicial relief shows how attention to dignity can spur creative judicial responses.

At the outset, the notion of dicta as dignitary relief is in tension with the Supreme Court's view of remedies. The Court in 2023, in analyzing the redressability prong of Article III standing, stated that a court must "be able to afford relief through the exercise of its power, not through the persuasive or even awe-inspiring effect of the opinion explaining the exercise of its power. . . . It is a federal court's judgment, not its opinion, that remedies an injury."[100] Despite the Court's view, the argument here is that dicta in opinions can provide meaningful relief (whether or not dicta can be formally classified as a "remedy").

How, then, can dicta in judicial opinions provide dignitary relief? "Dictum" refers to "[a] judicial comment made while delivering a judicial opinion, but one that is unnecessary to the decision in the case and therefore not precedential (although it may be considered persuasive)."[101] Dicta have many purposes: to clarify the holding of the case at bar or other cases, to signal the direction in which the law is moving, or to provide historical context for the holding. Dicta can also express a message about the moral dimensions of a case. Dicta can redress dignitary harm in a few ways.

First, dicta may bridge the gap between the demands of black-letter law and the call of fairness.[102] Sometimes judges are constrained to follow statutory language or judicial precedent they view as morally problematic, and they give voice to the tension through dicta. For example, in 2002, Judge Sullivan of the US District Court for the District of Columbia presided over a case brought against Iran by plaintiffs who were "held hostage, and at times tortured, for 444 days after being seized from the United States Embassy in Tehran by Iranian governmental officials" over twenty years earlier.[103] The

[100] Haaland v. Brackeen, 599 U.S. 255, 294 (2023) (internal quotation marks, citations, and emphases omitted).

[101] *Dictum*, Black's Law Dictionary (12th ed. 2024).

[102] Foster Calhoun Johnson, *Judicial Magic: The Use of Dicta as Equitable Remedy*, 46 U. S.F. L. Rev. 883, 889 (2012).

[103] Roeder v. Islamic Republic of Iran, 195 F. Supp. 2d 140, 143 (D.D.C. 2002).

district court held that the plaintiffs' claims must be dismissed because they were barred by international agreement. Yet the judge wrote:

> Were this Court empowered to judge by its sense of justice, the heart-breaking accounts of the emotional and physical toll of those 444 days on plaintiffs would be more than sufficient justification for granting all the relief that they request. However, this Court is bound to apply the law that Congress has created, according to the rules of interpretation that the Supreme Court has determined.[104]

The court's dicta did not provide a substitute for a judgment in plaintiffs' favor. Still, the judge's statements about justice in the opinion affirmed the plaintiffs' moral claims and conveyed respect for the plaintiffs. To give another example, a court may determine that an employer mistreated an employee but not to the extent required to make out a claim of a "hostile work environment" under Title VII or intentional infliction of emotional distress. The court might express sympathy for the plaintiff or note that the "conduct suffered by the Plaintiff is by no means trivial," without ruling in the plaintiff's favor.[105] In this way, the court can bolster the plaintiff's status even as it sides with the defendant.

Second, courts could provide relief for dignitary harm through dicta by expressing sympathy for a losing party in a case that was close. Instead of "sweeping [opposing chess pieces] off the table,"[106] a judge may convey some of the struggle and even anguish involved in coming to a decision. Such dicta could give the losing party a sense that its harms were acknowledged.

The forms of dicta mentioned thus far differ from traditional judicial remedies—which are directed at a winning plaintiff—because they express respect for the losing side, which may be either the plaintiff or the defendant. Whether or not dicta sympathizing with the losing party formally constitute "remedies," these statements can provide a measure of moral satisfaction and relief for dignitary harm.

A third dignitary role for dicta is to telegraph strong condemnation of the defendant's conduct even when the plaintiff wins. This approach makes it crystal clear that the plaintiff was treated in a way that was beyond the pale.

[104] *Id.* at 145.

[105] Stanfield v. Suntrust Bank, No. 815CV01472EAKTBM, 2016 WL 899279, at *6 (M.D. Fla. Mar. 2, 2016).

[106] Learned Hand, *Mr. Justice Cardozo*, 52 Harv. L. Rev. 361, 362 (1939).

Public condemnation of the defendant helps to rehabilitate the status of the plaintiff.

One might object that including dignity-affirming dicta is not genuine redress, and is often a cheap way to satisfy upset parties. Moreover, one might question whether it is really *judicial* for judges to include dicta expressing respect or sympathy in their opinions. In the Supreme Court's view, "psychic satisfaction" is not "an acceptable Article III remedy."[107] Judges are authoritative deciders, not therapists.

There are indeed limits on dicta's ability to provide judicial relief, and dignity-affirming dicta can misfire. Judges should not, for example, rule one way because ruling the other way would be unpopular, but then console themselves by inserting dicta favorable to the losing party. Yet dignity-affirming dicta cannot simply be dismissed as empty talk. Just as a party might be especially aggrieved by language in a judicial opinion gratuitously criticizing the party's conduct, a party might find satisfaction in dignity-affirming dicta. In fact, dignitary harm by its nature may be remediable through language and acknowledgment in a way that other forms of harm, such as financial or physical harm, are not.

The use of dicta to express respect may be most appropriate when there is a particularly sharp disconnect between doctrine and fairness, or when the case is especially close. Additionally, certain judicial settings may be more conducive to providing relief for dignitary harm than others. For instance, Edward Rock highlights the role of the Delaware courts of equity in articulating standards of appropriate managerial conduct in their opinions—wielding the tools of "public shaming or praise."[108] Thus, judges will need to use their discretion to decide when relief for dignitary harm through dicta is appropriate. Overall, however, judges ought to pay attention to the messages that their opinions send, and they should consider including language that recognizes and provides some relief for dignitary harm.

[107] Steel Co. v. Citizens for a Better Env't, 523 U.S. 83, 107 (1998). For discussion of the Supreme Court's view of proper federal judicial relief, see Bayefsky, note 4, at 1270–73.

[108] Edward B. Rock, *Saints and Sinners: How Does Delaware Corporate Law Work?* 44 UCLA L. Rev. 1009, 1103 (1997); *see also id.* at 1016 ("My intuition is that we come much closer to understanding the role of courts in corporate law if we think of judges more as preachers than as policemen.").

Judicial Relief for Dignitary Harm: Cross-Cutting Issues

Having analyzed the capacity of numerous judicial remedies to redress dignitary harm, it is worth taking a step back and looking more generally at the idea of relief for dignitary injury. I first address the question: Do all judicial remedies provide relief for dignitary harm, or are certain remedies distinctively likely to do so? I then take up three objections to remedies for dignitary harm: that many of these remedies are impermissible advisory opinions; that these remedies license unduly expansive relief; and that these remedies undercut personal resilience as a response to dignitary harm.

To begin, although this chapter has discussed several specific remedies, other forms of relief could also redress dignitary injury. For instance, an injunction against a discriminatory government policy could put an end to the violation of rightful status involved in discrimination. Perhaps, then, there is nothing distinctive about any given remedy in terms of its propensity to redress dignitary harm.

It is true that a variety of remedies could provide relief for dignitary harm. However, certain remedies are particularly likely to redress dignitary harm as compared to other forms of harm. Many of these remedies centrally operate through the medium of expression; they take effect by expressing respect for the party whose dignity was violated. For nominal damages and declaratory judgments, the remedy does not itself have a substantial physical or economic impact. Although the remedy may lead to physical or economic changes, a significant part of its influence lies in its ability to send a message. Dicta as relief for dignitary harm also operate through the medium of expression and may have no physical or economic impact.

For punitive damages, the remedy has a significant economic effect; but the monetary sum itself conveys a judgment of disapproval or outrage. Compensatory damages for dignitary harm are a trickier case. Compensatory damages often redress physical or economic harm. Moreover, one might argue that punitive damages, nominal damages, and declaratory judgments provide relief for dignitary harm precisely because it is clear they are doing something other than compensating. Why, then, do compensatory damages have a distinctive role in providing relief for dignitary harm? In response, compensatory damages specifically dedicated to dignitary harm convey that the dignitary effects of legal violations are significant and worthy of judicial attention. These compensatory damages indicate that wrongful departures from the rightful position are measured not only in dollars and cents, but also in dignitary terms.

Some remedies, then, are especially suited to providing relief for dignitary harm. Other remedies could perform this function too, and the list of remedies above is not meant to be exclusive. But those remedies usefully illustrate the ways in which courts can offer relief for dignitary blows.

I now take up the objection that many remedies for dignitary harm are actually illicit advisory opinions.[109] The concern about advisory opinions applies most directly to federal courts, for it is black-letter law that federal courts may not issue advisory opinions.[110] The Supreme Court has treated this prohibition as an outgrowth of Article III's restriction of federal jurisdiction to "cases" and "controversies."[111] Many state courts, however, are also prohibited from issuing advisory opinions, though by no means all.[112]

The federal prohibition on advisory opinions is often traced to a 1793 exchange between Secretary of State Thomas Jefferson and the Supreme Court justices of the time—the "Correspondence of the Justices."[113] In the Correspondence, the justices declined to answer questions that Jefferson had posed regarding the legal obligations of the United States during a war between England and France. The Correspondence has been interpreted to mean that separation-of-powers concerns prevent federal courts from answering hypothetical or speculative legal questions. Instead, federal courts (the Supreme Court has stated) must address only "litigation upon actual transactions between real parties, growing out of a controversy affecting legal or equitable rights as to person or property."[114]

Some judicial remedies for dignitary harm might be charged with being advisory opinions. This is especially true for remedies that take effect by expressing a message of respect. The Supreme Court has stated that "[t]he real value of [a] judicial pronouncement—what makes it a proper judicial resolution of a 'case or controversy' rather than an advisory opinion—is

[109] For discussion of the "advisory opinion" objection to remedies that express respect, see Bayefsky, note 4, at 1320–21.

[110] Flast v. Cohen, 392 U.S. 83, 96 (1968).

[111] Hewitt v. Helms, 482 U.S. 755, 761 (1987).

[112] *See* Helen Hershkoff, *State Courts and the "Passive Virtues": Rethinking the Judicial Function*, 114 HARV. L. REV. 1833, 1845–46 (2001); Lucas Moench, Note, *State Court Advisory Opinions: Implications for Legislative Power and Prerogatives*, 97 B.U. L. REV. 2243, 2246 (2017).

[113] *See Correspondence of the Justices*, *in* HART & WECHSLER, note 2, at 50–52.

[114] Marye v. Parsons, 114 U.S. 325, 330 (1885).

in the settling of some dispute *which affects the behavior of the defendant towards the plaintiff*."[115] Further, a federal lawsuit must "promise [a] concrete benefit to the plaintiff,"[116] and the court's judgment must resolve "a real and substantial controversy."[117] If a federal court issues a nominal damages award or a declaratory judgment that "makes a statement," or includes dicta expressing respect toward a party, has the court made a judicial pronouncement absent a "real and substantial controversy," and thereby rendered an advisory opinion?

The answer to this question depends on one's perspective on the nature of legitimate judicial relief. If dignitary harm is genuine harm, and an expression of respect is a real benefit, then judicial activity providing relief for dignitary harm by expressing a message of respect is not simply a pronouncement with no actual effect. This chapter, and the book more broadly, have argued that dignitary harm and its remediation have a normatively, legally, and empirically significant impact.

Consequently, relief for dignitary harm—including a remedy that takes effect by sending a message—is not merely an advisory opinion. The Supreme Court stated in 2023, as noted earlier, that "[r]edressability requires that the court be able to afford relief through the exercise of its power, not through the persuasive or even awe-inspiring effect of the opinion explaining the exercise of its power."[118] Yet the ability to provide relief for dignitary harm is *part* of a court's power. Power need not be understood in physical or economic terms. Of course, one could disagree with the idea that dignitary harms or judicial expressions of respect are legally weighty. But the ban on advisory opinions does not furnish an independent argument against the view that dignitary relief is proper and advisable.

Another objection to remedies for dignitary harm is the practical one that they license overly expansive judicial relief. If courts are authorized to grant remedies for dignitary harm, the argument runs, they might greenlight enormous punitive damages awards, or order nominal damages or a declaratory judgment in every case. The result would be ruinous liability for defendants and too intrusive a role for courts.

[115] Hewitt v. Helms, 482 U.S. 755, 761 (1987) (emphasis in the original).
[116] Steel Co. v. Citizens for a Better Env't, 523 U.S. 83, 103 n.5 (1998).
[117] Aetna Life Ins. Co. v. Haworth, 300 U.S. 227, 241 (1937).
[118] Haaland v. Brackeen, 599 U.S. 255, 294 (2023) (internal quotation marks, citations, and emphases omitted).

Relief for dignitary harm, however, is not a bottomless pit. Not all legal violations cause dignitary harm, and some dignitary harms warrant greater relief than others. For example, a data privacy breach resulting in the release of nude photographs warrants more extensive redress than a data breach resulting in the release of zip codes.[119] Certain criteria can help in making these determinations, such as the content of the legal violation, its intentionality, and the identity of the parties.[120] As to content, the question is whether the legal violation involves an infringement of dignity, understood as respect for status, nondomination, and denial of control over self-presentation. As to intentionality, greater intentionality on the defendant's part generally seems more likely to produce dignitary harm (as discussed in Chapter 4). As to the identity of the parties, lawsuits brought by individuals rather than corporations or state entities may have a particular propensity to involve dignitary harm, as individuals may have more direct experiences of disrespect. These types of criteria could be used to determine when relief for dignitary harm is especially warranted and to what extent.

Nevertheless, no abstract formula can answer the question of how much relief to provide for dignitary harm. The challenge is instead to devise suitable institutional arrangements for tackling this question. Various legal institutions properly play a role in determining the extent of relief for dignitary harm. Juries could help distinguish between violations that justify relief and those that do not. Judges could develop lines of precedent to determine whether and to what degree relief is warranted. These lines of precedent could then govern, for example, such questions as when a dispute over projected dignitary harm rises to the level of an "actual controversy" adequate to support a declaratory judgment. Legislators could set remedies by statute, in accordance with their assessments of the kinds of dignitary harm that justify redress. Dignity does not present the only complex line-drawing problem in the law of remedies, and the legal system contains tools to address this kind of problem. Indeed, some of these tools are already being deployed—in which case the account here offers ways to justify and systematize their use.

[119] *See* Spokeo, Inc. v. Robins, 578 U.S. 330, 342 (2016) ("It is difficult to imagine how the dissemination of an incorrect zip code, without more, could work any concrete harm.").

[120] *See* Bayefsky, note 4, at 1311–12.

Further, the scope of relief for dignitary harm can be limited by other values. If judges or legislators wish to restrict the availability of punitive damages because they are too costly, or to limit the availability of nominal damages because they keep too many suits alive, then they can do so. Relational dignity is not an absolute value (as discussed in Chapter 2), and providing relief for dignitary harm is not the only remedial goal. The efficiency of the court system also matters, for example. If legal actors choose to restrict relief for dignitary harm, however, then they should take this step with the awareness that the judicial system is not providing full relief—that the goal of redress has been subordinated, even if justifiably, to another normative or legal imperative.

A third objection to remedies for dignitary harm is that they detract from a model in which individuals are resilient in response to dignitary blows.[121] Perhaps judicial remedies for dignitary harm encourage people to overemphasize the ways in which they have been disrespected. At least when it comes to less serious forms of dignitary harm, it might be more advisable to encourage people to overcome experiences of disrespect without the intervention of courts. In response, judicial reactions to dignitary harm will be relatively rare in comparison to the vast number of dignitary violations inflicted in everyday life. Judicial remedies need not and should not "crowd out" the important value of resilience, and they ought to be cast as complementary to less formal ways of dealing with dignitary harm. But judicial remedies appropriately send the message that dignitary harms are societal problems in addition to individual ones, and that societal institutions also have a role in seeking to address them.

To conclude, this chapter has argued that courts can properly issue remedies for dignitary harm. These remedies are justified both as a way of restoring or maintaining the plaintiff's "rightful position" and as a response to the empirical interest in vindication. Relief for dignitary harm can take numerous forms, including compensatory damages for dignitary harm, punitive damages, nominal damages, declaratory judgments, and dicta in judicial opinions. Moreover, relief for dignitary harm need not expand indefinitely. Legal decision-makers can circumscribe remediable dignitary injury

[121] The resistance of some justices to "offended observer" standing sounds to some degree in this register, although that resistance also seems to emanate from skepticism about whether putative plaintiffs have suffered genuine dignitary harm. *See, e.g.*, Statement of Justice Gorsuch Respecting the Denial of Certiorari, Ocala v. Rojas, 143 S. Ct. 764, 764–65 (2023); Dissent from Denial of Certiorari, Ocala v. Rojas, 143 S. Ct. 764, 765–68 (2023) (Thomas, J.).

and permit other considerations, such as efficiency, to outweigh the aim of promoting dignity through the law of remedies.

Overall, dignity speaks not only to the "harm" side of the equation, but also to the "remedy" side. Courts are appropriate sites for the remediation of dignitary harm.

6
Dignity and Apology

The practice of apologies is familiar. We give and receive apologies frequently with respect to our family members, colleagues, and friends. We are also familiar with apologies that take place on a broader scale—for example, the US Congress apologizing in 1988 for Japanese internment during World War II,[1] or former British prime minister Gordon Brown apologizing "on behalf of the British government" for the treatment of Alan Turing, who was prosecuted for homosexual conduct after breaking Nazi codes.[2] In fact, some have said that we live in an "Age of Apology."[3] In the public sphere, we often hear calls to apologize, as well as disputes over whether someone has properly apologized. It is widely thought that a botched apology can make the situation worse.

Apologies are frequently understood to have dignitary impact. As Aaron Lazare writes, apologies effectuate an "exchange of humiliation and power": "Originally having had the power to hurt, the offender now gives the power to forgive or not to forgive to the offended party."[4] The apology releases the victim from domination and permits the victim to regain a sense of control. In other words, the apology reaffirms the victim's dignity.

Can apologies be a useful tool in the arsenal of courts seeking to provide dignitary relief? In particular, may a court compel the defendant to apologize? Take a lawsuit against an employer who has been cheating employees out of their wages in violation of labor laws, or against state officials for denying someone a permit in retaliation for the person's political beliefs, or against police officers for using excessive force. Could a court's order to a defendant to apologize, in these scenarios, do any good? Would such an order do substantial harm? Would it simply be "cheap talk"? From an American

[1] *See* Act of Aug. 10, 1988, Pub. L. No. 100-383, 102 Stat. 903.

[2] Caroline Davies, *PM's Apology to Codebreaker Alan Turing: We Were Inhumane*, THE GUARDIAN (Sept. 10, 2009), https://www.theguardian.com/world/2009/sep/11/pm-apology-to-alan-turing.

[3] *See* Roy L. Brooks, *The Age of Apology*, *in* WHEN SORRY ISN'T ENOUGH: THE CONTROVERSY OVER APOLOGIES AND REPARATIONS FOR HUMAN INJUSTICE 3 (Roy L. Brooks ed., 1999).

[4] AARON LAZARE, ON APOLOGY 52 (2004).

Dignity and Judicial Authority. Rachel Bayefsky, Oxford University Press. © Rachel Bayefsky 2024.
DOI: 10.1093/oso/9780197750322.003.0006

constitutional law perspective, there is also the question of whether court-mandated apologies are unconstitutional forms of compelled speech.

This chapter explores court-ordered apologies as a form of relief for dignitary harm. It grows out of Chapter 5's examination of dignity and remedies, but it focuses on a specific type of redress. Though courts in the United States rarely compel apologies as a formal remedy, litigants continue to request apologies, and the US legal system incentivizes apologies in certain ways without strictly requiring them. For example, judges routinely give longer sentences to criminal defendants who fail to show remorse.[5] The topic of court-mandated apologies thus sheds light on values underlying our legal system and forces us to confront the defensibility of existing legal practices. More broadly, court-mandated apologies are conceptually significant; they raise fundamental questions about the relationship between dignity and judicial authority. An apology might seem to be a logical response to dignitary harm. Yet apologies might also appear to be quintessentially private activities—suited to the sphere of personal rights and wrongs, but not to the world of judges and legally binding mandates. Judges, after all, are not parents or teachers. How, then, could they be authorized to order people to apologize?

The question whether court-mandated apologies are compatible with legitimate judicial authority raises the issue of how to demarcate such authority. Courts help to maintain social order in many ways, including ones that stretch traditional conceptions of the judicial role. Examples include "problem-solving courts" that oversee drug treatment or mental health programs,[6] as well as the field of restorative justice more generally. It should not be assumed, therefore, that the judicial role excludes the use of apologies to facilitate vindication or reconciliation.

This chapter analyzes court-ordered apologies in the following ways. First, I identify areas of American law in which court-mandated apologies are imposed or requested, including criminal law, civil rights suits, and attorney discipline proceedings. I then discuss connections between court-ordered apologies and other legal practices, such as the role of remorse in sentencing and restorative justice.

[5] Carissa Byrne Hessick & F. Andrew Hessick, *Recognizing Constitutional Rights at Sentencing*, 99 Calif. L. Rev. 47, 65 (2011).

[6] *See, e.g.*, N.Y. State Unified Ct. Sys., *Drug Treatment Courts*, https://ww2.nycourts.gov/courts/problem_solving/drugcourts/index.shtml; N.Y. State Unified Ct. Sys., *Mental Health Courts*, https://ww2.nycourts.gov/mental-health-courts-overview-27066.

Second, I analyze normative and constitutional considerations bearing on court-mandated apologies. Dignitary factors appear on both sides of the equation; court-mandated apologies can rehabilitate the plaintiff's dignity while risking a violation of the defendant's. First Amendment compelled speech doctrine helps to illuminate the threat to the defendant's dignity but should not result in a comprehensive ban on court-mandated apologies.

Ultimately, there is no one-size-fits-all response to the question whether court-ordered apologies are permissible or appropriate. Court-mandated apologies should not be rejected out of hand; they should be taken seriously but imposed with awareness of their drawbacks. This remedy should also prompt reflection on a broader range of legal practices. Examining court-mandated apologies raises fundamental issues about the nature of voluntary conduct, the impact of state action on individual conscience, and the challenge of pinning down which interests are protected by compelled speech doctrine.

Apologies in Our Midst

To analyze court-mandated apologies from a normative perspective, it is useful to have a sense of the lay of the land. Courts in the United States do not commonly require people to apologize, but the practice exists in certain settings. There is also a larger universe of practices "adjacent to" court-mandated apologies—practices that incentivize apologies from those involved in litigation even if the court does not technically mandate that a defendant say sorry. An example of the latter is that courts may impose a higher sentence on a defendant who does not show remorse. The chapter begins with court-mandated apologies "proper" and then examines adjacent practices.

Judicial Orders Requiring Apologies

When do courts compel apologies? There are examples outside the United States, including apology orders in discrimination and harassment cases in Australia[7] and court-ordered apologies as a remedy for defamation in

[7] *See* Robyn Carroll, *Apologies as a Legal Remedy*, 35 Sydney L. Rev. 317, 328 (2013).

Japan.[8] In the United States, court-mandated apologies are far from a frequent remedy, but they are not unheard-of.

In criminal cases, some courts have required the defendant to apologize as part of the sentence, including as a condition of probation. For example, a California federal district court in 2003 sentenced a defendant (Gementera) convicted of stealing mail to write letters of apology to all ascertainable victims of the defendant's crime "individually expressing defendant's remorse for the specific conduct that harmed that person."[9] The court also required the defendant to "deliver three educational lectures at three San Francisco high schools . . . in which the defendant shall describe the crime he has committed, express his remorse for his criminal conduct and articulate to the students in attendance how his conviction and sentence have affected his life and future plans."[10] To take another example: A Washington state juvenile court, in a decision upheld by the Washington Supreme Court, sentenced a 17-year-old convicted of sexual assault to "write a letter of apology to victim C.R. that is approved by the Probation Officer and the State."[11] In addition to requiring letters of apology, which might or might not be public, some courts have sentenced defendants to deliver a public apology. For instance, a California federal district court sentenced police officers convicted of perjury to publish an apology in the local newspaper and the police department's newsletter, with the words of the apology composed by the district judge.[12]

In academic literature, public apologies in criminal cases are often viewed as instances of a broader phenomenon called "shame sanctions": forms of criminal punishment that deliberately expose defendants to public

[8] Ilhyung Lee, *The Law and Culture of the Apology in Korean Dispute Settlement (with Japan and the United States in Mind)*, 27 MICH. J. INT'L L. 1, 39–41 (2005). Lee notes that a court-ordered apology in Japan, though allowed by law, "appears to be an infrequent remedy." *Id.* at 41. For further discussion of apology in Japanese law, see Max Bolstad, *Learning from Japan: The Case for Increased Use of Apology in Mediation*, 48 CLEVELAND ST. L. REV. 545, 555–61 (2000). For examples of court-ordered apologies in Switzerland, the Netherlands, and Latvia, see Wannes Vandenbussche, *Rethinking Non-Pecuniary Remedies for Defamation: The Case for Court-Ordered Apologies*, 9 J. INT'L MEDIA & ENT. L. 109, 115 & n.30 (2021).

[9] United States v. Gementera, 379 F.3d 596, 599 n.3 (9th Cir. 2004). The defendant does not appear to have appealed the apology conditions, though he challenged an additional requirement that he stand outside a post office wearing a sandwich board announcing his crime, and the Ninth Circuit upheld that requirement. *See id.* at 606.

[10] *Id.* at 599 n.3.

[11] State v. K.H.-H., 374 P.3d 1141, 1142 (Wash. 2016); *see also, e.g.*, State v. Lobato, 611 N.W.2d 101, 103 (Neb. 2000) (letters of apology as a probation condition for a defendant convicted of "theft by deception," in particular, stealing by pretending she would use donations for cancer treatment).

[12] United States v. Clark, 918 F.2d 843, 845 (9th Cir. 1990), *overruled on other grounds in* United States v. Keys, 133 F.3d 1282 (9th Cir. 1998).

opprobrium.[13] Other examples of shame sanctions are publication of offenders' names on billboards and requirements that offenders wear items of clothing announcing their crimes.[14] Though there is an overlap between court-mandated apologies and shame sanctions, the two categories are not coterminous. First, court-mandated apologies need not be public. Second, court-mandated apologies involve an order to the defendant to speak and therefore implicate issues related to compelled expression. Shame sanctions need not involve such a requirement; if the government publishes the name of an offender on a billboard, the offender herself need not speak.

Courts have cited multiple reasons to order apologies in criminal cases. One is to force defendants to acknowledge their crimes and the harm they have caused. In the California mail theft case *Gementera* mentioned earlier, for example, the Ninth Circuit observed that the district "court aimed to break the defendant of the illusion that his theft was victimless or not serious."[15]

A second and related justification is rehabilitation. For example, a former state judge was convicted in Pennsylvania state court of crimes including illegally using her judicial staff for her campaign and conspiracy to tamper with evidence.[16] As part of her sentence, the court required her to write letters of apology to her former staff and members of the judiciary.[17] (The court overruled, however, a requirement that the former judge write the apology letters on photographs of herself in handcuffs.) The apology letter mandate (minus the handcuffs), the court observed, "may force her to accept responsibility for the harm she caused and, as such, is consistent with the goals of rehabilitation."[18]

A third rationale for a compelled apology is to further the victim's interests. The Supreme Court of Washington stated in a case involving a juvenile convicted of sexual assault that an apology from the perpetrator "allows the victim to hear an acceptance of responsibility from the very person who inflicted the harm."[19]

[13] For debate about shame sanctions, see, for example, Dan M. Kahan, *What Do Alternative Sanctions Mean?* 63 U. Chi. L. Rev. 591 (1996); Toni M. Massaro, *Shame, Culture, and American Criminal Law*, 89 Mich.·L. Rev. 1880 (1991); James Q. Whitman, *What Is Wrong with Inflicting Shame Sanctions?* 107 Yale L.J. 1055 (1998).

[14] *See* Kahan, note 13, at 632.

[15] United States v. Gementera, 379 F.3d 596, 602 (9th Cir. 2004).

[16] Commonwealth v. Melvin, 103 A.3d 1, 9–10 (Pa. Super. Ct. 2014).

[17] *Id.* at 11.

[18] *Id.* at 55.

[19] State v. K.H.-H., 374 P.3d 1141, 1146 (Wash. 2016).

Turning to civil cases, courts in the United States sometimes (though not frequently) order apologies in the context of attorney misconduct in litigation. Courts have required attorneys to apologize to opposing counsel, their clients, or the court, including as a sanction in formal disciplinary proceedings.[20] Though these orders are not equivalent to requirements for a *defendant* to apologize, they too implicate a court's power to mandate apologies.

Court orders to attorneys to apologize may result from courts' assumption of a quasi-supervisory role over attorneys as officers of the court. There may be a kinship to courts' assumption of a quasi-supervisory role over juveniles ordered to apologize.[21] At the same time, some courts have suggested that it would be improper to order attorneys to apologize for their conduct. The Supreme Court of Washington, for example, stated back in 1905 that "[a]n attorney is under no obligation to apologize to a court under any circumstances, and the court exceeds its authority whenever it makes such a demand."[22]

Another category of civil cases in which apologies are requested are civil rights proceedings. These include suits brought in court (under, for example, the federal civil rights statutes 42 U.S.C. § 1983 and Title VII of the Civil Rights Act of 1964, or state antidiscrimination law), and actions before civil rights agencies.[23]

Some courts have ordered apologies in civil rights cases,[24] but most have declined to do so, stating they lack the "equitable" power to mandate an apology.[25] The US Court of Appeals for the Sixth Circuit indicated in 2002, for instance, that courts' "broad and flexible equitable powers to fashion a remedy that will fully correct past wrongs" did not extend to issuing an apology for gender discrimination in violation of Title VII.[26] "The law," the

[20] *See, e.g.*, Hubbard v. Kentucky Bar Assoc., 571 S.W.3d 90, 92 (Ky. 2019); Freeman v. Schointuck, 192 F.R.D. 187, 190 (D. Md. 2000); Matter of McCann, 669 A.2d 49, 59 (Del. 1995).

[21] *See, e.g.*, *K.H.-H.*, 374 P.3d at 1142; *In re* J.C., No. A135730, 2013 WL 1127777, at *1 (Cal. Ct. App. Mar. 19, 2013). I thank Rachel Anderson for this suggestion.

[22] State v. Pendergast, 81 P. 324, 325 (Wash. 1905).

[23] *See* Brent T. White, *Say You're Sorry: Court-Ordered Apologies as a Civil Rights Remedy*, 91 Cornell L. Rev. 1261, 1301–03 (2006).

[24] *See* Desjardins v. Van Buren Cmty. Hosp., 969 F.2d 1280, 1282 (1st Cir. 1992) (district court ordered an apology; Court of Appeals treated a First Amendment challenge as waived); Wells v. Lobb & Co., Inc., No. CIV. A. 97-WM-1011, 1999 WL 1268331, at *5 (D. Colo. Dec. 1, 1999) (ordering defendant employers in a sexual harassment suit to apologize to plaintiff); Villescas v. Abraham, 285 F. Supp. 2d 1248, 1256 (D. Colo. 2003) (ordering a defendant in an age discrimination and retaliation suit to apologize).

[25] *See* Clark v. Shrader, No. 20-CV-01410-DDD-KLM, 2021 WL 229283, at *3–4 (D. Colo. Jan. 22, 2021) (collecting cases).

[26] Woodruff v. Ohman, 29 Fed. App'x 337, 346 (6th Cir. 2002) (internal quotation marks omitted).

court explained, "is not usually concerned with procuring apologies to make morally right a legal wrong done to the plaintiffs."[27] A federal district court in a prisoner's Eighth Amendment lawsuit went further: "The remedy of 'apology' . . . is not cognizable, either within the meaning of a § 1983 action or as a general legal remedy that a court has the power to order, under any provision."[28] The view that courts have no power to order apologies is in tension with court-mandated apologies in criminal cases.

Judges have also confronted the question whether civil rights *agencies* have authority to order parties to apologize. The New York Court of Appeals answered "yes" in 1980, upholding a human rights commissioner's requirement that an employer apologize to an employee for anti-Semitic remarks.[29] In other cases, however, courts have concluded that ordering an apology exceeds the agency's statutory authority. For example, the Pennsylvania Supreme Court held in 1973 that the state human rights commission exceeded its remedial authority in ordering a cemetery to send a public letter of apology to a widow whose husband's remains the cemetery had refused to bury on account of his race.[30] A concurrence by Justice Pomeroy stated that the Commission, "an agency of democratic government, is without power to order the giving of a public apology."[31] For, Justice Pomeroy argued, "[a]n apology is a communication of the emotion of remorse for one's past acts," and "[t]o order up that particular emotion, or any other emotion, is beyond the reach of any government; to assert the contrary is to advocate tyranny."[32]

To summarize the overview of court-mandated apologies: Courts sometimes, though rarely, compel apologies in criminal cases, and they have also required attorneys to apologize. In civil rights cases, courts are generally more skeptical about whether a compelled apology falls within the bounds of their authority. The reason for the difference in approach may be that courts are more willing to assume a supervisory power over criminal defendants (particularly juveniles) and attorneys, or that courts are willing to accept more coercive measures against defendants in the criminal process.

[27] *Id.*

[28] Kitchen v. Essex Cnty. Corr. Facility, No. CIV.A. 12-2199 JLL, 2012 WL 1994505, at *4 (D.N.J. May 31, 2012).

[29] Imperial Diner, Inc. v. State Hum. Rts. Appeal Bd., 417 N.E.2d 525 (N.Y. 1980).

[30] Pennsylvania Hum. Rels. Comm'n v. Alto-Reste Park Cemetery Ass'n, 306 A.2d 881, 890 (Pa. 1973); *see also* City of Minneapolis v. Richardson, 239 N.W.2d 197, 205–06 (Minn. 1976) (rejecting a hearing examiner's decision to order city and chief of police to write an apology letter to a Black twelve-year-old whom officers had threatened with a police dog and called a racial epithet).

[31] *Alto-Reste*, 306 A.2d at 891 (Pomeroy, J., concurring).

[32] *Id.*

Practices Adjacent to Court-Mandated Apologies

The apologies discussed thus far are "court-ordered apologies" in the sense of apologies that a court formally orders a party or an attorney to provide. But there are other practices that might be described as "adjacent" to court-ordered apologies. For these practices, the legal system encourages or incentivizes apologies but does not formally mandate them. The existence of such practices demonstrates that apologies are not a mere curiosity or aberration in our legal system; the impulses behind court-ordered apologies extend more widely.

In general, an apology can be part of a settlement or a plea deal, including those approved by courts. To take a few examples, a lawyer for President Donald Trump in election-related cases, Sidney Powell, pleaded guilty in a Georgia court to conspiracy to commit election interference and assented to a plea agreement requiring her to write an apology letter to the citizens of Georgia.[33] As part of a settlement with the State of Washington over campaign finance violations, the Grocery Manufacturers Association issued an apology memorialized in a stipulated judgment.[34] Attorneys have agreed to write apology letters as part of settlements or "negotiated sanctions" in disciplinary proceedings.[35]

Although parties to a plea deal or settlement agree to apologize, they may face substantial pressure to do so, given the alternatives of a longer prison term or expensive and draining litigation. Apologies as terms of settlement highlight the murkiness of voluntariness in legal settings. And judges may well approve such settlements, raising questions about whether courts should sign off on heavily incentivized expressions of contrition.

In addition to the general role of apologies in plea deals and settlement, there are more specific scenarios in which the legal system encourages apologies even without formally mandating them. A few of these scenarios are now discussed.

[33] *See* Debra Cassens Weiss, *Trump Lawyer Sidney Powell Agrees to Write Letter of Apology as Part of Plea Deal in Election-Interference Case*, ABA Journal (Oct. 19, 2023), https://www.abajournal.com/news/article/trump-lawyer-agrees-to-write-letter-of-apology-as-part-of-plea-deal-in-election-interference-case.

[34] *See* Wash. State Off. of the Att'y Gen., *Grocery Manufacturers Association Apologizes for Campaign Finance Violations, Will Pay $9 Million and Drop Challenge to Washington Campaign Finance Law* (Mar. 2, 2022), https://www.atg.wa.gov/news/news-releases/grocery-manufacturers-association-apologizes-campaign-finance-violations-will-pay; Stipulation at ¶ 1, Washington v. Grocery Mfrs. Ass'n, Wash. Super. Ct. No. 13-2-02156-8 (Mar. 2, 2022).

[35] *See, e.g.*, Hubbard v. Kentucky Bar Ass'n, 571 S.W.3d 90, 92 (Ky. 2019).

Expression of Remorse as a Sentencing Factor

In criminal sentencing, judges may give longer sentences to defendants who have not shown remorse. Courts have held that the lack of remorse is a permissible sentencing factor "because it provides information about the likelihood of a defendant's rehabilitation."[36] Justice Kennedy stated that "[i]n a capital sentencing proceeding, assessments of character and remorse may carry great weight and, perhaps, be determinative of whether the offender lives or dies."[37] Judge Leventhal of the US Court of Appeals for the D.C. Circuit explained: "There is a natural, and I believe sound, disposition to adjust sanctions when an offender admits his responsibility. This blends in with a readiness to accept the conclusion that such a person has the stuff that portends future improvement."[38] Thus, criminal sentencing in American jurisdictions often permits judges to increase sentences for lack of remorse.[39] Because an apology is a plausible way to demonstrate remorse, criminal defendants face incentives to apologize.

Restorative Justice Processes

Restorative justice, broadly speaking, "is a process whereby all the parties with a stake in a particular offense come together to resolve collectively how to deal with the aftermath of the offense and its implications for the future."[40] Restorative justice plays a role in international conflict,[41] but it is also employed in criminal settings in the United States. A recent study found that forty-five states and the District of Columbia had "codified 'restorative justice' into their juvenile and/or adult criminal justice systems."[42]

Apology in restorative justice processes in criminal settings in the United States serves as a way for defendants to acknowledge the harm they caused victims and to move forward. As now-Judge Stephanos Bibas and Richard

[36] *See* Hessick & Hessick, note 5, at 66 & n.96 (collecting cases).

[37] Riggins v. Nevada, 504 U.S. 127, 144 (1992) (Kennedy, J., concurring in the judgment).

[38] Scott v. United States, 419 F.2d 264, 282 (D.C. Cir. 1969) (Leventhal, J., concurring), *abrogated on other grounds by* United States v. Grayson, 438 U.S. 41 (1978).

[39] This is true even if there are questions about whether judges consistently consider apologies in criminal sentencing. *See* Jeffrey J. Rachlinski, Chris Guthrie & Andrew J. Wistrich, *Contrition in the Courtroom: Do Apologies Affect Adjudication?* 98 CORNELL L. REV. 1189 (2013).

[40] John Braithwaite, *Restorative Justice: Assessing Optimistic and Pessimistic Accounts*, *in* 25 CRIME AND JUSTICE: A REVIEW OF RESEARCH 1, 5 (Michael Tonry ed., 1999) (quoting formulation offered by Tony Marshall).

[41] *See, e.g.*, Matiangai V.S. Sirleaf, *Beyond Truth and Punishment in Transitional Justice*, 54 VA. J. INT'L L. 223, 229–30 (2014).

[42] Thalia González, *The State of Restorative Justice in American Criminal Law*, 2020 WIS. L. REV. 1147, 1156 (2020).

Bierschbach have written, "[r]estorativists consider apology and remorse important as part of a holistic process," whereby "offenders will recognize the wrongfulness of their conduct, make amends with their victims and the community, and try to restore the moral balance by making actual or symbolic reparations."[43] A 2003 review of four restorative justice studies found that about 74 percent of offenders in restorative justice programs apologized, as compared to approximately 29 percent of offenders in court.[44]

Restorative justice programs are often voluntary but are sometimes mandatory.[45] Even when these programs are formally voluntary, offenders who do not reach a restitution agreement with the victim may find themselves back in court subject to the ordinary operation of the criminal justice system.[46] One might question, therefore, whether apologies offered as part of restorative justice programs are fully voluntary. Given that restorative justice processes generally take place outside the courtroom, however, there is little case law on challenges to apologies in these programs.

"Apology Shield" Laws

"Apology shield" laws enacted in many states prevent apologies (or a subset thereof) from being admissible in court. These laws are especially common in the medical malpractice context.[47] The theory behind apology shield laws is that people will be less likely to sue physicians or more likely to settle if they receive an apology, because they will already feel satisfied to some extent.[48] Apology shield laws are thus meant to facilitate settlement by reducing the risks to physicians of apologizing for medical errors. It is not entirely clear whether apology shield laws reduce malpractice claims, perhaps because many such laws protect only "partial apologies" involving expressions of sympathy or regret rather than admission of error.[49] Nonetheless, apology

[43] Stephanos Bibas & Richard A. Bierschbach, *Integrating Remorse and Apology into Criminal Procedure*, 114 Yale L.J. 85, 103 (2004).

[44] Barton Poulson, *A Third Voice: A Review of Empirical Research on the Psychological Outcomes of Restorative Justice*, 2003 Utah L. Rev. 167, 189.

[45] González, note 42, at 1184–86.

[46] *See* Richard Delgado, *Prosecuting Violence: A Colloquy on Race, Community, and Justice*, 52 Stan. L. Rev. 751, 760 (2000).

[47] *See* Gabriel H. Teninbaum, *How Medical Apology Programs Harm Patients*, 15 Chap. L. Rev. 307, 311–12 (2011).

[48] *See* Jennifer K. Robbennolt, *Apologies and Legal Settlement: An Empirical Examination*, 102 Mich. L. Rev. 460, 461–62 (2003).

[49] *Id.* at 505; *see also* Benjamin J. McMichael, R. Lawrence Van Horn & W. Kip Viscusi, *"Sorry" Is Never Enough: How State Apology Laws Fail to Reduce Medical Malpractice Liability Risk*, 71 Stan. L. Rev. 341, 342, 355–56 (2019) (noting that most state apology laws are partial and that, "on balance, apology laws increase rather than limit medical malpractice liability risk").

shield laws are relevant to the debate over compelled apologies because they aim to incentivize apologies through the medium of state law.

To be sure, apology shield laws might be viewed as fundamentally different from court-mandated apologies in the following sense: Apology shield laws remove a deterrent to an apology that the defendant already wants to give, while the defendant forced by a court to apologize may not wish to do so. But the dichotomy is not stark. A doctor may feel pressure to apologize if she believes that doing so will help to avoid a lawsuit, regardless of what she might have done otherwise.

The common thread in these practices "adjacent" to court-ordered apologies is that the law creates conditions favorable to apologies and unfavorable to their absence, even without directly forcing an apology. "Adjacent" apologies suggest, more generally, that voluntariness is a spectrum rather than an on–off switch. Individuals can face incentives that border on the coercive even if their decisions are still voluntary in some sense.

This chapter does not investigate the normative status of each adjacent practice in detail. The aim is to examine court-mandated apologies in order to shed light on the contours of judicial power to remedy dignitary harm. At the same time, I draw on adjacent practices in considering the normative benefits and drawbacks of court-mandated apologies.

After all, the existence of adjacent practices has ramifications for apologies that are formally ordered by courts. To the extent one is uncomfortable with court-mandated apologies, one may need to interrogate a wider set of legal practices. Or, to the extent one is comfortable with some of the adjacent practices, one might question critiques of court-mandated apologies. Overall, exerting some amount of pressure on participants in court proceedings to apologize is a feature of our current legal practices.

Court-Mandated Apologies: A Normative Assessment

I turn now to a normative assessment of court-ordered apologies from both a philosophical and a constitutional point of view. First, I consider the reasons why one would be in favor of court orders requiring or pressuring defendants into apologizing. Apologies can provide dignitary relief to those harmed and send a broader message about the egregiousness of the defendant's conduct. In suggesting that apologies can effectively serve these functions, I question the "sincerity objection"—the view that an insincere apology cannot be efficacious.

Second, however, I address the concern that apologies violate the dignity of defendants. That concern may be connected to a constitutional objection to court-mandated apologies, namely, that this remedy compels speech in contravention of the First Amendment. The First Amendment issue should affect the circumstances under which apologies are ordered, but it should not take these apologies off the table.

Court-Mandated Apologies and Vindication of Dignity

Why would one support a legal system in which judges could order—or even strongly incentivize—apologies? One reason is that an apology can reaffirm the dignity of the party judged to have been wronged. When one person diminishes another's status, the apology restores it. The apologizer, in humbling herself in front of the wronged party, relinquishes the higher status she arrogated to herself in causing the wrong.[50] An apology also reverses relations of control: The victim, previously put down by the offender, now gains the power to decide whether to respond to the apology with forgiveness or rejection.[51] In all these ways, apologies help to ameliorate dignitary harm.

One context in which apologies redress dignitary harm involves personal relationships. An apology can heal social rifts and bring people together. The capacity of apologies to heal wounds between offender and victim is part of why apologies are used in mediation—to effectuate "moral reconciliation."[52] But if moral reconciliation or repair of personal relationships is the goal, then one might question whether a *compelled* apology will advance the ball.

More broadly, one might level the "sincerity objection" at court-mandated apologies. According to this objection, a compelled apology is not sincere, and an insincere apology cannot be effective. A court-ordered apology, in particular, cannot deliver true relief to a plaintiff, because the plaintiff knows that the defendant is apologizing through gritted teeth. Some might even

[50] *See* LAZARE, note 4, at 52.
[51] *Id.*
[52] Deborah L. Levi, *Note, The Role of Apology in Mediation*, 72 N.Y.U. L. REV. 1165, 1179 (1997).

take the view that a compelled apology is morally problematic, a perversion of apology's genuine function of facilitating authentic healing.[53]

A vivid example of the sincerity objection comes from a case involving the use of the artificial intelligence tool ChatGPT in legal practice.[54] In federal court in New York in 2023, attorneys "submitted non-existent judicial opinions with fake quotes and citations created by the artificial intelligence tool ChatGPT, then continued to stand by the fake opinions after judicial orders called their existence into question."[55] The judge presiding over the case, Judge Castel, imposed sanctions on the offending attorneys and their law firm.[56] The sanctions included a $5,000 fine and a requirement to send transcripts of the sanctions proceedings to the judges that the offending attorneys had falsely identified as the authors of the fake opinions.[57] Yet Judge Castel declined to require the attorneys to apologize, "because a compelled apology is not a sincere apology."[58]

The sincerity objection, however, should not be dispositive. As an initial matter, it is not entirely clear that a compelled apology cannot be sincere. Sincerity may not be a "yes–no" proposition. Going through the process of apology might encourage people to confront the consequences of their misconduct and thereby make the apologizer's remorse more real.

But even if a compelled apology is not sincere, sincerity is not always a prerequisite for an effective apology. When it comes to certain types of apologies—for instance, a spouse's apology for infidelity—sincerity is critical. Further from the sphere of intimate personal relationships, however, sincerity is less clearly key.

After all, an apology is a social act in addition to an expression of individual conviction. In a range of contexts, an apology can serve a social function even if it does not reflect the speaker's true views or values. When the leader of one country apologizes to another for historical wrongdoing—even if the apology is undertaken under political or economic duress—the contents of the leader's heart are not necessarily critical. The point is that the world bears witness to the transmission of a certain message. When a student

[53] Lee Taft, *Apology Subverted: The Commodification of Apology*, 109 Yale L.J. 1135, 1138 (2000); *see also* Stephanos Bibas, *The Corruption of Apology*, Persuasion (Jul. 27, 2022), https://www.persuasion.community/p/the-corruption-of-apology.

[54] Mata v. Avianca, Inc., 678 F. Supp. 3d 443 (S.D.N.Y. 2023).

[55] *Id.* at 448.

[56] *Id.* at 466.

[57] *Id.*

[58] *Id.*

misbehaves on a school trip to a museum and the teacher orders the student to apologize to the museum staff, the apology can mollify the museum and smooth over the relationship between the museum and the school even if the student is not inwardly sincere.[59]

An apology can be effective, then, because it alleviates social tension, and an apology need not be undertaken free of compulsion to serve this function. To be sure, an apology in which the speaker openly states "I don't really mean this" would be unlikely to advance social reconciliation. But such an apology would not fulfill the social purpose of restoring the victim's status because the apologizer would be publicly flaunting the fact that he does not take the process seriously. In other words, the apologizer's mockery would alter the social meaning of the apology. An insincere apology unaccompanied by open disrespect need not suffer from the same flaw. Instead, such an apology could publicly telegraph that the victim was treated improperly and thereby reaffirm the victim's dignity, even if the parties do not truly make personal amends.

These points about sincerity and the social function of apologies apply to court-ordered apologies. An apology mandated by a court can reaffirm the plaintiff's dignity. It can transmit the message that the court system will not accept the defendant's conduct, and it can strengthen the societal norm against that conduct. And an apology may play these roles even if the apologizer is not inwardly remorseful. Apologies that occur as part of settlements—which may be approved by the court—can send similar messages. For example, plaintiffs alleging corporate misconduct may demand an apology as part of a settlement. In so doing, they seek dignitary relief independent of whether the corporate officer (or the corporation as a whole, to the extent corporations can have such views) "really means it."

An example of the public-facing aspect of court-ordered apologies comes from the New York case, mentioned earlier, in which the court upheld a civil rights commissioner's order that an employer provide a written apology for anti-Semitic remarks made to his employee.[60] Before administrative action was instituted, the employer had repeatedly refused to apologize to the employee.[61] The New York court noted that the employer's "contempt" for

[59] One might argue that the teacher, in this case, is sincerely remorseful. But an apology coming directly from the student (even if compelled) performs a social function that an apology from the teacher would not.

[60] Imperial Diner, Inc. v. State Hum. Rts. Appeal Bd., 417 N.E.2d 525, 527 (N.Y. 1980).

[61] *Id.* at 527–29.

the employee "was proclaimed crudely and openly, not only to her but to all within her hearing. This type of vilification is humiliating."[62] The court did not defend the apology remedy in great detail, but it observed that "in view of the commissioner's broad powers to fashion relief as well as the significance the employer's refusal to apologize had in this case, it cannot be said that ordering an apology was not essential to eliminate the particular discriminatory practice the commissioner had found."[63] The commissioner-mandated apology can be understood as a way to reverse the status relationship the employer created by insulting the employee in front of others.

Accordingly, the interest in providing a remedy for dignitary harm furnishes a basis for court-mandated apologies. There are other potential justifications, including one more focused on the interests of defendants—namely, that court-mandated apologies, in satisfying plaintiffs' desire for vindication, could take the place of seemingly harsher penalties for defendants. Yet the dignitary rationale for court-mandated apologies is an important part of the story.

Court-Mandated Apologies and the Violation of Dignity

Although court-ordered apologies can vindicate dignity, they could also be critiqued for violating dignity—the dignity of defendants. This critique captures a genuine intuition, but it is not straightforward to explain why court-mandated apologies violate dignity, and it is not clear that they do.

One possibility is that court-ordered apologies, or certain subsets thereof, gratuitously demote a person or expose her to ridicule. While apology mandates in criminal cases are usually upheld when challenged—given the deference extended to sentencing courts in the criminal context—some courts have invalidated these mandates on the ground that they exceed statutory authority. The explanation sometimes involves gratuitous humiliation. To return to the former judge convicted in Pennsylvania state court of crimes related to theft of judicial services: The appellate court upheld a probation condition mandating letters of apology but rejected the requirement that the letter be written on a photograph of the defendant in handcuffs.[64]

[62] *Id.* at 528.
[63] *Id.* at 529 n.*.
[64] Commonwealth v. Melvin, 103 A.3d 1, 55–56 (Pa. Super. Ct. 2014).

The handcuffs provision, the court explained, was not "reasonably related to rehabilitation" within the meaning of the applicable statute but was instead imposed "merely to shame and humiliate" the defendant.[65]

In another example, an Illinois court struck down a requirement that a person convicted of driving under the influence of alcohol place her booking photo along with an apology in a newspaper.[66] The applicable statute, the court reasoned, did not permit conditions of supervision to include "holding up a defendant to ridicule."[67] The Minnesota Supreme Court used similar reasoning in rebuffing a civil rights hearing examiner's decision to order a city and its police chief to write an apology letter to a twelve-year-old Black youth whom officers had threatened with a police dog and called a racial epithet.[68] "The writing of such a letter" of apology, the court stated, "is calculated to humiliate and debase its writer and will succeed in producing only his resentment—an emotion not particularly conducive to the advancement of human rights."[69]

These cases suggest that an apology mandate will likely be invalidated if it is understood as a form of gratuitous humiliation. On this view, a compelled apology violates dignity by exposing the defendant to ridicule for no good reason. This view leaves open, however, the possibility that a court-ordered apology is compatible with dignity when it is not gratuitous—when it is, for example, reasonably related to rehabilitation, as the Pennsylvania court ruled with respect to the photograph-free letters of apology.

Gratuitous humiliation, then, is one reason why a court-mandated apology might violate dignity. Another (related) reason is that these apologies constitute an unacceptable incursion on individual conscience. Here court-ordered apologies intersect with First Amendment compelled speech doctrine. A brief overview of that doctrine is therefore in order, though the doctrine currently seems to be in flux. The First Amendment protects not only the right to speak but also the right *not* to speak.[70] More specifically, an individual cannot be forced by the government to "'utter what is not in [her] mind' about a question of political and religious significance"[71] or "a

[65] *Id.* at 54–55.
[66] People v. Johnson, 528 N.E.2d 1360, 1362 (Ill. App. Ct. 1988).
[67] *Id.*
[68] City of Minneapolis v. Richardson, 239 N.W.2d 197, 206 (Minn. 1976).
[69] *Id.*
[70] Wooley v. Maynard, 430 U.S. 705, 714 (1977).
[71] 303 Creative LLC v. Elenis, 600 U.S. 570, 596 (2023) (quoting W. Va. State Bd. of Educ. v. Barnette, 319 U.S. 624, 634 (1943) (alteration in the original)).

significant issue of personal conviction."[72] Government-compelled speech appears to be either unconstitutional per se[73] or unconstitutional unless the government can identify a sufficiently compelling interest.[74]

Key precedents on speech compelled in violation of conscience are *West Virginia v. Barnette*[75] and *Wooley v. Maynard*.[76] In *Barnette*, the Supreme Court held that schoolchildren could not be required to salute the flag and recite the Pledge of Allegiance.[77] The Bill of Rights, the Court explained, "guards the individual's right to speak his own mind" and so did not leave "it open to public authorities to compel him to utter what is not in his mind."[78] *Barnette* included the well-known line: "If there is any fixed star in our constitutional constellation, it is that no official, high or petty, can prescribe what shall be orthodox in politics, nationalism, religion, or other matters of opinion or force citizens to confess by word or act their faith therein."[79]

In *Wooley*, the Supreme Court held that a New Hampshire resident could not be forced to display on his license plate a motto to which he was morally opposed: "Live free or die."[80] The *Wooley* Court, in its words, was "faced with a state measure which forces an individual, as part of his daily life indeed constantly while his automobile is in public view to be an instrument for fostering public adherence to an ideological point of view he finds unacceptable."[81] "In doing so, the State 'invades the sphere of intellect and spirit which it is the purpose of the First Amendment to our Constitution to reserve from all official control.' "[82]

In 2023, the Supreme Court in *303 Creative v. Elenis* invoked First Amendment compelled speech doctrine to uphold the right of a religious website designer to decline to create wedding websites for same-sex weddings, notwithstanding Colorado's antidiscrimination law.[83] According to the Court, "Colorado seeks to force an individual to speak in ways that

[72] *Id.* at 598.
[73] *See id.* at 596.
[74] *Wooley*, 430 U.S. at 716; *see* Eugene Volokh, *The Law of Compelled Speech*, 97 TEX. L. REV. 355, 359 (2018) (describing speech compulsion as "presumptively unconstitutional").
[75] 319 U.S. 624 (1943).
[76] 430 U.S. 705 (1977).
[77] *Barnette*, 319 U.S. at 642.
[78] *Id.* at 634.
[79] *Id.* at 642.
[80] *Wooley*, 430 U.S. at 717.
[81] *Id.* at 715.
[82] *Id.* (quoting *Barnette*, 319 U.S. at 642).
[83] 600 U.S. 570 (2023).

align with its views but defy her conscience about a matter of major significance."[84] That, the Court stated, Colorado could not do.

How does compelled speech doctrine—particularly the view that the state may not intrude in certain ways on individuals' consciences—apply to court-ordered apologies? Few judicial decisions analyze the relationship between court-mandated apologies and compelled speech doctrine in any depth.[85]

In criminal cases, First Amendment objections have not met with much success. The Washington Supreme Court, upholding a requirement that a juvenile defendant write a letter of apology to the victim of his sexual assault, rejected a compelled speech objection on the ground that "First Amendment rights are not absolute . . . particularly in the context of prison and probation, where constitutional rights are lessened or not applicable."[86] Courts have also been skeptical of claims that the practice of considering remorse in sentencing violates the First Amendment.[87] The Second Circuit Court of Appeals in 2012 treated it as accepted practice that courts could consider the lack of remorse in sentencing, given that "[n]early all the ways that defendants speak in court are heavily regulated and potentially punishable without raising First Amendment claims."[88]

In civil rights cases involving apologies, First Amendment concerns are visible in the background but are rarely addressed head-on. Courts have alluded to "the constitutional implications attendant to enjoining a party to make statements that may run contrary to his or her beliefs"[89] but have not engaged in detailed analysis of First Amendment issues. Perhaps this is because, as Brent White has noted, First Amendment compelled speech doctrine has less purchase against government actors, which are often the defendants in civil rights litigation.[90] Public officials carrying out their official duties have a weaker claim to be asserting their individual freedom of conscience.[91] Another reason for the relative dearth of case law on First

[84] *Id.* at 602–03.

[85] *See* Lee, note 8, at 45 ("[T]here is a surprisingly small number of cases in which a court refers to the First Amendment to deny a request for a court-ordered apology.").

[86] State v. K.H.-H., 374 P.3d 1141, 1143 (Wash. 2016) (footnote omitted).

[87] *See* Hessick & Hessick, note 5, at 68.

[88] United States v. Stewart, 686 F.3d 156, 172 n.19 (2d Cir. 2012) (quoting Alexandra Natapoff, *Speechless: The Silencing of Criminal Defendants*, 80 N.Y.U. L. Rev. 1449, 1484 (2005)).

[89] Clark v. Shrader, No. 20-CV-01410-DDD-KLM, 2021 WL 229283, at *3 (D. Colo. Jan. 22, 2021), *report and recommendation adopted*, No. 20-CV-01410-RMR-KLM, 2021 WL 11485638 (D. Colo. July 21, 2021) (internal quotation marks omitted).

[90] White, note 23, at 1298–1300.

[91] *Id.* at 1300.

Amendment objections to court-ordered apologies in civil rights cases may be that courts prefer to reject these apologies on nonconstitutional grounds.

Overall, then, existing case law does not provide much of a basis for a First Amendment objection to court-mandated apologies. Nevertheless, some judges have made this suggestion,[92] and it is worth considering the relationship between compelled speech doctrine and court-mandated apologies in greater depth. This relationship sheds light on the question whether court-mandated apologies violate individual conscience. In what follows, then, I identify values underlying compelled speech doctrine that raise questions about the appropriateness of court-ordered apologies. These values, however, do not provide sufficient reason to rule out court-mandated apologies. (I do not follow a purely historical approach to compelled speech doctrine here, but neither thus far has the Supreme Court.)

To reiterate, the Supreme Court has condemned government actions that "force an individual to utter what is not in her mind about a question of political and religious significance."[93] Court-ordered apologies may require individuals to say "what is not in their mind" about a matter of significance, though not necessarily political or religious. The case is not closed, however, from a doctrinal perspective. The contexts in which courts order apologies—such as cases of criminal offenses and attorney misconduct—may lessen the force of First Amendment protections. Further, the law of compelled speech is still being fleshed out. From a normative perspective, it is useful to ask about the values underlying compelled speech doctrine and their relationship to court-ordered apologies.

First Amendment compelled speech doctrine protects multiple interests, which vary in the strength of their connection to court-mandated apologies and dignity. One such interest, for example, is in promoting democratic self-government by encouraging the expression of a wide range of views.[94] An apology ordered by a court following legal process does not seem to have a substantial impact on democratic participation. Instead, court-mandated

[92] *See, e.g.*, Imperial Diner, Inc. v. State Hum. Rts. Appeal Bd., 417 N.E.2d 525, 529 (N.Y. 1980) (Meyer, J., dissenting in part) (objecting to an apology requirement on the ground that "the First Amendment protects both the right to speak and the right to remain silent"); Griffith v. Smith, 30 Va. Cir. 250, 1993 WL 945995, at *13 (Va. Cir. Ct. 1993), *rev'd on other grounds sub nom.* Roberts v. Clarke, 34 Va. Cir. 61, 1994 WL 16011491 (Va. Cir. Ct. 1994) (in a case involving sanctions on an attorney, "First Amendment concerns preclude the Court from ordering [an] apology.").

[93] 303 Creative LLC v. Elenis, 600 U.S. 570, 596 (2023) (internal quotation marks and alteration omitted).

[94] *See, e.g.*, Alexander Meiklejohn, *The First Amendment Is an Absolute*, 1961 Sup. Ct. Rev. 245, 255.

apologies more directly implicate a different First Amendment interest, namely, the interest in protecting individual conscience.

How? One might argue that forcing a person to apologize short-circuits the individual's deliberative processes, substituting court-approved views for the defendant's use of reason.[95] Yet, as Steven Shiffrin has pointed out, "compelled speech need not distort the thinking processes of the speaker."[96] People can say one thing and think another. Still, the deliberation objection might have most purchase with respect to children, such as children required to say the Pledge of Allegiance (in *Barnette*) or juvenile criminal offenders (in apology cases).

Another possibility is that court-mandated apologies violate conscience even if people do not end up believing what they are forced to say—precisely because people are forced to say what they do not believe. Perhaps, in the words of Vikram Amar and Alan Brownstein, "it is an affront to human dignity to be required to speak inauthentically."[97] In terms of relational dignity, authentic speech implicates the interest in control over one's self-presentation to others.

The view that compelled apologies violate conscience because they threaten authenticity, however, warrants interrogation. People routinely feel compelled to be not entirely "true to themselves" in numerous settings, including school and work. It is not clear that their dignity is being violated. To be sure, court-ordered apologies are more coercive than most everyday inauthenticity; but inauthenticity is not in itself a marker of a dignitary violation.

Moreover, the line between expressing an authentic message and speaking inauthentically is not precisely defined. Even at an interpersonal level, an apology offered primarily to defuse conflict, even if the apologizer is not entirely sure he is at fault, can play a positive social role. At the institutional level, the "adjacent" practices mentioned earlier—such as judges' consideration of remorse in sentencing, or the use of apologies in restorative justice processes—suggest that apologies can fall along a spectrum of authenticity. A person may "mean it" to some extent even if she is heavily incentivized to apologize. Whether a defendant delivers an authentic message or one resulting from pressure is not a binary matter.

[95] On distortion of deliberative processes, see Seana Valentine Shiffrin, *A Thinker-Based Approach to Freedom of Speech*, 27 Const. Comment. 283, 290 (2011); Steven H. Shiffrin, *What Is Wrong with Compelled Speech?* 29 J.L. & Pol. 499, 514 (2014).

[96] *Id.* at 505.

[97] Vikram David Amar & Alan Brownstein, *Toward a More Explicit, Independent, Consistent and Nuanced Compelled Speech Doctrine*, 2020 U. Ill. L. Rev. 1, 22.

Nevertheless, courts should take seriously the possibility that forcing inauthentic speech infringes dignitary interests. This is especially true when a person's motives are not mixed, and she simply does not believe what she is being asked to say.

In addition to the authenticity concern, another candidate to explain why court-ordered apologies violate dignity involves the Kantian idea that dignity requires persons to be treated as ends in themselves rather than as mere means.[98] Compelled speech could be critiqued as a way for the government to instrumentalize people by using them as mouthpieces—in Amar and Brownstein's terms, "the state's vocal puppet."[99] Just as one might object to the state's "requirement that someone's car be turned into the government's 'mobile billboard,'"[100] as in the Supreme Court case *Wooley* invalidating New Hampshire's license plate motto mandate, one might see coerced apologies as a practice that improperly harnesses a defendant to the government's purposes. This dignitary objection to court-mandated apologies sounds in autonomy: Individuals should not be reduced to instruments in the hands of the state.

A line of judicial opinions reflecting this kind of autonomy objection, though not directly concerning court-ordered apologies, involves the authority of the National Labor Relations Board (NLRB) to remedy violations of labor laws.[101] The question is: May the NLRB require a representative of an employer found to violate labor laws to read aloud to employees the NLRB's remedial notice listing the violations and the employer's commitment not to repeat them? Courts have taken different approaches; in 2016, for example, the D.C. Circuit upheld a notice-reading requirement as long as the company had "the option of punting the task to a Board employee."[102] Some objections to notice-reading orders sound in a dignitary register. For example, then-Judge Ruth Bader Ginsburg wrote in a 1983 dissent that "[a] forced, public 'confession of sins,' even by an owner-president who has acted outrageously, is a humiliation this court once termed 'incompatible with the

[98] *See* Christopher McCrudden, *Human Dignity and Judicial Interpretation of Human Rights*, 19 Eur. J. Int'l L. 655, 659 (2008).

[99] Amar & Brownstein, note 97, at 23.

[100] *Id.* at 22 (quoting Wooley v. Maynard, 430 U.S. 705, 715 (1977)).

[101] *See, e.g.*, HTH Corp. v. NLRB, 823 F.3d 668 (D.C. Cir. 2016); Denton Cnty. Elec. Coop., Inc. v. NLRB, 962 F.3d 161 (5th Cir. 2020); Conair Corp. v. NLRB, 721 F.2d 1355 (D.C. Cir. 1983).

[102] *HTH*, 823 F.3d at 678; *but see Denton*, 962 F.3d at 174–75 (vacating a notice-reading order based on the facts and expressing skepticism about such orders more generally).

democratic principles of the dignity of man.' "[103] "I would not," then-Judge Ginsburg continued, "single out the president here, or any other named individual, hand him lines, and make him sing."[104]

The objection to "making the employer sing" suggests that individuals should not be treated as tools or mouthpieces of the government. But it may not be improper for people to be "used" by a state actor. When courts order defendants to pay damages or send them to prison, they make these orders in the service of societal goals, to which the treatment of the defendant is a means. One might argue that in these cases, the defendant's autonomy is "truly" respected because he receives the penalty his conduct warranted.[105] But it seems more realistic to acknowledge that society often puts its own interests above those of the defendant. In other words, court-mandated apologies or compelled admissions are not the only practices that "use" individuals as means to societal ends.

To the extent court-ordered apologies are different, this may be a consequence of the kinship—either actual or symbolic—between these apologies and practices that are typical of antidemocratic regimes. Here I draw on arguments made by Dan Kahan and James Whitman in debates over "shame sanctions," which include not only forced apologies but also more physical forms of punishment such as wearing clothing or signs announcing one's crime.[106] A "forced, public 'confession of sins,'" in then-Judge Ginsburg's words,[107] may strike some as similar to the stocks, the pillory, scarlet letters, and public apologies imposed by antidemocratic regimes. As a result, court-mandated apologies might, as Kahan writes of shame sanctions, "conjure up the specter of hierarchy and coerced conformity."[108] In that event, court-ordered apologies would be unacceptable to some from an expressive perspective. They would send a message incompatible with dignity. Indeed, the relationship between court-mandated apologies and hierarchical regimes is not coincidental. Public apologies are a method of establishing and enforcing

[103] *Conair*, 721 F.2d at 1401 (Ginsburg, J., dissenting) (quoting Int'l Union of Elec., Radio & Mach. Workers, AFL-CIO v. NLRB, 383 F.2d 230, 234 (D.C. Cir. 1967)).

[104] *Id.* at 1402.

[105] Kant argued, for example, that criminal punishment was compatible with individual dignity in that it takes seriously the individual's moral choices. *See* Thomas E. Hill, Jr., *Kant on Wrongdoing, Desert, and Punishment*, 18 Law & Philosophy 407, 417–25 (1999).

[106] *See* Dan M. Kahan, *What's Really Wrong with Shaming Sanctions*, 84 Tex. L. Rev. 2075 (2006); Whitman, note 13.

[107] *Conair*, 721 F.2d at 1401 (Ginsburg, J., dissenting) (internal quotation marks omitted).

[108] Kahan, note 106, at 2088.

social norms, and hierarchical regimes may be more willing or eager to take these steps.

Yet we should hesitate before concluding that court-ordered apologies are unacceptable because they are reminiscent of undemocratic regimes. Other types of judicial rulings, notably imprisonment, can severely affect people's control over their daily activities, as well as their reputations. Of course, one might also oppose other types of judicial rulings, including imprisonment. But many are willing to live with imprisonment or some form of heavy judicial ruling—or, at a minimum, with the shame that an adverse judicial ruling often causes. In that case, the question remains why judicial apology mandates are distinctively likely to violate dignity in a manner that renders these mandates unacceptable. In fact, if a defendant's choice is between spending more time in prison and accepting a term of probation with an apology letter as a condition of probation, the apology letter might be the *more* dignity-enhancing choice.

Perhaps the instinct to criticize court-mandated apologies, while accepting at least some other forms of severe judicial treatment, reflects an unwillingness to directly confront degrading features of the judicial remedies that courts more customarily impose.[109] Moreover, undemocratic regimes are not the only ones that authorize court-mandated apologies, as the examples of Australia and Japan suggest. And an association with undemocratic regimes might not be sufficient to doom a practice. After all, "adjacent" practices that incentivize without strictly requiring apologies may also remind people of undemocratic regimes, yet courts could be wary about dismantling these practices.

Overall, court-ordered apologies risk violating dignity, and compelled speech doctrine reflects values that provide some support for that view. Nonetheless, the dignitary objection to court-mandated apologies is not a knockout blow. Inauthenticity and instrumentalization do not necessarily violate dignity. Court-ordered apologies, when viewed against the background of other judicial penalties, do not stand alone in their capacity to stigmatize. The dignitary objection to court-mandated apologies should prompt not rejection of the practice, but reflection on the acceptability (or lack thereof) of status-diminishing or reputation-damaging features of existing judicial systems.

109 *See* Kahan, note 13, at 609.

Evaluating Court-Ordered Apologies

Given that court-ordered apologies can both promote and violate dignity, how to assess their ultimate value? Court-mandated apologies should not be dismissed. They help rehabilitate the plaintiff's dignity, and they are part of a process by which society publicly articulates its commitment to respectful treatment. To condemn court-ordered apologies while endorsing other shame-inducing penalties is questionable. At the same time, the dignitary difficulties with court-ordered apologies should prompt substantial care about how this remedy is employed.

For example, not all defendants have the same dignitary interests. A government entity lacks a strong dignitary interest in not being used as a mere means to carry out judicial ends. Moreover, people are less likely to perceive apologies coerced from the government as tools of dictatorial regimes. Thus, the dignitary objection to court-ordered apologies is weaker when applied to the government.[110]

In addition, corporations arguably do not have the same dignitary interests as individuals. To be sure, the Supreme Court has treated the regulation of corporations as subject to conscience-based First Amendment objections. In *Burwell v. Hobby Lobby Stores*, for example, the Supreme Court rejected application of a contraceptive coverage mandate to a closely held corporation organized to act in accordance with its owners' religious principles.[111] Although the holding in *Burwell* was based on the Religious Freedom Restoration Act rather than the First Amendment, the Court stated that corporations could "further religious objectives,"[112] supporting the suggestion that an individual owner's dignitary interests could be advanced through the corporate form. Nonetheless, the dignitary interests would ultimately belong to the individual. And the corporate structure puts the individual's dignitary interests at some remove from an apology requirement imposed on the corporation. At a minimum, compelling an apology from a corporation would raise fewer dignitary concerns in the case of corporations that are not closely held.

Hence, the particular setting of a court-mandated apology influences its appropriateness. Beyond apologies procured from government or corporate

[110] On distinctions between government and non-government defendants in the realm of compelled apologies, see White, note 24, at 1299–1300.

[111] 573 U.S. 682 (2014).

[112] *Burwell*, 573 U.S. at 712.

actors, there are other examples of contextual factors. Court-mandated apologies may be more justified when the court has some kind of supervisory power over the individual compelled to apologize, such as when a court requires an attorney to apologize for violating the court's rules. Court-mandated apologies may also be more suitable and palatable when they express a broad-based social consensus, as distinct from a divisive or polarizing message.

The form of a court-ordered apology is also significant. An orally delivered apology is likely to be a harsher penalty than a written apology, as would an apology offered to a large audience. A harsher penalty may sometimes be warranted, but courts should take care not to produce gratuitous humiliation. In other words, judges should consider the dignitary and expressive goals that an apology can accomplish and ask whether the dignitary costs to the defendant must really be borne in order to accomplish these goals. If the answer is "no," then the apology would lead to gratuitous humiliation. Judges should further consider whether the dignitary costs are disproportionate to the dignitary benefits. These inquiries will not be exact sciences, but judges should at least aim not to produce unnecessary or disproportionate forms of status demotion, domination, or loss of control over self-presentation.

The most suitable attitude toward court-ordered apologies, therefore, is a contextually sensitive one. Additionally, characteristics of court-ordered apologies beyond dignity play a role in determining whether and how they ought to be imposed. One might argue, for instance, that court-ordered apologies are insufficiently serious as a remedy and do not have adequate deterrence value. The focus here is on dignity, and that focus provides all the more reason not to offer a final answer as to when courts should mandate apologies. This chapter suggests, however, that a rapid rejection of court-mandated apologies is unwarranted. The concept of a forced apology is not a contradiction in terms, and apologies have a place in public life in addition to personal relationships. Thus, the possibility that courts can order apologies to rectify dignitary harm should be taken seriously.

From an institutional perspective, which body would authorize court-ordered apologies? The analysis here is compatible with a variety of approaches. Legislatures could specifically authorize courts to mandate apologies in certain cases or in particular forms. But courts could also—as they have sometimes done—interpret their statutory authority to set conditions of probation or to discipline attorneys in a manner that permits apology requirements.

To conclude, this chapter has explored the practice of court-ordered apologies with a view toward illuminating their dignitary dimensions and evaluating their suitability as a judicial remedy for dignitary violations. Court-mandated apologies are worth considering, though it is important to remain aware of their risks, including First Amendment issues. Moreover, the chapter has urged attention to dignitary aspects of judicial practices adjacent to court-ordered apologies, as the law incentivizes expressions of remorse in a variety of settings. The idea of court-mandated apologies shines a light on corners of our legal system that contain both threats to dignity and relief for dignitary violations.

Conclusion

Dignity is an elusive concept. It has multiple meanings and applications. It is invoked by competing factions in high-stakes legal and political debates. It is situated at the apex of slippery slopes—where will dignitary claims end?—and beset by line-drawing problems.

And yet dignity is an essential concept. It speaks to the real-life experiences of countless individuals of varying backgrounds and walks of life. The sense that denigration and stigmatization are societal problems cannot be suppressed simply because dignity and related concepts are hard to define. The conceptual challenge of making dignity concrete is worth tackling head-on, instead of sidestepping.

This book has addressed a particular issue within the larger topic of how society should concretize dignity: the relationship between dignity and courts. To what extent should judges be in the business of rectifying violations of dignity? To embrace the task of dignity promotion is to take on the sensitive project of sifting meritorious from nonmeritorious claims about humiliation and degradation. To ignore dignity, however, is to miss an opportunity to advance an important value and to overlook the numerous ways in which judges affect status relations regardless of whether they are trying to do so. The role of dignity in adjudication raises questions about judicial competence, capacity, and legitimacy—in short, about the bounds of judicial authority.

This book has argued that courts should recognize dignitary harms as legally significant and seek to rectify them. It has presented a theory of relational dignity, understood in terms of respect for status, nondomination, and control over self-presentation. Violations of relational dignity are appropriate objects of judicial concern. Of course, the nature and manner of judicial responses to dignitary harm depend on the relevant institutional structures and legal regimes. Focusing on judicial structures in the United States, I have examined certain contexts in which judges confront the challenge of identifying and redressing dignitary harm.

In the law of constitutional standing doctrine, federal courts face the quandary of how to recognize the genuine effects of stigma without opening the doors wide to every claim of offense. Although the quest for a bright line between cognizable and noncognizable claims is unlikely to succeed, federal judges can fruitfully develop a body of precedent on dignitary harm as injury in fact. Tort law demonstrates that a concern for dignity is already embedded in legal regimes, albeit subject to some of the same worries about expansiveness and subjectivity that exist in the standing setting. Judges should not shy away from applying and developing tort doctrines that reflect the interest in promoting dignity, while erecting fences to prevent boundless recognition of dignitary claims.

The law of remedies also contains opportunities for judges to advance dignitary goals. Judges properly act within the judicial role when they issue remedies that telegraph respect or condemnation, as distinct from reallocating material resources or causing "tangible" effects. There are several mechanisms for judges to provide dignitary relief, including compensatory damages for dignitary harm, punitive damages, nominal damages, and declaratory judgments. Court-ordered apologies are another type of remedy that can redress dignitary harm. An apology, even when forced or heavily incentivized, can reverse status dynamics occasioned by the violation of dignity. Yet court-ordered apologies carry dignitary risks, including that of incursions on individual conscience. The idea of court-mandated apologies functions—like the exploration of dignity in this book more broadly—to illuminate judicial practices that affect status and stigma in consequential ways.

One general theme emerging from the analysis of dignity and judicial authority is as follows. There is a temptation in legal practice and theory to avoid concepts that seem subjective or difficult to apply. Perhaps, one might worry, legal recognition of these concepts will lead down a slippery slope, right past the guardrails carefully erected around the adjudicative process. But slippery slopes are an inevitable possibility. Pragmatism, common sense, and the willingness to act on the basis of less-than-clear-cut distinctions can prevent the descent into untenable results even when the relentless application of analytical logic would not. Or, in a line that Justice Ginsburg frequently quoted from a book by Judge Robert Bork, "Judges and lawyers live on the slippery slope of analogies; they are not supposed to ski it to the bottom."[1]

[1] *See, e.g.*, Nat'l Fed'n of Indep. Bus. v. Sebelius, 567 U.S. 519, 617 (2012) (Ginsburg, J., concurring

My hope is that this book will prompt further reflection, in a variety of areas of law, about how judges and other legal actors can instantiate concern for dignity in concrete institutional structures. Dignity is a powerful and volatile force in legal affairs, as in life. But dignity has an important place in law—in particular, relational dignity as defined by respect for status, non-domination, and control over self-presentation. Recognizing and embracing dignity's role in judicial decisions will help to create societies that better embody respectful social relations.

in part) (quoting Robert H. Bork, The Tempting of America 169 (1990)).

Index

For the benefit of digital users, indexed terms that span two pages (e.g., 52–53) may, on occasion, appear on only one of those pages.

www.ingramcontent.com/pod-product-compliance
Lightning Source LLC
Chambersburg PA
CBHW052302240825
31537CB00077B/177
9780197750322